Class & Gender in India

Patricia Caplan

CLASS & GENDER IN INDIA

Women and their organizations in a south Indian city

Tavistock Publications
London & New York

To Elizabeth and Linda, and all my other sisters

First published in 1985 by
Tavistock Publications Ltd
11 New Fetter Lane, London EC4P 4EE

Published in the USA by
Tavistock Publications
in association with Methuen, Inc.
29 West 35th Street, New York NY 10001

Filmset by Northumberland Press Ltd, Gateshead
Printed in Great Britain by Richard Clay
The Chaucer Press, Bungay, Suffolk

British Library Cataloguing in Publication Data

Caplan, Pat
    Class and gender in India: Women
    and their organizations in a south Indian city.
    1. Women——India——Social conditions
    I. Title
    305.4'2'06054   HQ1742

    ISBN 0–422–79970–X
    ISBN 0–422–79980–7 Pbk

Library of Congress Cataloging in Publication Data

Caplan, Ann Patricia.
    Class and gender in India.

    Bibliography: p.
    Includes indexes.
    1. Women——India——Madras. 2. Women——India——
Madras——Societies and clubs. 3. Women volunteers
in social service——India——Madras.
    4. Middle classes——India——Madras. I. Title.
    HQ1745.M33C37 1985   305.4'0954'82   85–17273

    ISBN 0–422–79970–X
    ISBN 0–422–79980–7 (pbk.)

Contents

Acknowledgements

Field-work for this study and a subsequent writing-up period were financed by a grant from the Social Science Research Council of Great Britain, between 1974 and 1976. My return visit in the summer of 1981 was made possible by the Nuffield Foundation and the Central Research Fund of London University. The SSRC also enabled me to have six months' sabbatical leave from October 1981 to March 1982, and the Nuffield Foundation gave me a further three months to June 1982; it was during this period that most of this book was written. I am extremely grateful to all these bodies for their assistance.

Many other people have helped me in various ways. First and foremost, I must thank the members of the organizations studied. I have tried to preserve their anonymity by changing their names and those of their organizations, but they will no doubt recognize themselves. For their kindness and willingness to put up with my presence at their meetings, my endless questions, and invasions of their privacy I can only offer my heartfelt thanks. Out of this study came not only a manuscript, but also numerous friendships which I value highly.

During the first period of field-work I received help from Mrs Sushila Krishnaswamy, who acted as translator and interpreter when needed, deputized for me in attendance at meetings, conducted her own interviews, and was a source of much useful information, as well as being a shrewd observer in her own right. During the summer of 1981 I was ably assisted by Miss Charubala, the daughter of one of my closest friends, who enabled me to make contact with the beneficiaries of the associations; without her help this vital part of the research would not have been possible.

Second, I must thank colleagues who discussed ideas with me at various stages, and particularly those who were willing to plough through this manuscript in its various incarnations: Janet Bujra, Lionel Caplan (many times), Girija, Olivia Harris, Brian Morris, Nici Nelson, and Hilary Standing. They have contributed greatly but are of course in no way responsible for any of its shortcomings.

Third, I thank those who helped in other ways: A. Violet and Mary Ponnamma, D. Padmanabahn and K. Selvarani who freed me from much domestic labour while I was in India, D. Samuel, K. Banumathy, Charleen Agostini, Joan Berry, and Jean Russell who did much of the typing at various stages.

Finally, thanks to Emma and Mark for learning to live in a south Indian city, which has not only enriched their own lives, but also enabled me to see things differently than I would have done without them.

Patricia Caplan
November 1984

Preface

In the early 1970s, having carried out two research projects in rural areas (Tanzania and Nepal), I decided my next area of research should be in a city. Furthermore, since by that time I was involved in the Women's Liberation Movement and an active member of several women's groups, it occurred to me that women's organizations might be a possible area of research. A few days in the India Office Library in London revealed that women's organizations did indeed appear to be plentiful in India generally, and in Madras city, the chosen study site.

It seemed that women's organizations in India had a long history, having been bound up in the nationalist struggle, and many appeared to be extremely active in the field of social welfare. The meagre literature that was available to me then pointed rather clearly to the domination of these organizations by women of the higher socio-economic strata. The existence and possible importance of women's voluntary organizations in India also seemed to highlight an apparent paradox – that while India had produced a female Prime Minister and numerous other political leaders long before any western country (including Britain), the ideology of orthodox Hinduism advocates an extremely subordinate role for women.

Thus the study of such organizations seemed to offer interesting possibilities and also to help solve the vexed problem faced by urban anthropologists: how to define their unit of study. Furthermore, the study of women's voluntary associations appeared to be a relatively new area of research for anthropology, in India or elsewhere.

Berreman has pointed out that historically anthropologists have emphasized studies of the 'remote, exotic and the powerless' (1981: 187). Like Laura Nader, he would support projects that 'study up'. Nader asks 'What if, in reinventing anthropology, anthropologists were to study the colonizers rather than the colonized, the culture of power rather than the culture of the powerless, the culture of affluence rather than the culture of poverty?' (1974: 289). But studying up raises complex ethical questions. Whereas one may fully concur with an ethic of 'informed consent' on the part of subjects who are, as Berreman puts it, 'powerless', how is it possible to work with such an ethic with the powerful? Are there different ethics for studying up and down?

The ethics of field-work and subsequent publication have been the subject of much discussion in the last few years. Given the increasing likelihood that anthropological subjects will read and react to material written about themselves, this is scarcely surprising. The twin traps of 'academic imperialism' and ethnocentrism here gape wide.

When I went to the field in 1974, I was not very sure exactly what I would find. I could only tell my informants what I knew myself: I was writing a book on women's organizations. I proceeded to make an intensive study of five organizations and to interview their members. They were mostly open and welcoming, and I became a member of them all. Some of the members became my close friends, offered me hospitality, and confided to me intimate details of their lives. However, I felt that few of them understood what I was trying to do.

Some viewed me as essentially the wife of my husband (who was carrying out research on Christians in Madras city at the same time) and they would explain to others that I had this little hobby of being interested in women's organizations in my spare time. Others saw me as the perpetual student and would ask me when I expected to finish my thesis. Still others saw me as a kind of glorified professional social worker, since I was so interested in social welfare. To some of these ladies, who were among the wealthiest in the city, I was very clearly a social inferior. Most women, however, were curious about me as I was often the first European with whom they had had a chance to experience prolonged social contact. They were anxious to know about life in the west, particularly about marriage and families. For many of them, this was the first time that a system different to their own had been coherently presented to them, although most had imbibed some of the wilder stereotypes about western women (cf. Chapter 8). One of the reasons many women gave for being glad of the opportunity to find out about a different way of life was that they frequently described themselves as 'frogs in a well' (cf. Jeffreys 1979) who think that the patch of sky above the well is the whole world. In other words, they saw themselves and their lives as circumscribed by custom, with a clearly laid down pattern, and with few opportunities for choice. While they may have complained about aspects of this situation, few questioned the system in which they found themselves – their socialization, arranged marriages, or lack of freedom to undertake paid work. For such women, there is little alternative but compliance; the family and its norms are their economic as well as psychological source of security, and there is no other. However, they are also members of a class whose interests are inevitably counterposed to those of the working class, particularly women with whom they come into contact either as servants or as clients of their social welfare activities. As individuals, members of organizations may seek to help poor women, orphans, and others in need by raising money, finding them work, and so on. Given the constraints on their lives, this is perhaps all they can do, and it may be argued that at least they are doing *something*. However, I suggest in this book that in many respects such activities may help to perpetuate and justify the very system that causes poverty and inequality in the first place.

This book is certainly not meant as a criticism of specifically *Indian* institutions. Indeed, much of my early thinking around this topic arose from discussions with people who were concerned about many of the issues discussed here – class, gender, and welfare – in a British context. Subsequent reading and work around these areas have only served to convince me further that the analysis I present here, while specific to Indian society in one sense, is yet applicable to most capitalist societies at certain stages of their historical development.

Laura Nader (1974) has argued that this kind of study should be carried out in the anthropologist's own society. I have often been asked why I chose to do this study in India rather than in Britain.

One of the reasons why this question is posed, I suspect, is that urban middle- and upper-class women and their organizations are not seen as exotic, but as familiar; had I been studying an Indian temple, for example, no one would have asked me why I did it there rather than here. Had I undertaken this study in Britain, most of the substantive conclusions would not, I think, have been very different. It is, as Berreman puts it, an attempt to contribute to the understanding of 'the institutions, the elite personnel, and the historical circumstances which limit human freedom, which control and repress people and societies *including our own*' (my italics) (1981: 187).

Glossary

Adi–Dravida term used in south India for untouchable or Harijan.
Appalam thin deep-fried pancake, resembling a large 'crisp' (called *poppadum* in north India).
Ayah nurse-maid.
Balwadi day-care centre for children.
Bhajan devotional songs or hymns.
Devadasi temple dancers (who also sometimes acted as sacred prostitutes).
Dhal lentil dish.
Dosai thin pancake of rice and gram flour eaten in south India.
Iddly steamed cake or dumpling made of rice and gram flour, specific to south India.
Karma fate or destiny.
Kolam geometric design of rice flour drawn by south Indian women on the thresholds of their houses.
Lathi steel-tipped baton with which Indian police are equipped.
Pilao dish of rice mixed with vegetables and/or meat and spices.
Puja religious worship.
Poriyal dish of fried vegetables with grated coconut.
Pottu mark on forehead (in north India – *tilak*); married women wear a red pottu; both men and women may receive a pottu as a sign of blessing from a religious officiant after a *puja*.
Rasam peppery soup specific to south India.
Ravai uppuma savoury semolina dish.

Salwar-kamiz tunic and trousers worn by some north Indian women (especially from the Punjab but now more widely adopted).

Sambar dish of highly spiced vegetables.

Sloka religious verses.

Stothra praises of a deity.

Tali necklace worn by married women, usually of gold; also sometimes called a *tirumangalyam* in south India.

Tiffin snack.

Vadam savoury snack made of deep-fried lentils.

Veena south Indian stringed instrument.

Abbreviations used

ADMK Anna Dravida Munnetra Kazagham (ruling political party in Tamilnadu in 1981–82; main opposition party 1974–75).

AIWC All India Women's Conference.

DMK Dravida Munnetra Kazagham (main opposition party in Tamilnadu in 1981–82; ruling party 1974–75).

CSWB Central Social Welfare Board.

IAS Indian Administration Service (top-ranking, all-India civil servants).

RCSW Report of the Committee on the Status of Women in India (1974).

SSWB State Social Welfare Board.

WIA Women's Indian Association.

Note on exchange rates

At the time of field-work between 1974 and 1975, the rate of exchange was fairly consistently Rs 18 = £1, In 1981–82, it fluctuated between Rs 15 and Rs 16 = £1. For most purposes of conversion in this book, I have used the 1974–75 rates.

PART ONE

INTRODUCTION
AND BACKGROUND

1
Introduction

During the Emergency in India, which lasted from 1975 to 1977, a prominent Congress Minister is reputed to have remarked that when his party announced its programme of socialism in 1955, 34 per cent of the population was below the poverty line, whereas Mrs Gandhi's *Garibi Hatao* ('away with poverty') programme had brought the number up to 70 per cent by 1975 (Lewis 1978: 181).

Exact figures may be disputed, but what is not disputed is that the vast majority of India's population lives in abject poverty, while a very small minority lives in relative comfort, even luxury. Inequalities in the distribution of wealth and resources in Indian society are enormous and probably increasing (cf. Bettelheim 1968; Davey 1975; Fonseca 1971; Guhan 1981; Thorner 1980).

Some social scientists who have carried out research in India have asked themselves how changes in the system that perpetuates such gross inequalities might be brought about. Lynch (1979) suggests that there are two possible ways. One is to study the poor and their consciousness and praxis in order to try and change it. This is what some have tried to do. 'The other option is more difficult, although probably more significant. This option is to study the rich and powerful' (Lynch 1979: 20). This book is an attempt to do the latter. At the same time, it is also a study of upper-class women and how they contribute to the construction and perpetuation of the class system.

In the first half of this chapter, I consider the question of what class means in the Indian context, and in the second, how it articulates with gender. I seek to show that it is only through an examination of reproductive as well as productive relations that an understanding of class, both as a dynamic process and as one having an important cultural content, can be achieved.

Outline of the argument

There are three dimensions of women's relationship to class among the urban elite. First, their relationship through their domestic role, which is examined in Chapters 3 and 4. Given the almost universal norm of marriage, the majority of women play roles as wives, mothers, and daughters-in-law, while also continuing to be the daughters of their parents. They are extremely important for the reproduction of the class system, not only in terms of their biological work of reproduction, but also through their domestic labour and their socialization of the next generation.

Second, a minority of women have a role as a paid worker. As will be seen in Chapter 5, women generally occupy specific niches in the labour market, even those in the minority of highly educated professional women who work outside the home. From this sector comes the phenomenon of the unmarried female professional, whose relationship to production is a direct one, unmediated by the occupation of a husband.

Third, many women at this class level, whether employed or not, belong to voluntary women's associations, which have a very important role in class formation. Such organizations help create a common culture, specific to a particular class level, through such activities as learning baking, practising English conversation, and through informal interaction between members, which helps standardize socialization of children and ways of running a household.

Even more significantly, women's organizations play a major role in the provision of social welfare facilities in India. Social welfare until recently has been largely of a voluntary nature, and the earliest state intervention immediately after independence was an attempt to channel this activity by injecting funds and creating Social Welfare Boards at the Union and state levels. The membership of the Boards has consisted largely of women prominent in women's social welfare associations, who have thus had a significant, albeit limited, involvement in the public and political sphere.

The second part of the book examines this sphere, beginning with a history of the women's organizations in Chapter 6, followed by a discussion of the relations between the women's voluntary organizations and the state, particularly as mediated by the Social Welfare Boards, in Chapter 7. Case studies of five such organizations in Madras city are presented in Chapters 8 and 9; their membership, activities, funding, and types of clients are examined, and their political significance in relation to class, caste, and gender is considered. The ideological functions of the women's welfare organizations are discussed primarily through an examination of their rituals and language in Chapter 10. It is shown that the women's organizations propagate certain norms regarding female behaviour and express class relations through their activities as dispensers of charity to the lower classes.

In the final chapter, I examine the politics of sex and class in the context of the women's organizations. The relationship of women to the class structure is a very complex one, which has to be viewed on the levels of reproduction (domestic labour), production (women as workers), and, in this case, voluntary public work in social welfare. I suggest that this is particularly important when the state is either unable or unwilling to provide such services directly. Furthermore voluntary organizations are able to perform certain ideological functions much more effectively than the state itself.

It is thus the argument of this book that women play an active part in class formation, not only as housewives and workers, but also as members of voluntary organizations and dispensers of social welfare. However, although in the process they gain a certain amount of political power, neither their membership of organizations, nor the kind of activities they engage in, much less the ideology they propagate, does very much to change the situation of women themselves. None the less, it is impossible to view them merely as passive recipients of a system not of their making. Many are strong and intelligent, seeking to make sense of a rapidly changing social situation and, above all, struggling to maintain the positions of their families within it. The very fact that the women with whom I worked were *joiners*, that they formed organizations and made and executed plans, indicates that they are far from passive or complacent.

Many women see clearly that there are problems in their own lives, in those of their families, their neighbours, and their friends. They see that there are enormous problems in Indian society, particularly the poverty of the great majority, and they seek to do something about these problems. By upholding 'tradition' and religion they feel that they are creating a haven of security in a too rapidly changing world, and yet by joining organizations and 'learning new things' that they are adapting to these changes, as indeed they are.

Class and production in India

India now has a large industrial capacity (ranking tenth in the world) but there are numerous contradictions in the form that capitalist development has taken. Much industrial development has not been in the heavy goods sector but rather in manufacturing luxury items such as cars, air conditioners, refrigerators, and so on for the middle-class market. Thus India's economic development has been distorted not only by the fact that it was for so long a colonial state, but also by the form of industrial development since independence. There is a small segment at the top of the socio-economic hierarchy that controls most of the resources in the economy, as well as receiving most of its income. For example, the top 10 per cent of the rural and urban population, comprising the bourgeoisie and the petty bourgeoisie, consumes approximately 36 per cent of the total supply of industrial goods (Sau 1981: 49). Kurien points out that the top 10 per cent of home-owners in the urban sector accounted (in the 1950s) for 57 per cent of the total wealth held in the form of owner-occupied houses and the top 20 per cent accounted for 73 per cent of the houses. This is scarcely surprising when such people are able to obtain government loans for house building or purchase. By contrast, the bottom 10 per cent owned only 1 per cent of house property (Kurien 1974: 53). The ownership of shares is even more concentrated than that of house building or property, with around 50 per cent of all private company assets being owned by the big bourgeoisie, consisting of about 75–100 business houses.

In contrast, at least 50 per cent of the urban poor and 40 per cent of the rural poor live below the poverty line, in terms of both their intake of calories and the quality of their nutrition (Dandekar and Rath 1971). There is evidence that in recent years the gap between the two ends of the economic spectrum has widened considerably and that this trend is increasing: 'The gains of development have remained largely confined to the upper middle class and the richer section constituting the top 40 per cent of the population ... the per capita consumption of the lower middle and poorer sections constituting the bottom 40 per cent of the urban population declined by as much as 15 per cent and 20 per cent' (i.e. in the two decades after independence) (Dandekar and Rath 1971). Kurien's study finds 50 per cent of the total population living below the poverty line (1974: 53).

Thus there is, at one end of the scale, a very large working class, but one which is extremely fragmented (ranging from the relatively well paid 'labour aristocracy', through those working in the informal sector, down to the lumpenproletariat), and, at the opposite end of the spectrum, a tiny but very rich and powerful bourgeoisie. In between these two classes is an intermediary 'new' middle class, very much the creation of the growth of capitalism in India, with a diversity of incomes and life-styles; poorly paid white collar workers may earn considerably less than skilled manual workers in a secure job with a big company, and the life-style of the top ranks of the middle class approximates very closely to that of the upper classes.

What must, however, be emphasized is just how small a proportion of India's population can be placed in the category of either upper or middle class. According to Sau, they constitute at most 10 per cent of the population, while the rural and urban bourgeoisie does not constitute more than 1.5 per cent (1981: 71–2). A monthly income of more than Rs 1000 per month in 1974–75 placed a household in the top 1 per cent in the country (Kurien 1974: 178).

Another point I wish to make here is that wherever the line between the classes is drawn, it has become, because of job shortages, increasingly difficult to cross in the last decade or so. Social mobility, in class terms, is almost non-existent. Furthermore, the standard of living of most working- and middle-class Indians has been eroded by inflation[1] while at the same time prices have risen considerably.

In short, then, an analysis of Indian society based upon production relations presents us with a picture of extreme inequality, and one whose polarization is increasing. Most have to struggle hard to maintain what they have, let alone improve the quality of their lives.

Women and class in India

Thus far I have sought to paint a picture of Indian society as one in which class formation is well advanced, and in which there are extreme inequalities. Both of these factors are very important. None the less, there are two lacunae in the analysis. One is that it does not give us a picture of what class *means*, of how it is formed and reproduced, nor of its cultures. The other problem is that I have said almost nothing about women and class.

In many respects, these problems are two sides of the same coin. A class analysis based primarily upon production will inevitably exclude women in a country where only a small minority of them work for pay outside the home. Although there are problems of definition with the term 'work', there does seem to be a general trend, at least until very recently, of women's declining participation in the labour force, particularly in the organized sector. In 1911, women's work participation rate was 34.4 per cent, but by 1971 it had steadily gone down to 17 per cent. Needless to say, for those women who do have jobs, their pay is much lower than that · of males.

Although there is relatively little information about women from the literature on class in India, this is not to say that there is no information from other sources. Indeed, there is no dearth of literature on the subject of women in India. Much of it is of indigenous origin. Even prior to 1975, when a torrent of new works began to appear, there had been a steady stream of publications (cf. Caplan 1979). Much of this dealt in the most general way with 'the status of women', a nebulous concept and one particularly ill-suited to understanding the lives of one half of the population of a sub-continent marked by its linguistic, religious, regional, and caste and class differences.

However, in the classic community studies carried out by anthropologists, both Indian and foreign, which began to be numerous in the 1950s and subsequent decades, women, except in their roles as wives and mothers, are conspicuous by their absence (cf. Caplan 1973). With a few exceptions, it is difficult to learn very much about women's productive role, which is considerable in the rural areas (cf. Nelson 1979). Nor do we learn much about women's political roles. The urban studies that began to emerge in the 1960s did little to redress the balance – women are viewed as members of families (Ross 1961), as 'traditional' wives of 'modernizing' husbands (Singer 1971), but rarely as workers, whether domestic or otherwise, much less as political actors, whether the context be a neighbourhood or some form of voluntary association. Nor do studies of caste or class have much to say about women; they only appear occasionally as the wives and mothers of the men on whom the studies focus.

Some have sought to explain the gaps in our anthropological knowledge about women in India by stating that it is difficult for male field-workers (and the majority are males) to achieve rapport with women, particularly in a society where segregation of the sexes is as marked as it is in most of south Asia. Others would maintain that since women are subordinate to men, they can be safely ignored in economic or political studies. Thus one noted anthropologist could remark that 'In the context of modernization in peasant India, it is usually appropriate to look at the cognitive maps of adult males' (Bailey 1971: 301). Even in 1977 it was not thought strange that another well-known scholar should publish a book on social inequality entitled *Inequality among Men* (Beteille 1977).

Although the issue is not as simple as deciding whether or not women are subordinate, or, to use the more popular term, as measuring the 'status' or 'position' of women through a number of variables, none the less, perhaps a useful way of beginning a book that deals with women in a particular section of Indian society is to compare women's situation with that of men.

Women in India

Some useful pointers can be obtained from the census figures, which have been taken in India for the past hundred years, although these need to be treated with caution.[2] Perhaps one of the most important trends to emerge from the census figures is that in India women do actually constitute a numerical minority of the population.[3] This is in contrast to most other countries where females, both because of their greater ability to survive the crucial early period of life and because of their propensity to greater longevity, usually outnumber males. In India, however, not only do men outnumber women, but census figures since the beginning of the century indicate that the proportion of women in the population has been falling steadily. The 1901 census gave a ratio of 972 females per thousand males; by 1971 this had dropped to 930. Various types of explanation for this have been offered. One would deny the validity of the figures, arguing that women tend to be under-reported in the census returns, which are usually made by males. This is, however, a grossly insufficient explanation of the declining as opposed to the consistently unfavourable ratio of women. Other explanations accept the sexual imbalance and seek to find reasons for its existence. For example, it is said that women are subjected to the risks of childbirth and maternal mortality rates are high, whereas men run no such commensurate risks, except perhaps in times of war. Another explanation is that female children are often neglected – they are not as well fed and do not receive as much medical attention as their brothers – and therefore fewer survive the early stages of life (cf. Miller 1981). Furthermore, it appears that the male rate of survival has improved considerably over the last several decades, while that of females has remained static, thus widening the gap (cf. Dandekar 1975).

It is also, argued that women suffer from neglect throughout their lives in many parts of India, particularly through the widely observed custom of sequential feeding. Women, who have usually processed and cooked the food and, in many rural areas, have also helped to grow and harvest it, eat after the men (and sometimes after the children) whatever is left over. Added to this is a very heavy burden of work, even among women officially classified as non-productive workers – food-processing (sorting, drying, winnowing, pounding), cooking (usually over dung or wood fires), fetching water, fuel, and fodder for animals, as well as caring for children and for the old or sick (cf. Nelson 1979). A recent article on work loads and nutrition in rural India suggests that the calorific needs of most women are, because of their heavy work loads, actually *greater* than those of men (Batliwala 1982).

Alongside the depressing demographic figures can be placed others such as the enormous disparity in the education of males and females (cf. Sopher 1980). In 1971, only 13 per cent of rural women and 42 per cent or urban women were literate, giving an overall female literacy rate of 18.7 per cent compared to 40 per cent of males. It is thus not surprising to find that more boys than girls go to primary school (77 per cent compared with only 62 per cent of girls) and that at the secondary level the disparity is even greater, with only 11 per cent of girls in school, compared with almost one-third of the boys.

A not dissimilar picture emerges from the statistics on employment. Among the upper castes in India the traditional norms are of female seclusion and, if possible, withdrawal from productive labour outside the household, as a sign of status. In rural areas, the women of families with large amounts of land never appear in the fields, for labourers are hired; families with smaller amounts of land may call upon women in particularly busy seasons, such as during planting or harvesting. But poor or landless families (of which there are a large proportion in Tamilnadu), whose members are obliged to work for others for a living, use the labour of both women and men and often of children too. In the urban areas, similar patterns are observable. High-caste and higher-class women are much less likely to work for pay than their lower-caste and class sisters, even though they are more likely to have received an education. Such women are likely to be married to husbands employed in the organized sector, whose wage or salary is expected to support both wife and children. In the last few years, the pay of urban middle-class males has not kept pace with inflation and there is some evidence of an increase in employment among their wives. However, women of the upper middle classes, except for a handful, usually remain outside the employment market.

Although the dominant ideological norms of both Hinduism and Islam can only be followed by the upper castes and classes, women are relegated, ideologically at least, to the domestic sphere – the private rather than the public; the reproductive rather than the productive. Women's work in this sphere, as has been frequently and forcibly pointed out, is not only unpaid, but is usually devalued too. In spite of this, a pronounced feature of recent literature on women has been to study 'modernizing' tendencies, usually through attitudinal surveys of particular categories, such as the small minority of middle-class working women and the 'role conflict' they are presumed to experience (e.g. Chakrabortty 1978; Kapur 1970; Rani 1976). Largely ignored in the literature is what middle-class women who are not employed do with their time. Some of the studies of families in urban areas (e.g. Ross 1961; A. M. Singh 1976; Vatuk 1972) do, of course, make mention of women, but it is primarily in their roles of wives and mothers, which are rarely examined in any detail. Their significance in the reproduction of the social system, their domestic labour, their biological work of reproduction, and the socialization of children is not examined in any detail, and certainly not in relation to class.

Thus in seeking to examine the relationship between class and gender in India generally, we are faced with the fact that most studies of class have been concerned primarily with production, and as a result have largely ignored women. But recent theoretical work in the west has begun to take account of this problem, and to approach class not only through a study of production, but also through that of reproduction.

Production and reproduction

'Marxists have rightly pointed out that any society must organise the production of food, clothing and shelter, but they have forgotten that it must equally organise the sexual and instinctual life of its members, and the process of human reproduction.'

(Zaretsky 1976: 134)

For example, Hindess and Hirst could state that: 'All that is required for the reproduction of the economic level is some system of social relations in which children are reared by adults' (1975: 74). This is scarcely surprising, given Marx's own summary dismissal of the reproduction of labour: 'The maintenance and reproduction of the working class is, and must ever be, a necessary condition to the production of capital. But the capitalist may safely leave its fulfilment to the labourer's instincts of self-preservation and of propagation' (1954: 537). None the less, Marx did state that reproduction has a historical and moral element, which indicates that he did not view it as entirely a 'natural' process, although he never elaborated on this in his writings.

The term 'reproduction' must be used with care, for production and reproduction take place in both the economy and the sexual system. Use values are produced and consumed in the home, just as reproduction takes place in the wider society, for example through schooling. Thus one cannot arbitrarily divide a social system into the productive sphere, which is public, and the reproductive sphere, which is domestic or private, although to some extent, of course, that is what *appears* to happen under capitalism. Furthermore, as Harris and Young point out, to substitute the categories of 'production' and 'reproduction' for men and women does not make for any greater understanding (1981: 11). In this work, as in their earlier article (Edholm, Harris, and Young 1977), these authors offer a number of definitions of the way in which the term reproduction may be used.

First, the term refers to *social reproduction*, that is the overall reproduction of a particular social formation, with its means of production and relations of production. Second, it refers to the reproduction of *labour*, which includes the sphere of biological reproduction. It is this latter meaning with which I am primarily concerned at the moment. Edholm, Harris, and Young (1977) distinguish a number of levels of reproduction of labour: (a) the reproduction of individuals within a specific class position; in other words the function of *allocation* which is carried out primarily through kinship and filiation, and in which marriage is particularly significant; (b) the reproduction of *adequately socialized labour*; this is the ideological level, and includes not only socialization within the home, but also the educational system, the mass media, and other forms of cultural production; and (c) the *material* dimension of reproduction including domestic labour, i.e. the material reproduction of labour. Third and finally, there is the process of *human or biological reproduction*, which, although it may be close to 'nature' still has to be viewed socially, for most societies that have been investigated culturally construct sexuality, fertility, and even birth itself.

This is something, of course, of which anthropologists have long been aware in their studies of pre-capitalist societies, but students of advanced societies have tended to accept the emic view that this sphere, above all others, is entirely 'natural' and that it is thus impervious to change. There is evidence that some scholars are beginning to use anthropology's insights into the nature of kinship in order to understand better the working of capitalist societies. A recent article by Bland and others at the Centre for Contemporary Cultural Studies argues that kinship is the site of biological reproduction (Bland *et al.* 1978: 156), and that 'it is precisely the economic and ideological effectivity of the family in the circuit of capitalist production and reproduction that is masked under capitalist relations and represented as unrelated to the specific demands of the capitalist mode of production' (Bland *et al.* 1978: 172). Stivens (1978, 1981), herself an anthropologist, has shown how fruitful the kind of analysis traditionally carried out in pre-capitalist societies by anthropologists, revealing kinship as having multiple and interrelated functions, can be for the study of capitalist society. Such recent work has moved beyond the earlier notion that in capitalist society kinship has no other functions than to organize and reproduce itself (e.g. Rubin 1975: 199).

Reproduction, then, like production, is seen to have a material base. Whereas for production this is the economy, in terms of reproduction it is women's sexuality, fertility, their domestic labour, and the products of all these – 'adequately socialized labour'. Some writers have in fact argued for the use of the term 'mode of reproduction', implying that reproduction too has its 'means' and its 'relations', although the latter are relations not between classes in terms of production, but between women and men (e.g. O'Brien 1981). Like the relations between classes, they are those of superordination and subordination.

The major question that arises out of all this debate is how does reproduction articulate with production? This problem has been examined in some detail by a number of authors who have looked at the position of women in advanced capitalist economies (e.g. Barrett 1980; Bland *et al.* 1978). Such women, if they are married, are seen by society primarily as housewives. They perform domestic labour for no pay, and if they work outside the home for pay, it is usually lower than the pay of their husbands. It is argued that this double subordination of women is highly func-tional for capital: women are performing unpaid labour in the home which would be extremely costly if it were paid. At the same time, the prevailing ideology states that their place is primarily in the home; it is their duty to do the housework and care for children. The primacy accorded to women's familial role results in their lesser preparedness for the job market – lower qualifica-tions, a more interrupted working career – as well as in the clustering of women in a range of 'caring' and 'servicing' occu-pations which resemble their work in the home, and all of which are low paid. This situation, however, is not thought to matter because women are also seen as dependants of a male (usually their husband) who is the bread-winner, earning a 'family wage' (cf.

Land 1980). As a result of this, women come to form part of a large industrial 'reserve army' of labour. When they are needed as workers, they are employed, albeit at lower rates of pay than men; when they are not, they go back to their homes.[4] Thus women's subordination is thought to be useful for capital, although it is widely agreed that capitalism has taken over pre-existing gender relations rather than creating new ones. The limitations of an approach of this kind are that it can become highly functionalist, and seem to offer simplistic explanations. Some authors, while seeking a relationship between production and reproduction, would argue that the latter also has its own independent dynamic, is autonomous, and may even be in contradiction with the former (e.g. Harris and Young 1981; O'Brien 1981). Others would still accord primacy 'in the last instance' to production.

Thus we must beware of accepting the emic view that there is a complete separation between the public world of production and the private world of the household. It is true that under capitalism this is what appears to happen, and yet in fact, each has important implications for the other. Indeed, it is part of the ideology of capitalism that there is a separate private sphere, uncontaminated by the public productive sphere, in which human emotions and subjectivity flourish (as Zaretsky 1976 has pointed out) and in which biological reproduction (as an entirely 'natural' process) takes place; this sphere is thought to be the province of women.

Like most ideologies, this contains both allusion to underlying reality, as well as illusion. Under capitalism the household largely ceases to be a production unit and becomes primarily a consumption unit. In most instances productive work is removed physically to another place. Thus in capitalist society there *is* a greater degree of separation between the household and the wider society than in pre-capitalist societies. Yet the household itself changes over time and in response to external pressures, i.e. it is socially constructed, as recent historical studies have shown for the west (cf. Flandrin 1979; Stone 1977). This is also the case in India (see Chapters 3 and 4).

Besides the family household, another important area of investigation in the relationship between production and reproduction is the state. For example, in Britain the systems of social security and tax payment operate on the premise that a woman is a housewife, dependent upon a male, and they act to reinforce such dependence (cf. Land 1976; Wilson 1977). Law, or the way in which it is administered, may differ considerably in its effect upon women and men (cf. Sachs 1978; Smart and Smart 1978). The state in advanced capitalist societies is also responsible for the educational system, which produces labour power with different skills, appropriate to different classes, as well as different genders (cf. David 1980).

Other reproductive activities of the state such as social welfare have also received a certain amount of theoretical and critical attention lately (cf. Ginsberg 1979; Gough 1979). It has been suggested that public welfare plays an important role in supporting capital. (Some of these arguments are discussed at greater length in Chapter 7.) However, most such works, based on western experience, tend to assume that social welfare is primarily a state activity. In less developed societies this is not necessarily the case and, even in Britain (as will be shown in Chapter 11), a very high proportion of social welfare is still carried out under voluntary auspices. In India, voluntary social welfare constitutes the bulk of such activities and most of it is in the hands of women's organizations dominated by bourgeois women.

Social welfare

Voluntary social welfare defines and mediates relations between the classes particularly effectively, for it consists largely of philanthropy carried out on behalf of the working class by the upper classes. On the one hand, the classes are defined in terms of givers and receivers of charity. On the other hand, class conflict is masked by giving, and vertical ties, which disguise the true nature of the relations between the classes, are created. Social welfare activities also enable the women of the bourgeoisie to inculcate their own ideologies of womanhood and the family into members of the lower classes. For poor women emphasis is laid on such solutions as marriage, family planning, and domestic training, rather than training in productive activities.

At certain historical moments most social welfare is voluntary and private, but with the growth of the state some of its functions are likely to be taken over. In many societies, however, the state and voluntary sectors have a complex and fluctuating relationship over time. The state may use the voluntary sector to implement its own policies, as happens in Britain. Or it may help to fund the voluntary sector, believing that in this way it is obtaining a cheaper service, as is the case in India today. Whatever the case, a good argument can be made that just as women form a reserve army of labour in productive activities, exactly the same is true of their reproductive activities in terms of welfare. Some mention of this has recently been made in comments on the effects of cutting government welfare services in the west – 'community care', as one observer acidly noted, usually means finding a woman to look after whoever it is (Barrett 1980: 232). This is then the other side of the coin – when the 'reserve army' is needed in production, then welfare services (such as day nurseries, day centres for the elderly) are made available. But when women are not needed as productive workers, they become a reserve army of productive labour but, at the same time, their reproductive tasks are increased, as geriatric wards are closed, special facilities for handicapped children withdrawn, and so on.

This view of women as a reserve army of socially reproductive labour is implied in recent works discussing the effect of cuts in welfare expenditure, but it is primarily about women as an unorganized reproductive army – women caring for others mainly in their homes. What has been ignored in the literature is the existence of a large *organized* army of carers: women in voluntary organizations. These organizations in the main continue to exist even when state provision is generous, but they flourish when there is a situation of crisis, perhaps aided by the state in a judicious mixture of some funding and a good deal of ideological input.

Women's social welfare activities, then, belong to both categories of reproduction. On the one hand, because of the way they construct class relationships, they are part of overall reproduction. On the other hand, because such activities help to produce labour power (or reserve labour power in the case of women) they are part of the reproduction of labour.

Class and gender

While much of the recent theoretical and empirical work on reproduction gives a useful framework for an analysis of Indian women's organizations, it has concentrated on the articulation between gender and class primarily in terms of the working class and the reproduction of labour power.

Some writers have claimed that it is not 'interesting' to look at the upper reaches of the class structure. McIntosh, for instance, states that since capital reproduces itself anyway, it is more useful to look at labour power and the way in which this is reproduced (1979: 153). Barrett makes a similar point: 'Unlike the reproduction of labour-power, which *depends* upon the reproduction of the living, human labourer, the reproduction of capital does not depend on individual ownership (of the means of production) in the same way' (1980: 133). She further notes, in the course of a discussion on whose interests the family-household system in western society serves, that 'It is not self-evident from Marxist theory that legitimacy and established paternity are in fact required for the reproduction of capital' (1980: 221). In other words, she appears to be arguing that the capitalist system could not continue without a supply of labour power, but it could continue without an established *capitalist class*. This obviously undermines the whole notion of a class *system*. It is, surely, just as theoretically interesting to know how capital is owned, and by whom, and what social mechanisms ensure its retention within a particular group, as it is to know how labour power is reproduced. It will be argued in this book that the bourgeoisie reproduces itself as a class, just as the working class does, and that in the work of reproduction of this class, women play a vital role. Plainly in this regard, it is necessary to look at kinship and marriage, in order to understand how people are allocated to positions in the class structure, and how boundaries are constructed and demarcated between classes. Studies of this area also help to explain the mechanisms by which ownership of private property, including capital, is transferred from one generation to another, and thus how the capitalist class perpetuates itself. The sphere of kinship and marriage also, as some anthropologists have maintained, goes a long way towards explaining how women are subordinated in most societies, since they are the objects of male exchanges in marriage.

An understanding of bourgeois women thus gives us an important insight into the way this class reproduces itself and, therefore, into the dynamics of the class system as a whole. Yet it is often in their work of reproduction of their own class that women of this level collude in their oppression as women.

Some Marxist feminist writers have dismissed the oppression of bourgeois women, seeing it (if it is conceded to exist at all) as so far removed from that of working-class women as to be of a different order altogether. However, Engels (1972) saw clearly that it was in their dependence upon men that bourgeois women were oppressed (although he contrasted this with a rather romanticized view of working-class women whom he saw as relatively emancipated by their earning capacity). Indian women of the upper classes help to create a culture that differentiates them from the working class in a number of ways, ranging from baking cakes to coaching their children in academic work. Yet such cultural production requires an ideology of female domesticity, and by maintaining such an ideology and inculcating it into their children women perpetuate their own subordination. Paradoxically, although such an ideology of domesticity may initially serve to differentiate the upper classes from the working class, it frequently comes to be imposed on the working class also, as has been well documented for Victorian England (cf. Prochaska 1980; Summers 1979; and also Chapter 10) and as is happening in India today.

It is argued here then, that it is important to look at the upper classes and to understand how they operate in order to see how the class system as a whole works. Frequently, the way in which power is maintained by a particular class is not immediately visible; the system may appear to be open and democratic, and yet plainly economic and political power remains, generation after generation, in the hands of the same small number of families, with relatively few new entrants. Why is this so? And why do the majority of people who do not benefit by such a system accept it? In the final instance, of course, it is control of the use of force which may be the explanation. But there are many steps along the way, and many other mechanisms for ensuring hegemony. It is only through examining class in terms of both its material base in production and reproduction that we can begin to answer such questions, and also what it means – how it is formed, perpetuated, and of what its culture consists.

In short then, in considering both production and reproduction we need to have regard not only to the material level, that is, economic and sexual relations, but also to the ideological. It is particularly important to understand the process by which gender identity and sexuality are socially constructed. It is obvious that approaches such as these make it impossible to ignore women, or render them invisible, and the political relations between the sexes become as important as those between classes. Such an approach is one to which anthropological techniques lend themselves well, and it also helps solve the vexed question of women's relationship to the class structure, for the creation of a culture specific to a particular class is largely the work of women.

Such an approach, indeed, which considers culture as much as production makes it quite impossible to ignore women, either empirically or theoretically. It thus begins to help us formulate a study of society which is that of the 'total ensemble of social relations entered into in the social production of existence' (Marx 1968: 184).

Notes

1 The Consumer Price Index for industrial workers (using 1960 as a base line of 100) rose from 170 in 1970–71 to 454 by January 1982 in Madras, while in Bombay over the same period it rose from 182 to 468, and the all-India index rose from 186 to 459 (*Hindustan Chamber Review*, March 1982). To some extent, those in the formal sector are protected by regular salary increases tied to the cost of living index, although it is widely recognized that this index does not reflect the true rate of inflation.

  Real wages in manufacturing industries for employees earning less than Rs 400 per month (who are over half of the total workforce) have gone down severely. Using 1961 as a baseline, real wages had gone down from 100 to 67 by 1975 (Sau 1981: 81).

2 There are good critiques of statistical techniques regarding women in Boserup 1970; Rogers 1980; and specifically for women in India in Dandekar 1975; S. D'Souza 1980; Government of India 1974; A. M. Singh 1975.

3 For a further discussion of women and demography in India cf. Bose 1975; Chen 1982; Dandekar 1975; Desai 1967; Miller 1981; Mitra 1978, 1979b; K. P. Singh 1979; Visaria 1967.

4 There is evidence, for example, that a higher proportion of women workers than men have been made unemployed in Britain in the last few years, but few of them are registered (since they cannot claim benefits) and so do not appear in the statistics (Counter Information Services 1981).

2
Background to field-work: Madras city and its women's organizations

In this chapter I consider women's organizations in Madras city and the sample of organizations studied. First, however, some background is given on two areas: the historical development of the city and its occupational structure; and the politics of caste as well as class in the city. Both these are necessary to obtain an understanding of the class and caste background of the women who were studied, and of their organizations.

Historical background[1]

Madras was established in the seventeenth century by the British East India Company. Over the next two hundred years it developed primarily as a trading centre, serving British and other European interests. Madras became more important as a centre of services and administration during the nineteenth century, particularly after the assumption of direct power in India by the Crown in 1857. By this time, the city was capital of the Madras Presidency, which covered most of south India. In the latter part of the nineteenth century it increasingly became a centre of road and rail networks, as well as being the site of a new harbour. By the end of the century, the headquarters of all important commercial firms and banks in south India were located in Madras. In addition it was recognized as the main educational centre of the area, with a university (started in 1857) and various colleges. The 1901 census revealed that Madras had a population of just over half a million and was the third largest city in India after Calcutta and Bombay. Between 1891 and 1911, the population grew by 16.5 per cent with immigration being responsible for 70 per cent of this increase. Although cotton mills were established in the city during this period, Madras was much less industrialized than the northern cities of Bombay and Calcutta. Its importance depended primarily upon trade and its locus as a seat of government. This remained the case for the rest of the colonial period. When in the immediate post-independence period the decision was made by the Indian government to place priority on industrialization, Madras was favourably situated to benefit from the policies of the Five Year Plans, being already a market centre with reasonably good lines of communication, and possessing a ready labour supply. While the pace of industrialization quickened in most Indian cities, this was particularly noticeable in Madras, with the establishment of such industries as automobiles, bicycles, machine tools, electrical equipment, railway wagons and coaches, chemicals, fertilizers, sugar, cement, leather goods, scientific equipment, and many others. As a consequence, Madras has one of the highest concentrations of engineering industry in India. The changes in the occupational structure between the 1951 and 1961 censuses are revealing: in 1951, just under a quarter of the city's workers (24.8 per cent) were engaged in manufacturing and similar industries. Ten years later, the proportion had risen to almost a third (32.6 per cent), while in the metropolitan area the proportion rose from 22.8 per cent to 31.7 per cent (Hyma 1971: 201).

In spite of the rapid industrialization it has undergone in the last few decades, Madras still retains much of its character as a collection of villages which have been gradually absorbed by the growing city. With few exceptions, high-rise buildings have not been encouraged in Madras. Some areas, like Mylapore and Triplicane, centre on their ancient temples, surrounded by crowded bazaar areas, while others still retain their spacious 'garden' houses built during the period of the Company and the Raj. Many open spaces have, however, been taken over by poor migrants to build huts. In the early 1960s it was reported that a quarter of the city's population was living in over 550 such small and large slum areas (Nambiar 1961). Ten years later, a study by the Tamilnadu Slum Clearance Board (TNSCB), a State government undertaking, showed that the proportion of slum dwellers was one-third of the city's population.

The rate of population growth in the city reflects its historical expansion. The first census of 1871 showed a population of 400,000 living within its twenty-seven square miles. By the end of the century it had increased by 25 per cent to just over half a million. Over the next forty years the population grew by a further 50 per cent (a rate of increase much lower than that of the other Presidency towns of Bombay, Calcutta, and Delhi, and one which demonstrates its lack of industrialization during that period). However, since independence the rate of growth has been much more rapid, and by 1961 the population had risen to 1.73 million, by which time the city limits had been expanded, bringing the total area to just under fifty square miles (Hyma 1971: 90). Over the next ten years the city increased by 40 per cent to 2.5 million in 1971. The latest census of 1981 reveals a further large increase of 25 per cent to 3 million persons. The growth rate in the surrounding area, which together with the city is now known as the Madras Urban Agglomeration (and contains forty-eight satellite towns in addition to the city itself), has been even higher over the last decade, at just over 33 per cent, adding a further million persons.

Much of this spectacular increase in the size of population in Madras and its surroundings is due to immigration from both rural and other urban areas in south India (cf. L. Caplan 1976). The 1961 census revealed that almost 70 per cent of migrants were from within Madras State, and that migrants at that time constituted a third of the city's residents. Over the last eighty years the percentage of urban population in Tamilnadu has increased from 14 per cent to 33 per cent; Tamilnadu is now, after Maharashtra, the second most urbanized state in the Indian Union.

The politics of caste and class in Tamilnadu

Madras has, then, over the last one hundred years, attracted a large number of different immigrants, many of whom came to seek work and/or education. A large number of those who initially came primarily for the latter purpose were Brahmins (the highest stratum in the Hindu caste system). A study in 1886 found that 73 per cent of Brahmin boys of school age were under instruction, but only 18 per cent of Vaisya and Shudra boys (cited in A. M.

Singh 1976). Similarly, Barnett states that the proportion of students at Madras University between 1870 and 1918 who were Brahmins ranged between 64 per cent and 71 per cent (1976: 20), and Bhatia notes that in 1890–91, Brahmins formed 81 per cent of the total number of students attending college (1965: 353).

Athough members of this caste have always formed a very small proportion of the population in south India – in Madras Presidency during the period of the British Raj they numbered approximately 3 per cent – none the less, from the latter part of the nineteenth century they came to dominate the government and professional sectors not only in Madras city, but in the Presidency as a whole. It was reported by the Public Service Commission in 1887 that in Madras Presidency Brahmins held 202 out of 297 posts in the executive and judicial services (quoted in Misra 1961: 322).

Even as late as the period between 1930 and 1933, Brahmins constituted almost 40 per cent of gazetted officers in Madras Presidency and over 50 per cent of the higher paid, non–gazetted officers (Barnett 1976). And although the legal profession at the senior level long remained in the hands of Europeans, the only Indians who became lawyers practising in the High Court at Madras were also Brahmins (Rudolph and Rudolph 1966).

In addition to their dominance of the civil service sector, Brahmins were among the first to become politically conscious, resenting bitterly the fact that colonial rule denied them the top-most posts in either the civil service or commercial firms, both of which were reserved for Europeans (cf. L. Caplan 1977: 199–201). They were active from the end of the nineteenth century in the Congress Party in Madras Presidency; indeed, for many, Home Rule was identified with Brahmin rule. By supporting the Congress Party and being among the most active of nationalists, the Brahmins undoubtedly consolidated their political dominance.

This Brahmin dominance did not, however, go unchallenged indefinitely. A Dravidian Association was founded during the First World War with the purpose of advancing non–Brahmin political power and establishing a Dravidian state. Although the association never really became important, it was succeeded by the South Indian Liberal Federation, commonly known as the Justice Party, which contested the elections in 1921 and won. Although the Justice Party did not remain in power for long, over the next half century various Dravidian nationalist, often anti-Brahmin, parties

contested elections, employing a populist rhetoric and using Tamil
nationalism. The party formed in 1949 under the name of Dravida
Munnetra Kazagham (DMK), which denounced the economic
hegemony of northerners and Brahmins in the economic life of
Tamilnadu and received substantial financial support from non-
Brahmin south Indian business communities (such as Chettiars and
Naidus), finally won outright in the 1967 elections, ending a
period of thirty years' domination of Tamilnadu politics by the
Congress Party.[2]

Parties that may be loosely termed 'Dravidian nationalist' (i.e.
the DMK or its off-shoot the ADMK) have thus been in power
in Tamilnadu since 1967. Congress has been further weakened by
its tendency to split, and seems unlikely to be able to come to
power again in the state.

What have been the implications of these political changes in the
last two decades? The first point to be noted is that while
Tamilnadu has had a regional party in power, the Centre, with the
exception of the brief period of Janata rule (1977–80) following the
1975–77 Emergency,[3] has continued to be governed by Congress,
which also has a majority in most states of the Union. Relations
between the central government and the Tamilnadu State governments have shown a marked unevenness, ranging from electoral
alliances between both DMK and Congress, and ADMK and
Congress at various times, to the appointment of commissions of
enquiry by the Centre to look into allegations of corruption on
the part of the Tamilnadu government.

The second point, which is important for the argument of this
book, is that many of the policies pursued by the DMK and more
latterly the ADMK governments have had important repercussions on access to jobs and education. The central government,
after independence, adopted a policy of 'positive discrimination'
for members of 'Scheduled Castes and Tribes' (mostly untouchables or Harijans, and tribal people). The Tamilnadu State government has extended this principle even further by creating a
category of 'Backward Classes' (mostly low-caste, although not
untouchable, people) who are also given a fixed proportion of
college places and state government jobs. 'Forward communities',
like Brahmins, have found it more and more difficult to get
places in colleges for their children, or government jobs for
themselves.

Although many have voiced their resentment at these policies, paradoxically, it has not necessarily led to a decrease in the economic power of the Brahmin community. For this happened at the time when, as related earlier, industrial growth was accelerating in Madras. Denied government posts, Brahmins went into industry. Their high level of education plus the know-how and skills acquired from a background of government service or the professions enabled them rapidly to achieve a strong position in this field.

The other path that Brahmins who found their way blocked in Tamilnadu State have chosen is to enter central government service – entry is by open competitive examination – where many of them occupy senior positions. A. M. Singh's study of south Indians in Delhi, for example, reveals that the majority of them are Tamil Brahmins and that 82 per cent of the adult males are in service and administrative occupations (A. M. Singh 1976).

The history of the development of Madras city thus shows a strong congruence between caste and class. In the early period it was the higher castes, and particularly the Brahmins, who formed what may be termed the 'bureauratic bourgeoisie', and it is from their ranks that most of the relatively new 'industrial bourgeoisie' have also been drawn. At the bottom end, there has been very little social mobility of the members of untouchable castes who are still concentrated in unskilled and poorly paying jobs in the city. Only in the middle ranges do the lines become more blurred. Caste politics is, to a large extent, also class politics – Congress still tends to attract a larger proportion of wealthier and educated people, and the DMK a smaller number.[4]

Women in Madras city

It is difficult to glean much information about women in Madras city. The only studies that relate specifically to women are one on white collar working mothers by the Madras School of Social Work (1970) and the work of Egnor (1977, 1980) on the religious lives of women. For further information it is necessary to go to the censuses and to the publications of the women's organizations.

From the 1981 census we learn that women in Madras city are slightly outnumbered by men (males 1,688,547; females 1,577,487) although less so than in other large Indian cities. The proportion of males to females is not purely an urban phenomenon, for it applies to the district of Chingelpattu, which surrounds Madras, and indeed to the whole of Tamilnadu State, although the ratios are much less unfavourable to women than in most of the other states of the Indian Union.

The literacy rates in Madras city are higher for both sexes than in India as a whole, but again, more favourable to men, 57 per cent of whom are literate, compared with only 34 per cent of females. Fewer girls attend educational institutions at all levels – for instance, only 39 per cent of all college students in Madras city are women.

As far as participation in the labour force of the city is concerned, women are enormously disadvantaged. Only 7 per cent of women are categorized as 'main workers' in the 1981 census, although this is an improvement on the 1971 census where only 5 per cent so qualified. In comparison, 46 per cent of males were classified as 'main workers' in the 1981 census, a slight decrease on the 1971 figure of 49 per cent. On the whole, the index in work participation for women has shown a downward trend since 1901, when 11.6 per cent of women were said to be in the labour force.

Women's organizations in Madras city

Field-work for this study was mainly carried out between summer 1974 and summer 1975 in Madras city. An initial attempt was made to survey as many women's organizations in the city as possible by contacting the Registrar of Societies and the Social Welfare Department of the Tamilnadu Government, as well as by following up leads. Contact was made with a total of fifty-three organizations. Following on this, a selection of eight organizations was made, of which five were studied very intensively and the other three less so.

It is not easy to give a precise total of the number of women's organizations in Madras city. When I arrived to begin field-work in 1974 I used the register held by the Registrar of Societies which listed seventy-four organizations calling themselves women's associations (using such terms as *mahila sangam* or *mahalir mandram*). On checking some of these it became apparent that the list did not cover all organizations, but only those that had registered themselves. Many organizations had become defunct since registration.

An attempt was also made to survey women's organizations through the Directorate of Women's Welfare, which proved useful. However, their contacts were primarily with women's associations that carried out social welfare work. Their list yielded about forty such organizations. Here, however, a definitional problem arises. What exactly is a women's organization? On the one hand, there are organizations of women which may be set up to carry out social welfare for children or the handicapped, that is, not necessarily for women. On the other hand, there are organizations with mixed-sex membership whose primary purpose is to provide social welfare services for women. Both types may be called women's organizations.

On my return in 1981 I came across another useful source of information: the *Directory of Social Welfare Services in India* (CSWB 1978a). The two volumes for Tamilnadu list several hundred social welfare organizations, of which sixty are in Madras city. Twenty-four of these are women's organizations in the sense that they are run by women (including several run by orders of Catholic nuns), but they often cater for males as well as females (e.g. orphanages for children). Seventeen organizations cater specifically for women, but some of these have members and officers of both sexes, as for example the 'rescue home' run by the Vigilance Association whose chief officer is a man.

During the course of my initial surveying in 1974 I made contact with fifty-three agencies, which fall into the following categories:

Table 1 *Categories of women's organizations in Madras city, 1974–75*

1 women's welfare (including voluntary institutions)	14
2 working women's associations	5
3 communal (caste or regional) women's associations	3
4 political organizations	6
5 religious associations	3
6 women's counterparts to male organizations	6
7 mixed-sex associations for women's welfare	6
8 neighbourhood associations	10
total	53

In addition, there are numerous more or less informal women's groups, some centred on particular temples, others on neighbourhoods. Many consist of groups of women who meet once or twice weekly to sing *bhajans* (devotional songs);[5] others carry out certain charitable work, such as a group of women who attended a particular temple on certain important days of the month and who also collected money to buy 'poor and deserving brides' a *tali* (marriage necklace).

Many such associations are highly ephemeral and do not bother to register themselves, so that their existence is difficult to track down. However, they must be extremely numerous, because in virtually all the suburbs with which I was in contact such groups are in existence.

Organizations can be divided not only according to their aims and functions but by other criteria too. One of the most important of these is language. Almost all associations use either English or Tamil, except for the communal ones which use such languages as Hindi. Generally speaking, most of the city-wide associations concerned with social welfare use English, as do the professional women's associations and the women's counterpart associations. These organizations attract the top socio-economic stratum, whose members are fluent in the language having generally attended English-medium schools. Neighbourhood organizations, on the other hand, as well as the political and religious organizations, tend to use Tamil. These organizations often attract women who come from a slightly lower class level (i.e. the middle rather than the upper classes), and not all of them are necessarily quite so fluent in English, although most have a good working knowledge of it.

Thus language to a large extent coincides with class. It is also the English-medium, city-wide organizations that tend to have overlapping membership; their officers and committee members are part of a small elite which shares many ties in the city. Most of these people know each other personally and belong to the same set of prestigious recreational clubs. Their husbands interact in their jobs and their children attend the same small range of elite schools and colleges.

By the time I returned in 1981–82, a number of new organizations had been formed, including a Women Doctors' Association. Two new organizations which were particularly interesting were the Working Women's Forum (cf. Jeffers 1981), a credit union modelled on SEWA in Ahmedabad (cf. Jain 1975, 1980) and Penn Urimai Iyakkam, a women's liberation organization. Both had memberships mainly of working-class women but were organized by upper middle-class women. The former worked primarily with petty traders and producers, such as street and market vendors; the latter campaigned around such issues as liquor shops, organizing women construction workers, consumer issues (prices and ration shops), and rape, particularly in police custody. It was at that stage too early to make any assessment of the impact of such organizations on the existing 'establishment' women's organizations with which this book is concerned, but it seems likely, from what has happened in Delhi and Bombay, that more radical women's organizations are likely to be formed and to attract support in Madras. Furthermore, issues such as rape and 'dowry deaths', as well as obscenity in films, were issues which the establishment women's organizations were beginning to talk about.

The sample of organizations and their members

The organizations studied intensively were as follows.

The Institute for Women   An organization founded soon after independence, with its own premises on which took place various classes, a dispensary, and a nursery school. Approximately half of the active members were interviewed – a total of thirty-six women.

The Housewives' Association   A charitable organization that collected money for various worthy causes and later established a residential institution. Just under half of the members were interviewed – forty-nine women.

The Neighbourhood Club   This was situated in a suburb close to where I lived and all the members were interviewed, a total of sixty women.

The Wives' Auxiliary Association   Counterpart of a men's international 'service' organization. All fifteen members were interviewed.

The Professional Women's Association   Also a branch of an international 'service' organization, with a total of seventeen members, all of whom were interviewed.

The organizations which were studied less intensively consisted of two more professional women's associations and one for women graduates, most of whom were also professionals: from these three organizations data on another forty-nine professional women were obtained.

I became a member of all the five intensively studied organizations, attended almost all of their meetings over the 14-month period, read their minutes, annual reports, and any other available data, and interviewed many of their members in their own homes. From this interviewing I was able to gather information on household composition, educational level of respondents, their parents, husbands, and children, occupations, income consumption patterns, marriage practices, standard of living, domestic division of labour, friendship patterns, leisure activities, membership of other associations, and religious activities. Furthermore, I attended various rituals, such as weddings and sacred thread investitures, went on visits to temples, and spent time just talking in people's houses. In addition, selected persons kept diaries or prepared detailed household budgets, while others met regularly in a small group to discuss various topics; these discussions were tape-recorded and transcribed.

The second set of organizations was studied chiefly through the use of questionnaires administered by a research assistant; some of the meetings of these associations were also attended by one or both of us.

In addition to studying organization members, a complete census was made of the neighbourhood women's club's locality. Women in a further seventy-four households who did not belong to the club were interviewed, although this data is not included in the statistical material in this book unless specifically stated. In addition to members, I also interviewed employees of the organizations. What I neglected to do during that period was to gather information about people who used the services provided by the organizations – parents of creche children, dispensary patients, women who came for classes, and so on. Fortunately, I was able to return to the field again in the summer of 1981 and one of the major purposes of this re-visit was to gather more data in this area. The second purpose of my re-visit was to see what had happened to the organizations in the interim. By this time I was also interested in the political economy of women's organizations, and was able to gather a good deal of material on the relationship between the central government, state government, and voluntary sector over a period of several decades which enabled me to put my own empirical material, which is primarily of the micro variety, into a wider context.

There are two main types of women in the total sample. First, there are those who are primarily housewives who do not work outside the home and who are members of the first four organizations listed above – a total of 160 women. Second, there are 66 professional women belonging to four other associations.

In the first category of 'housewives', the vast majority of women are married and almost all have children. In the other category of professional women around half are unmarried. The occupations of the husbands of all married women, whether housewives or professionals, are prestigious and well paid. The husbands include senior civil servants, managers in public and private industry, professionals such as doctors and lawyers, and men owning their own medium to large businesses; such men are highly educated, at least to degree level. The professional women themselves tend to be drawn from a narrower range of occupations, with teaching at a senior level (secondary school heads or college lecturers), medicine, and law the most highly represented; other women are government servants, social workers, bankers, and businesswomen. All these women have degrees and many are postgraduates.

The housewives too tend to be well educated; almost three-quarters are matriculates and around a third hold degrees, although younger women are more likely to have a degree than older ones.

I have termed these families either upper middle or upper class. In upper-class households, the chief earners are owners or directors of medium to large companies and very senior government servants (including such professionals as judges), while in upper-middle-class households they are engaged in such occupations as the professions (law, medicine), government service, banking, and middle-level management in business and industry. Generally speaking, the income of upper-class families at the time of field-work in 1974–75 would be at least Rs 2,000 per month net (over £100) while the income of upper-middle-class families ranged from Rs 1,000 to 2,000 per month.

The upper middle and upper classes in Madras are a very small proportion of the population. Many of them are Brahmins, whose representation at this class level is totally disproportionate to their numbers (about 3 per cent) in the population as a whole. Thus a striking characteristic of the members of both the housewives' and the professional women's organizations is the predominance of Brahmins among them. For the housewives' organizations, Brahmins constitute an absolute majority of over 60 per cent, while for professional women they constitute over 30 per cent, the largest single category. High-caste non-Brahmins of Tamilnadu origin tend to be few in numbers in both categories, but high-caste women from other states in southern India, particularly Kerala and Andhra Pradesh, are particularly numerous among professionals, ranking almost as high as Brahmins (35 per cent). In my sample there are also women of north Indian origin, almost all of whom belong to the Women's Auxiliary Organization; there are very few north Indians in the other organizations. Low-caste, untouchable, and tribal women are hardly represented in the sample at all; this is not surprising given the near perfect correlation of class and caste at this level.

Joiners and non-joiners

A frequent finding in both British and American studies which take account of voluntary organization membership is that the higher the social status of the respondent, the more likely that person is to belong to a voluntary organization. In many respects, my data from Madras do not contradict this view (cf. also Driver and Driver 1982). Although it is difficult to obtain a complete picture of how typical or atypical are the women who join voluntary organizations, some indications do emerge from my census of the whole of the suburb in which the Neighbourhood Club was located (cf. P. Caplan 1980). Here the households were (in 1974–75) almost equally divided into joiners and non-joiners, with just under half (60 out of 134) represented in club membership.

Brahmins were much more likely to join the club (over half the 'joiner' households were Brahmins), whereas only one-third of 'non-joiner' households fell into this category. 'Joiner' women also tended to come from households where the educational level of both themselves and their husbands was higher than for the non-joiner category. Sixty per cent of joiner women had received higher education, compared with only 30 per cent of non-joiner women. The difference in the educational level of husbands was also significant, although somewhat less marked – 95 per cent of joiners' husbands had had a higher education, compared with only 80 per cent for non-joiners. Although the husbands did not differ very greatly in the kind of work they did, the households of the joiners appeared to have a higher income and standard of living: joiners were more likely to live in owner-occupied accommodation, and their houses were slightly larger. Joiners had more servants per household (an average of 1.5 each, compared with only one for non-joiners), and over 70 per cent of joiners' households had cars, compared with only 50 per cent of non-joiner households.

There were other differences too between joiners and non-joiners: the latter were likely to have more children (3.24 each) compared with the former (2.5 each), and to live in larger households, not only for that reason, but also because they were more likely to be living in a joint family household. It is not surprising to find that women with more household commitments and fewer servants gave their main reason for not joining the club as 'lack of time'.

The chief factors, then, that would seem to predispose a woman to joining a women's association are sufficient time and money, which are linked to her own and her husband's educational level, and, in the case of women in Madras, her caste background.

In this context it is not unimportant that the women's organizations are not only middle and upper class in their membership, but that they also tend to be heavily Brahmin-dominated, and politically supportive of the Congress Party. In many respects they serve as a vehicle for a minority community, which was once dominant but is now eclipsed numerically and politically, to continue to wield a certain kind of power. In short, then, caste is an important political dimension of a study of women's organizations, as well as class.

Notes

1 For further information on the history of Madras, cf. Hyma 1971; Lanchester 1918; Lewandowski 1980; Ranson 1938.
2 For further information on the rise of the DMK see Hardgrave 1965; Irschik 1969; Rudolph 1961; Spratt 1970. For more recent events see Forrester 1976.
3 Emergency rule was imposed on the country by Mrs Gandhi's govern-

ment in 1975, on the grounds that there were both internal and external threats to the country. The chief precipitating factor seems to have been the impending court case against her for misuse of election funds. The state of emergency lasted for two years, at the end of which elections were called and her government was decisively defeated, only to be re-elected in 1980.

4 Barnett's 1976 study reveals that 13 per cent of DMK leaders had incomes of less than Rs 500 (£30) per annum compared to 0.8 per cent of Congress leaders; at the opposite end of the scale, only 1.5 per cent of DMK leaders had incomes in excess of Rs 10,000 (£600) per annum, while 15 per cent of Congress leaders fell into that category. A similar pattern emerges for education: more than 20 per cent of Congress leaders are educated up to degree level or beyond, but only 0.9 per cent of DMK leaders have a degree (Barnett 1976: 193, 198).

5 In his article on Radha-Krishna *bhajans* of Madras city, Singer (1971) does not mention the existence of women's *bhajan* groups at all. The impression given by his article is that these are groups for men. Certainly at the level of upper middle and upper classes I would estimate that women's *bhajan* groups are far more numerous than those for men.

PART TWO

THE WOMEN

3
A woman's life cycle

This and the following chapter are concerned with women's role in the reproduction of the labour force, in human reproduction, and in the production of a culture specific to a particular class. In them I look at the domestic lives of the members of the four organizations composed of women who define themselves primarily as 'housewives', that is who do not engage in paid labour outside the home. Such a group is not, of course, a random sample. None the less, a study of their domestic lives does give an insight into the lives of women of the higher class levels in Madras city.

In this chapter I consider a woman's life cycle, from birth to death, including marriage, relations between husband and wife, motherhood, and old age.

Childhood and adolescence

In south India it is customary for a woman to return to her natal family when she gives birth, particularly for the first child. For this reason, many respondents had been born in areas different from those in which they subsequently grew up. Even then they did not usually remain as children living in one place, particularly those in the younger age group whose fathers were likely to have been employed in 'modern' occupations and who therefore moved every time the father was posted to a different area.

Only a third of my respondents had spent their early childhood in Madras. In general, the older women in their late forties and fifties were less likely to have done so than younger women in their thirties. The majority of them had grown up in other parts of Tamilnadu, sometimes in villages, but more often in small towns and district capitals.

Although a large number of respondents' fathers were in government service, and thus liable to be posted to different areas, they still retained links with their father's 'native place' (*sonda ur*), where the family might own lands and have its temple. Among the older women, particularly the Brahmins, between a quarter and a third stated that their family still owned rural land. Other fathers had their own businesses or else practised law, again especially if they were Brahmins, who (as already stated) had a virtual monopoly of the legal profession in Tamilnadu during the period of British rule (cf. Rudolph and Rudolph 1966; and Sastri's 1972 biography of Srinivasa Iyengar).

Almost all the respondents had attended school, although a small minority of elderly women had been tutored at home. This was common among the wealthy classes early in the century, a time when there were very few girls' schools, and all of them were run by missionaries; for this reason orthodox parents were reluctant to send their daughters to school.

Thus the standard of formal education varies very much depending on age – younger women are much more likely not only to have completed matriculation, but to have attended college, whereas even those older women who did go to school rarely continued their education afterwards. Another important factor is caste background, for Brahmins are much more likely to have received a college education than their non-Brahmin sisters.

Almost all the private schools in south India were and continue to be single sex establishments, and this also applies to institutions of higher education. It is thought to be improper for boys and girls to mix together freely, as it might lead to undesirable liaisons which would interfere with the pattern of arranged marriages.

An important event in the life of a south Indian girl is her first menstruation or her 'coming of age' (*chaddangu*) as it is known. In earlier days, for a high-caste girl this would soon be followed by the consummation of her marriage (the ceremony itself having taken place earlier) but this is now rarely the case for the urban middle classes. Few girls, even today, are prepared for menstruation, as it is thought that the less they know about any matters pertaining to sex, the better. A young woman in her early twenties, with a degree, and daughter of parents both of whom also had degrees, told me 'When my first period started, I didn't know what had happened. I was really frightened and ran crying to my mother.' This event is, however, soon made public knowledge, for often the family distributes sweets to relatives, friends, and neighbours to announce the news, and the girl herself is presented with a new set of clothes in a ritual termed *poopunirattudal* (cf. Reynolds 1980).

From then on, the girl has to observe two forms of restriction. One is that during her monthly period she is considered ritually impure and, in many families, may not enter the kitchen either in her own house or anywhere else (cf. Ferro-Luzzi 1974; Krygier 1982). In addition, considerable restrictions are placed on her behaviour, for it is considered that she is now an adult and circumspection in her behaviour is vital for both her own and her family's reputation. Girls are not allowed out in the evenings, unless with suitable adult chaperons, and can only go out on legitimate business – to college for example. Parents display great anxiety about a daughter, whom they regard as in need of protection, for the slightest breath of scandal can spoil not only her own marriage prospects, but also those of her sisters and brothers.

Marriage

Marriage is almost a universal norm in Indian society, and these urban middle- and upper-class families are no exception. There are various reasons for this – one is the fact that most women are economically dependent and therefore could not choose to remain unmarried, except in the case of a very tiny minority who are discussed in Chapter 5. The ideology of female sexuality in Hinduism is a complex one, but basically it is believed that a woman's sexuality is dangerous unless it is controlled by a male (cf. Allen 1982; Fuller 1980; Wadley 1975, 1980). Women's power (*sakti*) must be 'tamed' and then channelled into useful purposes, namely the bearing of children, particularly sons.

Earlier in the century and in preceding centuries, such an ideology led to the phenomenon of extremely early marriage for women (cf. Forbes 1979a), especially among Brahmins and to some extent among other high castes, where it was thought a sin for a girl to be unmarried at the time of her first menstruation (although marriage was rarely consummated until afterwards). However, by the early days of independence the climate of opinion had changed, and it was considered reprehensible at this class level to marry off a daughter before she had completed her schooling. Today, few girls marry before finishing their BA degree at the age of twenty. There is in fact a clear rise in the age of marriage. Women aged fifty and above had an average marriage age of sixteen, whereas those whose average age is ten years younger had married at eighteen or nineteen, and their daughters, many of whom were getting married at the time of my re-visit in 1981, were all above twenty at the time of marriage.

Marriage in Indian society is considered to be the responsibility of the parents, and many of them find it weighty indeed. The vast majority of the marriages of my respondents were arranged, although a small minority of 'love' marriages – around 7 per cent – had taken place; the lowest proportion of such marriages was among older women and the highest among the youngest. Love marriages are thought to be highly dangerous – they imply that the behaviour of the couple had not been circumspect, or they could not have got to know one another in the first place. They usually provoke considerable parental disapproval. Given the norms of extended family support in south India, if a couple marries in defiance of their families and has support withdrawn, it is very difficult for them to manage alone. Without emotional, financial, and other help, the marriage may founder, thus providing yet another dire example to romantic young people that 'arranged marriages are best – love marriages just don't work'.

Most Indian girls of this class do not in fact rebel against the norm of arranged marriages. In a survey carried out at one of the leading women's colleges in Madras in 1975, the vast majority of young women said that they expected and wanted to make arranged marriages. Many writers (cf. Roy 1975a) have commented that this phenomenon results in a situation of relative lack of anxiety for young women – it is not their job to find themselves husbands. For this reason they can concentrate far more on their studies, and many do outstandingly well.

It is true that young Indian women do not continually have to worry about dating or whether they are being 'a success', and, since they are not usually educated with boys, about playing down their abilities in order to fit in with stereotypes of being a popular girl (cf. Sharpe 1976 writing on Britain). None the less, marriage does occasion anxieties if a girl does not fit in with certain require-ments − if she is dark-complexioned, for example, or even if she wears glasses − and particularly if she knows that her parents are going to find it difficult to put a suitable dowry together.

Marriage patterns are very different in north and south India. In the north, clan and village exogamy is the rule, and women usually face their early days of married life among complete strangers. In south India, however, there are various preferential forms of marriage between relatives − either between cross-cousins or else a woman may marry her mother's younger brother (cf. Good 1980). Such marriages are possible in a number of south Indian castes: Brahmins most frequently, but also Vellalas, Mudaliars, and Nadars. In my sample, 30 per cent of women were married to men already related to them including eight to their mothers' younger brothers. Informants often felt defensive about uncle−niece marriage practices and sometimes condemned them by asserting that 'of course, nowadays we wouldn't do that', being aware that both north Indians and Europeans consider such prac-tices incestuous. Even so, I came across several cases of such marriages being arranged in 1981.

Marriages with relatives do not, of course, mean that they are exclusively arranged as opposed to love marriages. In several instances women told me that they had fallen in love with a cousin or an uncle and persuaded their parents to go through the formali-ties of 'arranging' the marriage. Given the fact that the only men with whom young women come into contact are relatives, it is not surprising that they sometimes form romantic attachments to them.

Marriages that take place outside the family are arranged in a variety of ways, but generally speaking, it is the responsibility of the girls' parents to initiate negotiations. Fathers and mothers are always on the look-out for a likely match for their daughters. When they consider a daughter is ready for marriage they dis-creetly spread the word among their relatives and friends, who may be able to suggest 'suitable parties'. Initial enquiries are about the 'boy's' occupation, salary, and prospects, as well as his family and his height (he must be taller than his wife); whereas for the girl, her complexion (fairness is highly prized), height, education, and accomplishments are considered important. In the vast majority of cases, horoscopes are exchanged at an early point and if they do not agree negotiations are broken off. If matters look favourable, the two sets of parents meet for a discussion at the house of the girl, who is usually introduced. Then, if all goes well, a 'girl-viewing' is arranged, when the prospective groom, his parents, and perhaps brothers or sisters come to 'see' the girl. It is a considerable ordeal for both parties, but more particularly so for the girl. This is how one Brahmin girl, who was fortunate enough only to have to go through it once, described the occasion:

> 'The boy came with his brother and brother's wife, his sister, and one classificatory brother [this boy's father was dead, and his mother, as a widow, could have only minimal involvement with a wedding]. I had to do *namaskaram* [prostration] to their feet, to greet them as my elders. I sang for them [since she had vocal training], and they gave me a blouse piece and some betel nut. The singing and the greeting gave them a good chance to look at me. I didn't speak to him. I felt very nervous. I think he was also nervous – he was sitting so rigidly. When he was leaving, I watched (through the window) to see how tall he was. The women folk had said there and then that they liked me, but he wouldn't commit himself until he'd spoken to his mother, and got her formal consent [this was a mark of respect to her].'

On this occasion, all went well, and the boy agreed to the match. The girl herself had resolved to abide by her parents' choice, although she had earlier specified certain requirements – that she wanted to live in a rural joint family – which her parents duly took into account.

Some families consider themselves more 'modern' and arrange a 'girl-viewing' in a restaurant. One of my informants described how her marriage had been arranged.

> 'I told my father "If you like the boy, I don't need to see him," but my father replied that the boy wanted to see *me*! We had tea at 4 p.m. in one of the big hotels in town (he wanted to see me in daylight!). I went with my parents, he went with his two sisters. They made us sit together. He

asked me a few things and I replied. Then he asked me to go and see an exhibition which was showing in that hotel; I knew this was an excuse to get me alone. We talked a bit, and we both came back smiling. He ordered more tea – and my father knew that it was OK!'

Other girls are less fortunate. One woman, now in her forties, told me bitterly that she had been subjected to no less than twenty-five 'girl-viewings' and been rejected each time 'because I was a little bit dark'. She finally married a man of her own choosing. But in other cases if no suitable match can be found through the usual channels, then resort may be had to newspaper advertisements. Many Indian papers have a matrimonial column carrying advertisements from the families of both boys and girls, and also a column for exchange marriages (i.e. brother and sister marrying brother and sister). Essential information is given in the advertisements, such as caste and sub-caste, educational level, occupation and salary (boy) and looks and character (girl), and sometimes an indirect mention of dowry expectations.

The subject of dowry is an extremely important one and merits some discussion. Although the giving and taking of dowry has been illegal in India for many years, there are few marraiges among the middle and upper classes that take place without it, and even castes which formerly gave bridewealth have in the last few years switched to dowry. On several occasions I participated in discussions on dowry, and the following extracts from a taped conversation in 1975 help to explain the varieties of situation, and the ways in which it is changing.

BRAHMIN WOMAN

'In our caste, the girl's side has to give dowry to the bridegroom. If she comes from a rich family, the groom's party will demand something like Rs 8–10,000 in cash, and perhaps a car, or a house. It depends upon the boy's education and all that [i.e. his career prospects]. If he is like my husband, who has a PhD and has been abroad, then it will be a great deal – even in 1955 at the time of my marriage, we had to give Rs 5–6,000 in cash, and then the diamonds and other jewellery [for the bride] which cost between Rs 15,000 and

Rs 20,000. All of that was without the marriage expenses. Then we had to arrange for the marriage celebration which cost around Rs 30,000 for feeding the guests, and for hiring performers to entertain the bridegroom's party. The groom's mother will ask for a pair of diamond earrings [for herself] and a diamond ring for the bridegroom, and a suit for him, costing Rs 1,000 or more, and then saris for the groom's mother and his sisters.

'In a recent marriage in our family, instead of giving cash, they gave a Fiat car, which cost Rs 18,000. If you give cash to the groom's parents, then they say it is to cover *their* expenses – in fact the groom's side won't spend more than Rs 3–4,000, and they pocket the rest.'

KALLAR (NON-BRAHMIN) WOMAN

'In our community the groom has to give money, or he won't get a bride. It is the groom's party which celebrates the marriage, although the custom is changing now, and expenses are more likely to fall on the bride's parents. Nowadays, the bride's parents are even willing to pay dowry (to get a suitable match), but even if they do, we still feel that we must receive something from the groom's side, otherwise it is a disgrace. And in the villages, still the payments all come from the groom's side – the money and the wedding expenses. The only expense for the bride's side is after the marriage, when at the Pongal (new rice) festival, the bride's father has to give vessels, saris, and a year's supply of food. But only for the first year.

'The reason why things are changing in our community is that it is very difficult to get educated bridegrooms, so doctors, teachers and other occupations each have their price.'

MUDALIAR (NON-BRAHMIN) WOMAN

'In our community, we don't have to pay any cash. The bridegroom's side gives the bride some jewels and a sari, but the bride's parents have to provide jewels, clothes, cooking vessels, furniture, and in addition, bear the expenses of the wedding. In the case of my daughter who is getting married now, we have to give her a pair of diamond earrings, a gold necklace, and several pairs of bangles. She is highly educated and has a job as lecturer. Then after she is married, the first Pongal and Deepavali festivals, we have to give cooking vessels and other gifts to her – this goes on until the first child is born, and on that occasion, we have to give the groom a ring.'

Here we have a number of strands which must be disentangled. First, among high castes we have the traditional form of dowry – *stridhanam* – which consists of gifts, mainly in the form of gold jewellery, given by the parents to the bride. This has been regarded by some as a form of pre-mortem inheritance (cf. Goody 1976), and is widely thought in India to represent a woman's security (cf. Jacobson 1976). Even so, nowadays the amount of jewellery given to a bride is usually determined more by the groom's family than by the bride's. A Brahmin woman who married in 1975 told me 'My mother-in-law said that all her daughters-in-law had jewellery worth 70 sovereigns [then worth £6,000], so I must have the same, so my father had to get it for me.' The bride's jewellery remains her inalienable property, which she will only sell in case of dire need, although she may later give some to her daughter on the occasion of her marriage. Likewise the cooking vessels, usually made of stainless steel or sometimes in a rich family of silver, are given by her parents to the bride, and remain her property.

The second element that must be distinguished is the cash (or sometimes car, house, or trip abroad) that also goes from the bride's side to the groom's. It is this people mean when they speak of the 'social evil' of dowry, which is much discussed in the Indian press and preached against on many public occasions. In fact, this form of dowry might more appropriately be described (following L. Caplan 1984) as 'groom-price', with a price tag on each occupation. The parents of brides feel that they must agree to pay this to get their daughter 'well settled', while the parents of grooms argue that they have spent lavishly on their son's education and since he is now going to support his wife well, they should be recompensed – in any case, it is argued, they had to pay out dowry to get their daughters married, so why shouldn't they receive in return when their sons marry?

The payment of large cash or kind amounts to the groom's family has undoubtedly increased in recent years – in terms of both the amounts demanded and given and the numbers of sub-castes observing this practice. The Kallar woman informant shows clearly that such a form of dowry (groom-price) is an innovation in her community and is primarily an urban phenomenon. In the case of the Mudaliar woman, her daughters are all highly educated and earning, and she has not attempted to try and make matches with very 'desirable' grooms such as IAS (Indian Administrative Service) officers, who command a huge amount. For this reason she has not paid this form of dowry, only the traditional *stridhanam*. She does however speak feelingly of the continuing obligation of a bride's parents to continue to provide even after the marriage.

What is often problematic is that expectations shift over time. The parties may come to an agreement on the financial transactions in the early stages, only to disagree later, when the groom's side makes extra demands, or the bride's side finds itself unable to fulfil its commitments. If matters have gone too far the marriage takes place anyway, but it may leave a great deal of rancour.

The new forms of dowry have to be considered in context. They are primarily an urban phenomenon and are very much tied in to class formation. Parents buy their daughter's way into a family of suitable status, as determined by her husband's occupation and income level. In their anxiety to see their daughter 'well settled', many parents bankrupt themselves, for the rapid rate of inflation in dowry of all kinds means that calculations made when a girl was young rarely prove sufficient when she is of marriageable age. One woman, mother of five daughters, said that she had saved what she thought would be enough to marry them all off. In the event the money was only enough for the first three, and the remaining two had to earn part of their own dowry.

If all the negotiations prove satisfactory and the 'girl-viewing' goes well, the betrothal follows shortly afterwards. Even once engaged, few girls have much contact with their fiancés. They may perhaps be allowed to write to each other, but it is extremely rare for them to be allowed to go out together. In any case, the marriage usually follows soon after the engagement.

Marriage (appropriately termed a 'potlach' by Hanchett (1975)) is an elaborate and expensive affair, as the following account of wedding arrangements in 1975 in a middle-class, non-Brahmin family shows:

'Now we have to book a *Kalyana mandapam* [marriage hall] which will cost around Rs 1,500, and then nowadays, they don't just want a reception in the evening, they want music too. We said we could afford Rs 250 for a Carnatic music performance but they wanted a well-known light music group which costs Rs 750 – finally they agreed to pay the difference themselves. Then we have to pay the cook – he wants Rs 600 for two days' work, and to buy the food. I've bought a diamond ring for the groom which cost me Rs 700 and we have to give him a suit.

'Later, the bridegroom's side gives a reception for us – but by that time, most of the crowd will have gone away and only a few people will be there, so the expense isn't very great, not like the wedding proper with 800–1,000 people. Their only other expense is to buy a sari and some gold jewellery for the bride at the time of the betrothal.'

The number of guests at a marriage is rarely less than a thousand, even in the case of a fairly modest one, such as that just described. The proceedings last for thirty-six hours, beginning with a ceremony of blessing in the evening and the marriage itself early the following morning at an auspicious hour determined by the astrologers. The essential elements of a clean caste Hindu marriage are the 'giving of the bride' (*kanyadan*) by her father, the exchange of garlands between bride and groom, the tying of the *tali* around the neck of the bride by the groom, and the seven steps around the holy fire by the bride and groom with their clothes tied together. Different castes have various other embellishments, but the central elements are always present, and the ritual is conducted by Brahmin priests. The ritual emphasizes that marriage is a sacrament (not a contract) and is indissoluble.

Marriage changes the status of a couple greatly. The 'boy' becomes a man, while the girl becomes an 'auspicious' person – a married woman (*sumangali*) (cf. Reynolds 1980). As a symbol of her auspiciousness she wears not only the forehead mark (*pottu*) but also the red *kumkum* (powder) in the parting of her hair and diamond earrings; these diacritical signs clearly proclaim her marital status.

Relations between husband and wife

Immediately after the marriage, it is common nowadays for the couple to go away for a short honeymoon together. This may be the first occasion on which they have been alone, for the formal 'girl-viewing' and equally formal visits during engagement do not allow much privacy or a chance to get to know one another. Soon after the marriage, the couple begins a series of semi-formal visits to relatives, beginning with the bride's family, after which the bride's parents also visit the groom's family. After this round of visiting is over, the bride usually returns to spend some time with her parents before finally joining her husband's household.

The majority of young women who undergo arranged marriages are very ready to fall in love with their husbands. They are like the Bengali women so sensitively described by Manisha Roy (1975b) who read romantic novels and see films and dream of the 'ideal man' they will marry. Yet this romanticism is always tinged with a certain levelheadedness – young women are often quite clear about the kinds of families they want to live in (specifying a preference for either nuclear or joint) and often about their husband's occupation too. One woman told me 'I don't want an engineer, their promotion is too slow, but we don't mind a doctor, or an officer [i.e. a senior government servant, such as IAS].'

The type of occupation followed by males of this class level in Madras has shifted over the last several decades, as *Table 2* shows.

Table 2 *Occupations of respondents' husbands' fathers, fathers, and husbands compared*

Occupation	1 husband's father %	2 father %	3 husband %
own business	18.8	23.10	27.8
government service	30.0	17.95	15.8
law	13.7	25.64	9.8
industry	6.8	6.00	31.6
bank	0	2.56	3.0
landlord	17.1	8.55	0
medicine	6.84	8.55	9.0
army/police	4.27	4.27	1.5
teacher/lecturer	2.56	3.42	1.5
total	100.00	100.00	100.00

It should be noted that husbands' fathers will tend on average to be somewhat older than respondents' own fathers, owing to the earlier age of marriage of women, and also to the fact that men do not usually marry until all their sisters are married. Thus for most occupations, the greatest contrasts are between columns 1 and 3 in *Table 2*. Almost a third of husbands' fathers were engaged in government service, and a substantial proportion of them were rural landlords. But the proportion of husbands engaged in government service has dropped by a half, none of them is a landlord, and almost one-third are employed in industries; the proportion of those engaged in their own businesses has also risen. A generation ago, the largest participants in the 'modern' sector were Brahmins, whereas now members of all communities are involved. It is also now rarer to find men listing their sole occupation as 'landlord'.

To a large extent, the type of occupation engaged in by the husband determines the family's life-style in a number of respects. First, most household income comes from this source. Very few women work outside the home for pay, although a small number find ways of making money from within the home. One woman, for instance, had bought a big electric mixer, and for a small remuneration used to grind her friends' batter for *dosai* (rice pancakes) or *iddly* (rice cakes). Another made fruit juice, and a third fancy candles. Women who engage in such activities say it is largely because they find it very difficult to maintain the extremely high standard of living expected of them on their husband's pay, relatively good as it is. One IAS officer's wife, who made handicrafts to sell, told me 'You have no idea how problematic it is. We are always overdrawn at the bank. People expect IAS officers to have a lavish life-style, but in fact they don't get paid that much. My little contribution helps quite a bit; my husband was reluctant at first, and I had to get government permission (as a government servant's wife), but then he agreed.' Women themselves usually understand perfectly the reasons for such petty enterprise and, far from condemning it as a loss of face, are often envious and admiring of the few who manage to find the time, skill, and capital to conduct such activities.

The second way in which the husband's career determines life-style is his degree of mobility. Government servants, for instance, are subjected to frequent transfers. Often when the children's schooling becomes an important factor, the wife remains with the children in the city while the husband works away from home. In such circumstances, the wife's responsibilities are greater than if the husband is present to share them. Even husbands who are not transferred often may work long hours, and have to undertake business trips if they work in industry or commerce. Women whose husbands are in this category do not see a great deal of them and also make most of the day-to-day decisions themselves.

Relationships that develop between husbands and wives vary enormously. To begin with, very few brides move into a separate home with their husbands – they usually begin life in a joint family, or 'with my mother-in-law' as they express it. So to a large extent, the mother-in-law stands between the husband and wife. Women's relations with her exhibit a considerable range, from affection to loathing, but as Das puts it 'a girl in India is obliged to love and honour her husband's relatives in much the same way as she is obliged to love and honour her own parents', for 'marriage creates ties for a bride which are as binding on her as the ties of blood' (1976: 85). The reality may not quite fit the ideal, as the following extract from a taped discussion with a group of women (A, B, C, and D) demonstrates.

A: 'It depends upon the family – if your mother-in-law is a good lady, you can manage to live in a joint family. But if she is difficult, then you can't. I stayed with my mother-in-law for two years after my marriage, and after that I [i.e. she and her husband] came away, because I find it difficult to live with her – she is so short-tempered.'

B: 'We are afraid of our mothers-in-law. If she is doing any work, we have to help her. We can't go off out and enjoy ourselves. Only if she goes out can we do so.'

C: 'But my two married daughters have adjusted themselves so nicely to joint family living. If the husband doesn't want to come out [i.e. separate] how can you do so? Your husband has to co-operate with you [i.e. it must be a joint decision to separate].'

A: 'My husband is very attached to his mother, that is why I stayed with her for two years. After that I couldn't manage any more. She said I had not brought enough dowry – she wanted Rs 8,000 and my father only gave Rs 5,000 [this was in 1955].'

D: 'We should be kind to our mothers-in-law, I feel. I am lucky, both my mother- and father-in-law died a long time ago. But my husband's sister used to come often. I don't like it when she interferes, and criticizes me for giving the servants too much food. I am a short-tempered person, and if I had had to live with my in-laws I don't know what would have happened.'

C: 'I lived for 12 years with my mother- and father-in-law. A joint family also means sisters, sisters-in-law and brothers-in-law, not just the mother-in-law which is what we have been talking about. It is the duty of the son to keep his mother with him, and it is our [women's] duty to obey her, and put up with her short temper. I would like to have my sons live with me when they are married. I can get used to their wives. My eldest son is married, but he is posted out of Madras. If you ask his wife, I am sure she will tell you she likes her mother-in-law very much, and she is lucky to have such a nice one! But if when they come back to Madras they want to continue living separately, I won't interfere, I won't mind.'

To some extent, the comments in this discussion are coloured by the fact that it is public. No one dares to state too openly their feelings, except perhaps for A. Some women admitted privately that they found living with their husband's parents, particularly his mother, very difficult. But others do get on very well. Girls are taught from an early age that they must 'adjust' in their husband's home, and until their position is strengthened by the birth of children, and they and their husbands are in a financial position to acquire a house of their own, this is what they do.

One young woman, married for about a year and expecting her first baby, told me:

'At home, I never used to go into the kitchen, my mother did everything. Even now I wake up sometimes feeling sleepy, but something tells me that I must get up and go and help my mother-in-law. She would not be angry if I did not, but I do. And I have learned so much from her. I am a good cook now and my mother is surprised. I think that is how it is, only after going to the mother-in-law's house does one *want* to learn these things. So most days I get up by 7 and go and help. But occasionally I sleep until 8 – she won't mind.'

However, the fact that most husbands tend to be mobile because of their occupations means that there will often be a residential separation from the husband's parents fairly early in the marriage. This may only happen on a temporary basis and joint family living be resumed when he is posted back to Madras. However, with the passage of time, most couples try to construct their own houses and eventually move out to live separately, although they may remain living near to kin.

Some husbands and wives do develop very close relationships with each other, with husbands expressing great solicitude for their wives, and vice versa. Others, in spite of living together for many years, achieve what might be described as a *modus vivendi*. The ideals of marriage are not such that husbands and wives expect to be companions. On the contrary, the division of labour and the norms of sexual segregation tend to mean that women and men have largely separate spheres, and interact mainly with members of their own sex. Even so, husbands and wives do participate in some activities together, such as attending concerts or the cinema.

The norms of marriage are clearly, frequently, and forcibly stated in Hindu society. A husband has authority over his wife, indeed, she should worship him as a god. She should do nothing without consulting him, and she should always put his needs before her own. For instance, she should eat after him, no matter how late he comes. While couples are highly aware of these norms and careful not to deviate from them too publicly, the amount of latitude practised in husband–wife relations is in fact considerable. Very few women that I know eat after their husbands, although most will wait to eat with them if they are expected home. However, many women fast regularly once a week or more and perform *pujas* in order to ensure their husband's longevity. They also perform numerous personal services for their husbands, apart from cooking and child-rearing, such as fetching things that they need (some women said their husbands would not even get a glass of water for themselves).

Where relationships between husband and wife do not work out very satisfactorily, they remain living together as a couple although they may lead very separate lives. Divorce is virtually unheard of, even though legally it has been possible and indeed relatively easy to obtain since 1955. Women who are badly treated by their husbands may complain to their kin and may even go and stay with them for extended periods, but formal divorce is out of the question. This is partly because women are economically dependent and partly because of the very strong norms against such a step; not only would it result in disgrace for the woman, but for her family too – the chances of her younger brothers and sisters or her own children making a 'decent marriage' would be 'spoiled'.

Chastity is a virtue which is very much prized by women – it encompasses not only technical fidelity, but devotion in thought, word, and deed to the husband, no matter how unsatisfactory he may be. Women often say that a perfectly chaste woman could cause the rain to fall, if she prayed for it. They admit that they themselves are imperfect in this respect, but they all uphold this ideal as one to strive for (cf. also Egnor 1980; Reynolds 1980). Jacobson has beautifully conveyed the social power, as well as the self-respect, that the upholding of such virtues brings to a woman: in the words of her informant Bhuribai 'Virtue is what's holding up the world', and thus she 'feels herself to be an embodiment of age-old goddess-like virtue and a vital support of the very firmament' (Jacobson 1978: 135). Such sentiments would certainly be echoed by my informants.

Children and motherhood

Children are passionately desired by most couples and very few take any contraceptive precautions at the beginning of their marriage, with the result that children tend to arrive quickly. For a woman, the birth of her first child establishes her in that most secure of statuses – that of a mother. The rituals surrounding the birth of a first baby, whether boy or girl, are more elaborate than for any other. In several senses it marks a rite of passage from married couple to parents. Sons are more desired than daughters, for they are still thought to provide economic support to parents in old age whereas daughters will marry away, and also because sons have to perform the funerary rites (*sraddha*) for their parents. None the less, daughters are very much loved and cared for – indeed, they may be indulged and petted during childhood because of the knowledge that they are to leave home and go and live with strangers.

Barrenness is a terrible fate and causes women much emotional suffering. On one occasion I was interviewing a young woman in her late twenties who had been married for several years but had no children. As it happened, a second older woman, herself childless, was present. When I asked the interviewee if she had children, she said not. At this point, the older woman interrupted, and asked for a glass of water. As soon as the interviewee left the room, I was told by the older woman not to mention that subject again, as it would upset the woman terribly. Women who do not conceive will, of course, go through medical tests to try and rectify matters, but in addition many of them go on pilgrimages, visit temples, and make vows to gods and goddesses in the hope of getting a child.

However, while couples of this class level want children, the number they want is very small. There has been a revolution in motherhood over the last generation. Whereas the grandmothers and, in some cases, the mothers of my respondents had large numbers of children – with six to ten live births being not uncommon – these women themselves have rarely borne more than three, and more usually two children. The most widely expressed ideal is two children, a boy and a girl, but even if two daughters are born few couples will risk a third pregnancy for 'who can find a dowry for *three* daughters?'

When a woman is pregnant, particularly with her first baby, she usually returns to stay at her parents' home at around the sixth month. In the seventh month, a ritual is held called *poochootal*, during which the woman's mother gives her a gold and a silver bangle and a black sari. Other gifts may also be given by the wife's parents to her and her husband and possibly to his parents. In the sixth or eighth month, the husband's parents perform *seemantham*, a ritual which is supposed to link the child in the womb to its ancestors.

After the birth, which usually takes place in a hospital or nursing home, the mother and child return to her parents' home. On the eleventh day after the birth the *punya vachanam* or cradling ceremony is held, when the mother is ritually purified from the pollution of childbirth, the child receives its name, and presents are brought by all the relatives. The new mother usually only returns to her husband after several months and on this occasion her parents must send her with many presents.

Most women of this class do not breast-feed their babies for long (although most of them do breast-feed); around six months seemed to be the average, and then the children were put on to the bottle. Although there is an official ceremony of giving of first rice at around one year, in fact most children have been put on to solid food long before that.

Women are more cosseted during and immediately after pregnancy than at any other time. Most help is given by female kin, particularly their own mothers, but even mothers-in-law in joint families do not expect women who have recently given birth to work as hard as usual. Some wealthy families hire special ayahs (nursemaids) to help with the baby; others expect their regular servants to lend a hand. Fathers have little to do with their new children until the mother returns to her husband's house. After this they are usually eager to cuddle and play with their children, although rarely to feed or bathe them.

Babies and small children are treated with a great deal of attention and affection by all members of the household, even when their demands might appear to a western observer to be excessive. They are rarely separated from adults, especially their mothers, asleep or awake, and are generally taken everywhere with parents (e.g. to concerts, rituals, even meetings).

Mothers are expected to put the needs of their children first. Some women told me they had given up their hobbies, at least for a time, because their children demanded all their attention. Even so, they sometimes get impatient with them. One woman who had a third child unexpectedly in her thirties admitted to slapping her sometimes (she was then aged two) for not eating her food and for 'not allowing me to do *anything*'. On the whole, however, children tend to receive very little punishment of any kind.

Middle age and old age

For many women the process of marrying off children begins while they themselves are scarcely in their forties, because their daughters will marry in their early twenties. Women speak anxiously of the need to get them 'well settled' – a word that has the connotations of 'settling down', and of marital matters being finalized. By the time I returned to the field in 1981, many of my informants were going through this process. I asked some of them whether they regretted 'losing' their daughters. Several daughters had married men who lived abroad, for at this class level in south

Indian society there is scarcely a family that does not have a close
relative who has migrated, usually to the USA but also to Canada,
Australia, and the UK. Their response was that yes, they do miss
them, but that this is mitigated by a sense of relief in having done
their duty satisfactorily in making a suitable match for them and
thus no longer bearing the same weight of responsibility. On my
previous visit I would hear parents say 'If she wants to study
further/go abroad/take a job, let her get married first, then if it is
her husband's wish, she can do so.'

In certain respects, acquiring a daughter-in-law is more trau-
matic for a woman than marrying off her daughter. The latter visit
frequently, especially in the first few years. But the son's wife
usually moves into the family home, and is seen as a threat to the
mother–son relationship. On one occasion I went to visit a friend
and found her closeted with a neighbour who appeared upset. My
friend later told me that this woman's son had recently married.
'Previously, he was so affectionate to his mother, but now he only
thinks about his wife.' For a woman whose major source of
fulfilment is her role as mother of a son, this can be difficult, and
it is small wonder that many women are tyrannical mothers-in-
law.

Many women become grandparents in their early forties and
this adds a new dimension to their domestic roles. Daughters come
home for their confinements, and stay for long periods. If they live
in Madras, they visit frequently; indeed, I found from women's
diaries that visiting the wife's family was much commoner than
visiting that of the husband (if the couples were not living with
them already of course). Most women welcome and accept eagerly
their role as grandmothers and if they have grandchildren living
with them devote a great deal of time and attention to them.

Women tend in middle age and later life to become more
ostensibly pious and pray and visit temples more often. In part
this is because with their children grown they have more time
available, but also because of the Hindu ideal that in the declining
years of life, one should turn one's thoughts to death.

As Vatuk (1975) has pointed out, 'disengagement' is not just a
way of coping with old age, for Hindus, it is a cultural ideal too.
But not all elderly women are able to 'let go' – some still seek to
retain their control over the family, even if they no longer are in
charge of food. Their power particularly manifests itself in

marriage arrangements, when the approval of elderly grandmothers is always sought. Indeed, I came across several cases where
an old lady's desire to 'hold a great-grandchild before I die' resulted
in a young woman being married off at an earlier age than she
might otherwise have been.

The majority of women are more likely to become widows than
to die before their husbands, who are usually older than them.
Widowhood is considered a great misfortune. Formerly, and to
some extent even today, it was thought to be the result of some
sin on the part of the woman, perhaps committed in a previous
life. Formerly, high-caste widows shaved their heads, ate only the
simplest foods (and that only once a day), and observed various
other restrictions. Today, a woman dons a white sari, dispenses
with most jewellery, and ceases to use the red *kumkum* in her hair-
parting or the forehead mark (*pottu*), but she is not ill-treated or
believed to be a mystical threat as in some areas of India (cf. Harper
1969). Widows rarely remain living alone; even if all their children
have left home, they will usually move in with one of their sons.
If they have more than one son, they may divide their time
between them. Widows occasionally go to live with their
daughters if they have no sons, and this seems to be a growing
pattern. Otherwise, they may move nearer to a son or daughter.
A woman moving into her adult son's house is in a quite different
position *vis-à-vis* her daughter-in-law than a woman living in her
own house to which a new bride comes as daughter-in-law; she
is far less powerful, and likely to play a much less important role
in the household.

In examining the life cycle of Indian women we can note a
considerable contrast between their roles as wife and as mother.
The position of a wife is one of subordination, that of mother is
much more powerful. It is through her status as a mother that a
woman is able to ameliorate her position as a wife. As a mother,
she controls the socialization of children, the running of the household, and later, her daughters-in-law. This pattern is not peculiar
to middle-class urban women. It is deeply embedded in Hindu
thought and shows little sign of change in an urban middle-class
environment. As many writers have pointed out, motherhood is
deified, not fatherhood; mothers are seen as strong and powerful.
In the sacred scriptures of the Shastras it is said that the father is
a hundred times more venerable than the teacher, and the mother

a thousand times more venerable than the father: 'There is no shelter like the mother. There is no refuge like her. There is no defence better than her. There could be no one dearer than her.' The mother of children, especially sons, who are grown-up and married with children of their own, can, if she retains her physical and mental health, command their allegiance and respect. Mina Swaminathan (1975) presents a convincing portrait of such a woman, 'not so much to be looked at, as reckoned with', a good description of many of my informants.

4
Women in the household

In this chapter I look first at households and their developmental cycle, the composition of the households in which my informants were living, and the allocation of resources within them. This section includes information on different kinds of family household and their changes over time, as well as a discussion of the financial resources available on this class level and the ways in which they are used. The second section of the chapter examines the division of labour within the household, and looks at domestic labour and its implications.

Households and their resources

HOUSES

The vast majority (70 per cent) of informants live in houses that are owner-occupied. Less than a third live in flats or rented houses. Most houses are modern, built or purchased during the last few years, although a minority of people live in older houses which usually have been inherited. Modern houses are more likely to have been built by the owners themselves, for Madras has seen a great deal of building during the last few years and 'building a house of one's own' is seen as a good investment, a source of security, and a status symbol.

Modern houses usually consist of several bedrooms, living room and/or dining room, kitchen, and several bathrooms. They have electricity, hot and cold water, and ceiling fans. Kitchens have gas cookers, fridges, and often electric mixers/grinders. The average number of rooms, apart from kitchen and bathrooms, is five, but some houses are considerably larger than this, and set in spacious grounds. Three-quarters of informants live in households with telephones, which are both difficult to obtain and expensive to rent in India. Furthermore, almost 80 per cent of households own a car (and a few own more than one), and most who do not are likely to own a motor-bike or a scooter (which are also expensive to buy).

To a western reader, such a standard of living does not sound particularly grand, but it must be remembered that most 'luxury' items in India cost more than they do in the west (electricity, phones, cars, petrol, etc), and that average wages and salaries are considerably lower. Thus this sample of informants represents the tiny urban elite – the top of the socio-economic hierarchy – which lives in comfortable, spacious houses, with modern conveniences.

In addition, all households have servants. These range from one part-time maidservant to a full complement of cook, maidservant, children's ayah, gardener, watchman, and driver. The average number of servants is two per household.

HOUSEHOLD COMPOSITION

The average household size is just under five persons. Only 12 per cent of households fall into the classic joint pattern, that is with either two married brothers and their wives and children, or, more commonly, a married couple and their married son, his wife and children. A further 4 per cent of households, however, are made up of a married couple and their children, with the widowed brother or sister of one of them (usually the husband), and their children.

The bulk of households, therefore, consists of nuclear families. Simple nuclear families account for 55 per cent of total households, but a further 21 per cent are what I have called 'supplemented nuclear', that is where there is another relative living in the household apart from the focal couple and their unmarried children. In most cases this other relative is the husband's widowed mother. For women this is an important consideration and many women used the term 'joint family' to mean that they were living with their mothers-in-law; in fact about a third of the informants are living in households that contain their husband's mother. Five per cent of households consist of widows and their unmarried children, while only 3 per cent consist of women living alone; the latter might of course contain resident servants, but these have not been included in household totals.

HOUSEHOLD INCOME AND EXPENDITURE

I was not able to obtain detailed information on property-holding or salaries for all informants because this is such a delicate topic. However, the vast majority of husbands were earning over Rs 1,500 (around £85) per month at the time of field-work and some were earning well over Rs 2,000 (£100). In addition, about half the households in the sample have either a husband or wife, or occasionally both, who owns either rural or urban property apart from the house in which they are living or the husband's business.

The fact that women own property of this type is a relatively recent phenomenon, which has come about as a result of two changes in the law. First, the Hindu Succession Act (1955) gave women equal inheritance rights with men for the first time. Second, various laws have been passed since independence regarding land ceilings in both rural and urban areas. These have resulted in a tendency to formal partitioning of land, and often in land being given to women so that total amounts held by individuals do not exceed the limit. Although in some cases this is a way of getting around the law and the land in fact remains largely under the control of a woman's brothers, often the woman does receive proceeds from the land (and of course it is in her husband's interest to ensure that she does). A substantial minority of households receives paddy from the rural lands of either husband or wife, which are either managed by members of the extended family still living in the village or else given out to share-croppers. There seems today, however, to be a greater tendency to invest money in the urban areas by buying land or houses, for either rent or re-sale, rather than maintaining rural land.

I suspect that the amount of property-holding is probably greater than this, partly because people may have been reluctant to disclose their total assets, and partly because of the way in which property division takes place. Frequently it appears that people living in nuclear family households (i.e. who have separated residentially from the husband's parents) have not yet received their share of the family property and this is not likely to be done until after the death of the husband's father, or even in some cases of his mother. Technically, then, the property may still be owned by the joint family as a co-parcenary unit and, until it is divided up, it may not be counted as part of their assets by the constituent nuclear families which are already living as separate households, although the latter may derive substantial benefit (e.g. in the form of paddy) from it.

I was able to obtain detailed budgets from a small sample of households which fall into the upper middle-class category: the husbands' salaries were between Rs 1,500 and 2,000 per month, and their occupations were senior management in industry or they had their own small businesses, with a sprinkling who were doctors and lawyers. The average net monthly household income of this sub-sample in 1975 was Rs 1,845 (£100), which was made up primarily of the husband's salary, plus income from shares or rent from other property owned by husband or wife; the latter accounted for an average of Rs 375 per month, or 20 per cent of the total monthly income.

The highest single expenditure was on food, accounting for an average of Rs 530 per month, or 30 per cent of the total income. (This was a period shortly after food prices had risen considerably, and most women complained about this.) The next largest single item was transport, at 15 per cent of total expenditure. The major costs would be for petrol, although many husbands employed in private industry received a car and a mileage allowance as one of the perks of their jobs. Insurance policies and other forms of saving accounted for Rs 243 per month, or a further 13 per cent of the total expenditure. People spent Rs 190 per month on average (10 per cent) on house rent or loan repayments. However, one-third of households owned their own house outright and paid nothing; those who did pay averaged Rs 278 per month.

Most households reckoned to spend a further 7 per cent on clothes, although these were generally bought at the major festivals such as Deepavali, or on special occasions like marriages. School or college fees for children accounted for another Rs 85 (4.6 per cent) per month on average. If those households with no

children or with children too young to attend school are dis-
counted, the average rises to between Rs 90 and Rs 100 per month.
Similar amounts were spent on household bills such as electricity
and gas. Servants constituted only 3 per cent of household expenditure, which is indicative of the extremely low salaries they receive
– maidservants at that time would be paid around Rs 15 per month
plus some food, cooks around Rs 100 plus food, and drivers
around Rs 150 without food. Households spent an average of
Rs 36 per month (2 per cent) on entertainment (cinema, concerts).
About the same amount went to help relatives; just over half the
respondents said they made regular payments averaging Rs 63 per
month. A further 2 per cent of all budgets went on telephone bills.
These categories account for 95 per cent of expenditure, leaving
5 per cent in the 'miscellaneous' category. Most households lived
within their means, that is their reported expenditure equalled or
was less than their reported net income, but just over a quarter of
households appeared to overspend. It is possible they had other
sources of income they did not report, or that with the recent rises
in food and petrol prices they had suddenly found their income
inadequate, a complaint I heard often in 1974–75, and even more
frequently in 1981–82.

All these households maintain bank accounts and, in the vast
majority of cases, husbands and wives have joint accounts. Wives
know very precisely what their husbands earn and in many households women have the major share of responsibility for expenditure and financing. One woman recorded in her diary: 'My
husband came home with his salary and handed it over to me. I
put it in the *puja* [prayer] room.' On one occasion I had to give
a large sum of money to a couple; we were sitting in a room and
the husband was next to me and, unthinkingly, I handed it to him.
He immediately gave it to his wife, remarking that 'she takes care
of all that'.

In addition, as already stated, some women have their own
income from property; generally this is put into the household
account and helps maintain the standard of living. Most women
feel free to take money from the household budget if for example
they have to give a gift at a marriage. Many women keep secret
small amounts of money which they consider their own, and for
which they do not have to account to anyone (husbands are
generally aware of this, but most are wise enough not to ask about

it). This means that women can give gifts, lend small amounts, or buy small luxuries if they want to (cf. Vatuk 1971).

Domestic labour and its division in the household

Not all domestic labour is necessarily carried out by the women and there are various complex forms of division of labour between the following pairs: wife–husband; wife–servants; wife–children; wife–husband's mother. These vary according to household composition (e.g. whether the husband's mother is living in it), the class level of the household (e.g. richer households will have cooks, others not), the age of children, and finally, the relations between individuals.

In recent years domestic labour has been much debated in the west. The main issue has been its contribution to the economy – for instance, whether or not it produces surplus value. There appears to be a lack of consensus on what exactly falls under the rubric of domestic labour. Most agree that 'housework' (i.e. cleaning and cooking) is included; many also include childcare and socialization as part of domestic labour. Some would include the sexual services provided by the wife to the husband (although usually not vice versa). The point about all these services is that they reproduce labour power. However, while most attention has been on the way they reproduce the labouring class for capitalism, much less attention has been given to the way in which the capitalist class itself is reproduced or to the manifestation of its particular culture. For this reason I have included in this chapter a number of activities which seem to be very important in the broad context of reproduction, but which are not usually seen, certainly not by protagonists, as 'work'.

The women in my sample saw themselves primarily as 'housewives', with their roles of wife and mother being the most important aspect of their lives. I discuss the ideology of the norms of these roles in Chapter 10, but here it is sufficient to note that this is a view shared by the wider society, as well as being internalized by the women themselves. They define their main work in the household as connected with food, personal services to the husband, and childcare. Cooking is clearly recognized to be work (and hard work at that); looking after husbands and children is not necessarily so defined, because it is done from a mixture of love and duty. Nor are religious activities, such as domestic rituals, defined as 'work'; people tend to define them as a mixture of duty and pleasure. At the opposite end of the continuum of the emic definition of work is 'leisure'. Activities that women perform in what they conceive of as their leisure hours are of their own choosing, and thus are the antithesis of 'work', which is a necessity. Hobbies, membership of organizations, and so on would fall into this category. None the less, it is many of these activities that contribute to producing the culture of a particular class level, and it is for this reason that I would include such activities under 'reproduction'. The concept of reproduction is thus a wider one than that of domestic labour.

However, this is not to say that everything these women do must be regarded as work in exactly the same sense. The point about a materialist analysis is that it enables one to look at activities in terms of their contribution to class formation – it does not deny the validity of other interpretations. A woman may love her children dearly and *want* to care for them; none the less, the way in which she does this inevitably reproduces another generation at a particular class level.

If then we use an emic definition, we would arrive at a continuum beginning with 'work', which is seen unequivocally as such. It is usually unpleasant and menial and includes cleaning the house and washing clothes. Next comes food preparation – a necessity, an arduous chore, but one that may be enjoyed by some women who use it as a vehicle for their talents; it is also, in the Hindu context, of important ritual significance (cf. Appadurai 1981; Khare 1976). Third comes caring for children, which most women would not describe as work because they value children very highly. Next comes religious activities, which might be described as a 'duty' although with elements of pleasure ('peace of mind' as some put it). Finally, under the emic concept of leisure, come such activities as handicrafts, reading, or joining an association.

If we think of these activities as forming a continuum in this way, then we can state that the likelihood of a task being delegated is greater the nearer it approaches the 'work' end of the continuum.

CLEANING AND WASHING

All the households in this sample employ a part-time maidservant at the very least, and therefore women in the household are not responsible for cleaning the house or for heavy washing of clothes. However, orthodox women wash some clothes themselves so that they might be ritually pure (*madi*) for performing *puja* (worship).

Maidservants generally work for several households, coming for a couple of hours in the morning to wash up the dishes and to sweep and swab the floors, and returning again in the evening to wash dishes. They may also wash clothes, although some families use a professional *dhobi* (washerman). Relations with maidservants vary considerably. In some households, where the servants are old-timers, they might be trusted to work on their own; in other households, probably the majority, constant supervision of their work (and honesty) is thought necessary.

FOOD PREPARATION

Shopping for food is done sometimes by women, sometimes by husbands, and sometimes by servants. Grains and pulses are bought in large quantities and stored, and in those households that still have links with rural areas they may be brought from there to the city. Vegetables are bought almost daily and for these either husband, wife, husband's mother, or servant may be responsible. Items of household equipment and clothing are purchased more sporadically, by either husband and wife jointly, or the wife alone. It should be noted that this male participation in shopping activities does not betoken any particular change in the division of labour, since in many parts of south Asia it is more common for men to do the marketing than women.

Almost all food is bought in its unprocessed state. Grains, for instance, have to be picked over to remove dirt and stones, and then ground to make particular dishes (such as *iddly* and *dosai*) which are eaten daily in most households. In very few households is bread purchased regularly, partly because most people prefer the traditional foods, and partly because it is much more expensive. Most of the work of cleaning grains and pulses is done by a maidservant. Grinding may be carried out by hand (in which case it is the servant's task), by use of a local mill (to which the servant goes), or by an electric grinder. A large proportion of households own grinders and/or mixers, but these are only used by a woman or her mother-in-law, never entrusted to a servant. Vegetables have to be washed and chopped and, here again, women have help from their maidservants. Even where they are of relatively low caste, they can still handle food while it is in its raw state without risk of pollution. Maidservants are also responsible for clearing up after cooking and washing the dishes and pots.

Only a minority (40 per cent) of households have a cook who actually prepares food; these are all upper-class families. Cooks are usually male and Brahmin and are paid considerably more than maidservants. Women who do not have cooks rarely spend less than four hours in the kitchen preparing food, and some spend up to six hours.

The following are some accounts of how women spend their day.

Woman of Kallar caste, aged forty, husband a civil servant, three teenage children:

> 'Usually I get up at 5.30 and say a few words of prayer. Then I make breakfast – *iddly* or *dosai* or something like that. Then I go for a walk. After that I do *puja* for 10–15 minutes; on Tuesdays and Fridays we have special *pujas*, especially on Friday, when the *puja* lasts for about an hour. Then I prepare lunch which is eaten at around 1 p.m. My husband and son both come home for lunch – my son is at a nearby school. The other children take their food with them. Then I listen to the radio and have a rest. After that I have to prepare tiffin (snacks) [i.e. for when everyone comes home in the late afternoon]. Sometimes I make a heavy tiffin and we eat it in the evening, rather than cooking a [rice] meal again. Sometimes we all go out for a walk, or my mother or sister (who live together nearby) may come and visit. When I go to bed I read for some time. So I am in the kitchen from 7–9 in the morning, again from 10.30–12.30, then again to make tiffin, and finally for the evening meal – a total of about five hours. On Sundays the family wants meat, which involves longer preparation, so I spend more time in the kitchen; Sunday is a heavy day for me.'

Brahmin woman, husband a college professor, two teenage daughters:

> 'I get up very early at around 4.30 a.m., have my bath, and then make coffee. If it is a school day I have to have cooked lunch by 8 a.m. so that the children can eat it before going to school or else take it with them. My husband only has tiffin in the morning, but he comes home for his lunch at 1 p.m. When they have all left, I read the paper, and do some washing. My husband comes home at 1 p.m. and stays for a couple of hours. The children come home after 4 p.m. and I make something for them. Then my husband comes back in the early evening, and I make tiffin for him. At night we eat curd rice, so I don't have much cooking to do for that. I generally prepare all the food first thing in the morning and keep it in the fridge, so only the actual cooking has to be done during the day. I suppose I spend around two hours cooking, excluding making sweets (which are very time-consuming).'

Food then is seen as central to the role of the wife and mother. Many women begin the day by making coffee at around 5 or 6 a.m. Then they start to prepare breakfast which is eaten by different members of the family at different times, depending upon when they leave the house for school, college, or work. Many women prepare a full cooked meal in order that husbands and children can take their lunch with them in a 'tiffin carrier' (a series of interlocking dishes) or else they send the tiffin carrier later by a 'boy' who works in this way for a number of households. If husbands or children are nearby during the day they may return at midday for lunch – as yet, the provision of a midday meal in schools or workplaces is a relative rarity. Children returning from school expect tiffin which is also time-consuming to prepare. Finally, the whole family eats supper together at around 8 p.m.

There are several points which should be noted about these patterns. First, the cooking and serving of food may be spread out throughout the day, so that if a woman is solely responsible for it she has relatively little uninterrupted leisure. Food must not only be cooked, but also *served* – preferably by the wife/mother, or her husband's mother, or by a cook, but never by a maidservant, and never in the form of people helping themselves. On numerous occasions I was told 'I think that mothers should give food, even when the children are big. If I go out my son and my husband will get angry if I'm not there to serve them even if I've left it ready. Only my daughter will eat if I'm not there.'

One woman, whose daughter was studying at medical college, commented that the latter would not even prepare coffee for herself; her mother had to be there to prepare it for her. At first I found this statement surprising, for I had expected that girls would be more 'domesticated' than boys. However, I soon learned that very few girls actually participate in cooking, and many have to begin to learn immediately prior to or even after marriage. One reason for this has already been stated: they are extremely busy with school and college work. But another is that mothers put very little pressure on their daughters to help. Partly this seems to be because the preparation and serving of food are associated with the role of wife/mother, not of daughter. Some women state quite categorically 'She'll be doing it for the rest of her life when she gets married, so let her enjoy and not do it now.'

Some women share responsibility for cooking with their husbands' mothers. Often in the early stages of marriage a new bride does little but carry out instructions. Gradually, she assumes more and more responsibility for buying food, planning menus, cooking, and serving. The stage at which a mother–in–law 'retires' from the kitchen depends upon various factors: her own inclinations, her state of health, relations between her and her daughters-in–law, and whether either of them has other activities. Mothers-in–law who turn to religion in their old age and spend much of their time visiting temples, singing *bhajans*, and listening to religious discourses may be happy to leave domestic work to their sons' wives. But other older women find their chief fulfilment in cooking food and refuse to give it up. In those families where women are paid workers it may be convenient that mothers-in–law continue to cook. I also came across cases where mothers and daughters-in–law shared the cooking – one doing the evening and the other the morning meal.

In all cultures, cooking and giving food are loaded with emotional significance, but in India food has extra dimensions, those of purity and pollution. It is the duty of the cook to ensure that food is cooked and served in a ritually pure way. In quite a large number of households the women are vegetarians, the men non-vegetarians. Men say with pride 'My wife is a *pure* vegetarian', whereas they themselves admit to eating eggs and even meat outside the home. Some women will cook eggs or even fish and meat for husbands and children, but will not eat them themselves. It is as if somehow this marks the family as 'modern' and the husbands as 'men of the world' for their lapses from vegetarianism, whereas its sanctity and purity are ensured by the abstinence of the wife from such foods. Similarly, women never smoke or drink alcohol which men quite often do.

In many households, particularly those of Brahmins, women observe ritual pollution during their menstrual periods. If they do not have a mother-in-law living with them or employ a cook, then someone else must do the cooking during this time. Not infrequently, this is the husband, and it is said that most Brahmin males know how to cook for this reason. For most women, the 3- or 4-day period during which she is polluted and polluting does provide a break from an otherwise fairly arduous routine of cooking.

A third dimension of food relates to class levels. Obviously the wealthier the family, the more it can afford to spend on food, and the chances of having a varied and nutritious diet are greater. But it is primarily women of the upper middle and upper classes who have begun to innovate in food preparation and to go to classes where they learn to bake western-style cakes and puddings, and make fruit juice and jam; only women of such a class level would be likely to have either the time or money for such activities.

Similarly, it is mainly women of this class level who are highly concerned about the nutritional aspects of food. They read articles in books and magazines about vitamin and protein levels and many give their children extra vitamin drops or tablets in addition to their ordinary food. Advertisements in the mass media play upon this; one which advertised a malt drink showed a mother giving food to her husband and children with the caption 'Are you *sure* they're getting enough?'

But families demand variety as well as 'good' food. Many women sighed as they told me of their efforts to think of 'something different' each day – a particular difficulty for vegetarians, since vegetables can only be seasonal. Here is an extract from one woman's diary:

'Started to cook. Here begins my headache – to think, to programme the day's menu. For instance, every day we require three types of vegetable; one for curry, one for *sambar* [hot vegetable stew] and one for salad or *raitha* [raw vegetable in yoghurt]. If we have one for *sambar*, I can't have it for curry for that day or the next or my daughter will be saying "I've been eating ladies fingers for *days* now" or "Is this drumstick [type of vegetable] week then?" So I plan ahead and buy the vegetables in the market the previous day.'

Attempts are usually made to satisfy the whims of the family. Here is another woman with three children (aged 2, 7, and 9): 'My son will say he does not want rice (for breakfast) he only wants toast, and my daughter will say she only wants omelette, not rice with curds. Though I get angry, I immediately prepare what they want.'

A final aspect of food distribution which should be mentioned is that it is the woman's job to distribute food as she thinks fit. If a *sadhu* (holy person, ascetic) comes begging to the door, the woman will decide how much food should be given, and the same is true of beggars, some of whom are regularly fed by housewives.

In short, then, the preparation of food demands time and effort in order to ensure that it is nutritious, varied, and conforms to the canons of ritual purity; in addition, it must be served by an acceptable person, usually the wife and mother.

CHILDCARE AND SOCIALIZATION

The primary responsibility for childcare lies with the mother. None the less, she will receive help from other members of the household – her husband's mother and even husband's father, with whom her children usually have an affectionate relationship. Indeed, some women complain that the grandparents 'spoiled' the children by indulging them too much. Only a minority of households have full-time children's ayahs, and like those which have cooks, they are from the upper rather than upper middle classes. Few men have much to do with babies when they are small, but later they play and interact with them a great deal. The uninhibited joy with which men greet their own (and other people's) children in this culture is very striking to a western eye. But during the week most men work too late to be able to have much to do with small children. Furthermore, they are not responsible for feeding them, or for cleaning up after them.

An important aspect of children's socialization is their religious education. Again, this is predominantly a female task. Women tell their children the stories of the Sanskrit classics *Ramayana* and *Mahabharata* from an early age (often as a bribe to get them to eat) and they also gradually begin to explain to them the meaning of various rituals and to encourage them to participate and to pray. If the husband's mother is in the household, she too will participate in the children's religious education. One of the roles that Indian grandmothers are supposed to fulfil is that of story-teller to grandchildren.

Another extremely important aspect of socialization of children is of course gender formation. Mothers play a most important role in this, partly in the way that they respond to their sons and daughters, and partly in the role model that they themselves offer. Girls are dressed with an emphasis on 'prettiness', with bangles, earrings, and long hair. Boys are encouraged to do sports; girls to be interested in dance. Rough noisy behaviour is tolerated much more from boys than girls. When their future is mentioned, girls are constantly told they will get married and have to 'adjust' to their husband and their in-laws.

None the less, given the very different role sets for women and men in evidence at this class level, I was surprised at how little gender differentiation was made between small children and particularly how little it affected the division of labour. Many women assured me that there was little difference in rearing boys and girls, and that they expected their young sons as well as daughters to help with certain chores. One woman with five adult children said 'No, I don't think there are differences between boys and girls. They both used to help me, but now the boys won't help because they are grown-up.' Another woman with three teenagers (one daughter, two sons) reported,

> 'Yes, my daughter helps, and even my sons. Yesterday I went out and my younger son cleaned the kitchen. It is mostly my younger son and daughter who help. They make their own breakfast ... There are some differences between boys and girls – my daughter fights with her two brothers; it's a pity she hasn't a sister to support her. They mostly fight over clothes – since the fashion is for bell-bottoms at the moment they try to borrow each other's clothes. But the boys are

untidy and she is tidy — she always gets her school things ready the night before, whereas my younger son is always rushing round the house in the morning looking for his things. But not all males are like that; my husband was always neat as a child, so his mother told me, and even now he is a very tidy person.'

There is a considerable difference in the extent to which children are encouraged to be independent. Some women speak fondly of their teenage children's incompetence in the household, but others are quite clear that they expect their children to fend for themselves to some extent. One woman whose children (a daughter aged twelve and a son, ten) regularly make their own breakfasts was glad of their help and efficiency when she needed them:

'I don't think there's any difference in bringing up boys and girls. Last week my servant left, and I was helping out for a few days at the neighbourhood school. My daughter practically ran the house. She fed the toddler, washed dishes and clothes, while my son did all the ironing and shopping. He is always a good help — he washes up and sweeps, and makes his own bed, and he likes gardening too. I think boys should help in the house.'

Another woman with three teenage children commented that her daughter did nothing during term-time, and that she was a very untidy girl, but her younger son was quite different:

'He will tidy up. He has made a chart of his daily routine. I don't ask him to do anything, he does it all voluntarily. This holiday he has tidied up all the cupboards and overhauled two bikes. My daughter will only do anything if I ask her to.'

The situation in these families seems to be that boys and girls are not treated very differently until they reach adolescence. Certainly the rules about division of labour do not apply to them until then. At this time, in any case, most become very busy with the demands made upon them by school and college and do very little to help in the house. However, even if children do give a modicum of help in the house, the major burden of housework falls upon the mother. Furthermore, it is primarily women who are responsible for child-rearing and socialization. The traditional, almost mystical, notions about the bond between mother and child have been reinforced by ideas from the west. These ideas, which have been imported via women's magazines and the medical profession, are that children 'need' their mothers with them all the time and that mothers are the ones best fitted to take care of children.

Another aspect of women's role in the rearing of children is their responsibility for academic success. They do this in two ways. First, to a large extent women choose their children's schools. As one woman said to me, 'My husband says that I meet other women, and we talk and compare schools, so I know more about it than he does.' If the father is living at home in Madras and is not posted elsewhere, he, either alone or with his wife, may go to a particular school to seek admission for a child, but the major business of comparing the merits and demerits of schools is the wife's responsibility. It is also primarily mothers who attend school functions and maintain relations with class teachers.

Second, it is mainly women who are responsible for 'coaching' their children. Although all the children of this class level attend private schools – usually English medium, with high fees – the classes are often very large and the competition fierce. From the age of five or even earlier when the child enters school, its life is dominated by examinations. The educational system demands a great deal of memorization and rote learning, and most schools impose a considerable burden of homework. Most women sit with their children every evening, not only helping them with home-work, but also going over the day's lessons and explaining points which the children do not understand. In the periods preceding and during examination time, they spend even longer with them. Few fathers participate to any great extent in this chore, so it is not surprising that a reason given for wanting educated brides is that 'educate a woman, and you educate a whole family'. This is true more literally in India than elsewhere.

What is very striking about the role of mother in middle-class urban south Indian society is that the relatively fewer children of today's generation are seen to need more care than the more numerous children of previous generations. In part this is due to the demands of modern schooling and in part to the influence of western psychological ideas about 'maternal deprivation'. Women feel acute responsibility for their children's development – morally, academically, and even physically.

RELIGIOUS ACTIVITY

As is made plain in the accounts of their day given by women earlier in this chapter, religious activities play an important part in women's daily, weekly, and annual routine. In one sense this is paradoxical, for according to Hinduism a woman should not study the sacred scriptures nor perform any independent sacrifice. Even in temples dedicated to goddesses, the priests and officials are always male. Similarly, the majority of life-cycle rituals (*samskaras*) are for males and not females, particularly the important *upana-yanam* (investiture with the sacred thread for boys of twice-born castes) (cf. Pandey 1969).

Domestic ritual emphasizes such observances as prayers and devotions and in these women play important roles. Indeed, women spend far more time every day performing religious activities than men do. Women pray when they get up and many draw *kolams* outside their front door before dawn. One woman described them thus:

> '*Kolams* are drawings or patterns made either at the gate of the house, or in front of religious pictures (in the *puja* room). It is a custom in south India to draw a *kolam* daily before dawn. They are done in rice flour, and are later eaten by ants and crows, which ask the sun-god on our behalf that our lands in the village will be fertile.'

When all the members of the family have left the house most women pray for about half an hour in the *puja* room. On religious festival days, which occur very frequently, they pray for longer periods. The third time of day for performing religious duties is at dusk, when a short prayer is said as the lamps are lit.

In addition, on religious festival days women may be expected to cook special food, often in larger quantities than usual to offer to visitors and to send to the neighbours. They also take special baths instead of ordinary ones. Most women have what is called an 'oil bath' at least once a week. It consists of massaging the scalp and body with oil, followed by a bath with warm water. It is considered more purifying than an ordinary bath. Women are also responsible for ensuring that their children have regular oil baths, as well as their daily or twice daily baths. Women visit the temple more frequently than men, often going in the evenings to participate in the *puja*. Some go in the very early morning if there is a temple nearby. Most women go to the temple at least once a week – Fridays and Tuesdays being the most popular days. They also observe both the Tamil and lunar months with special rituals for new moon and full moon days. For example, one woman recorded in her diary:

'Today is the first Friday in the Tamil month of *Adi*; it is an auspicious day. Usually we prepare *malivakku* [flour lamps] on one of the four Fridays in *Adi* – we prepare a mixture of sugar, rice flour, cardamom, etc., and put the mixture on a plate. Then we insert two wicks into holes in the dough, and pour in ghee, and light the wicks. As we pray, we keep pouring more ghee, so that the flames do not go out. When we have finished we do *puja* in the usual way by offering flowers to the gods.'

Another woman who kept a diary over the same period records for that date:

'I woke my daughter to take an oil bath. For in this Tamil month of *Adi* unmarried young girls and *sumangali* [married women whose husbands are still alive and thus are auspicious] should take oil baths and pray to the Goddess Lakshmi [of wealth and prosperity] ... Then we [she and daughter] went to a nearby temple and offered *puja*.'

What is important to note about much of this religious and ritual activity is that women do not only perform it for their own good or individual merit, they perform it on behalf of their families (cf. also Singer 1971). When there is some problem in the family it is usually the wife/mother who takes appropriate action in the religious sphere; she may undertake a fast as part of a vow, go on a pilgrimage, or go to a temple where there is a medium who specializes in divination and can give information about the causes of misfortune (cf. Egnor 1977).

MAINTENANCE OF KINSHIP RELATIONS

Women interact more frequently with kin than men and thus carry a major responsibility for maintaining existing kin links, with both their own and their husband's family. They also initiate new relationships through the important role they play in arranging marriages.

In one woman's diary she records the following incidents: 'A friend of mine came to discuss a marriage proposal between my neighbour's daughter and my friend's cousin. She had come to find out some details about the girl.' Two days later the same woman wrote in her diary: 'I wrote a letter to my auntie who is in Bombay regarding the girl we interviewed on Sunday (as a prospective bride) for her son.' The very next day she noted 'copied four or five horoscopes from my file to my friend's niece.' Later she writes that, 'A friend of my husband and his wife came to invite us to his niece's marriage. They wanted the same photographer as I had arranged a year ago for the wedding of my cousin. I rang the photographer and fixed it up.' Thus in the space of only two weeks, this woman had been involved in negotiations or preparations for no less than four marriages.

Most of the initial soundings in finding suitable partners are done by women, and this is a frequent topic of discussion in gatherings of relatives, neighbours, and friends. Women also carry most of the subsequent burden of organizing the marriage arrangements in their family. Women attend more marriages than men and they usually stay for the whole duration of the marriage ceremony and feast, whereas men may just come for a short time, unless they are closely connected with either bride or groom.

Another important way in which kin links are maintained is during sickness or pregnancy. Women are the ones who visit and help most regularly, and for the longest periods. One woman recorded in her diary how she went every day to the hospital to visit a sick affine of her husband, taking food and drink for him; this is by no means untypical.

LEISURE

Women who completed a time budget questionnaire said they had between two and five hours' leisure a day. As has already been shown, this is unlikely to be a continuous period unless they employ a cook, so such women would have to choose leisure activities that would not take them away from home for long periods. Women frequently read books, magazines, and newspapers in both English and Tamil in their homes. Some magazines are expressly designed for women and form an important source of new ideas on cooking, childcare, marital relations, and so on. Books are generally romantic (particularly popular are Mills and Boon romances and Barbara Cartland) or detective novels (Agatha Christie), or sometimes, especially for older women, religious works.

Another favourite activity is handicrafts, with 65 per cent of informants stating that they practised at least one of a very wide range: embroidery, knitting, crochet, paper-flower making, fabric-painting, bead-work, tatting, doll-making, and so on. Most women have attended classes to learn such skills but subsequently continue to practise them at home. Almost all south Indian homes at this class level are adorned with the wife's handiwork. Only a few women turn their skills in this line to productive ends, either by selling their handicrafts or by holding classes for other women and charging a small fee.

It was apparent from the diaries kept by the women that a good deal of their leisure time is taken up with visiting and being visited by kin. Although some of this is done in evenings and on weekends when other family members also participate, women visit or telephone relatives during the day, when husbands and children are at work or school.

It is striking that younger women seem to pay a lot of visits to friends and/or neighbours as well as to kin, whereas older women seem to have most of their contacts with kin. If I visited a house in the early afternoon it was common to find one or two neighbours or friends sitting talking to the woman whom I had come to see. It is on such occasions that women compare their children's progress and discuss their schools and careers. Unless the friends are of the same sub-caste, however, marriage is not likely to be discussed except in general terms. Such contacts are of course both the result of and assist in the creation of a common life-style (cf. Cohen 1978).

Frequently a group of neighbours form a *bhajan* group – sometimes these are formal classes, meeting in outside premises, at other times they are semi-formal groups that meet in members' houses. *Bhajans* are religious songs which may be sung in Hindi, Tamil, or other Indian languages. Women regard singing them in a group as a form of religious as well as musical experience; joining a *bhajan* group also provides for a pleasant social experience. Because *bhajans* are part of the Hindu *bhakti* (devotional) tradition, they override caste distinctions and hence *bhajan* groups may be composed of a variety of castes. Some women – particularly Brahmins – join classes to learn Sanskrit verses. Around 10 per cent of informants mentioned specifically going to *bhajan* groups as part of their leisure activities. This is certainly an underestimate, as some who spoke of spending time on 'music' or 'religion' included *bhajans* in that category, while women who had previously participated in such activities but were not doing so at the time of interview did not always include it in their current list of activities.

Evening and weekend leisure is often spent with the family members in such activities as going for a walk, or visiting the cinema, or a concert. Concerts of classical Carnatic music tend to be arranged by musical associations (*sabha*) which usually are very Brahmin-dominated. Interest in music is noticeably higher among Brahmins than members of other castes. A large number of women from this caste reported that they are *sabha* members.

Many families at this class level take an annual holiday, or even two. Some visit relatives in either the husband's or wife's native place, particularly if they still have lands there and/or if it is in an area with a pleasant climate. Sometimes a woman goes with the children for an extended period during the school holidays whereas the husband may only go for a short time. Another sort of holiday is a pilgrimage to a famous temple or shrine; there may be a particular reason for visiting this place, such as a request to a particular deity or the fulfilment of a vow. Some families go to a hill station for a few weeks during the very hot season from May to June, when the temperatures in Madras become unbearably high. Seventy-eight per cent of respondents said they went away from Madras regularly or often, and only 22 per cent said they did so rarely or never.

Finally, of course, all my informants belong to at least one women's association. Many of them belong to other voluntary associations as well, averaging 1.32 each (including the one being studied). In this respect, they are more likely to be multiple joiners than their husbands, who only average one association each. Whereas women tend mainly to join women's associations (most of which perform social services), men are more likely to join one of the prestigious recreational clubs in the city, such as the Madras, Boat, Gymkhana, or Cricket club. In such cases, members of their families also attend club functions, such as the weekly or fortnightly film show, or have dinner there occasionally. Only a small minority (18 per cent) of husbands also belong to men's 'service' clubs, such as Rotary, Lions, Round Table, or Jaycees. 'Social service' at this class level is by and large a female activity and men are content to delegate this task to their wives.

Conclusion

In the context of reproduction, it is analytically difficult to separate the emic categories of 'work' and 'leisure' activities, since many leisure activities make an important contribution to reproduction. It is also not always useful to distinguish between public and private activities since much of what is done in the home demonstrates the family's class position to the society at large.

Papanek (1979) has suggested that these 'family status production activities' become more elaborated the higher the class position. This is a historically specific process, as has been shown elsewhere (cf. Ehrenreich and English 1979). For India, the Report of the Committee on the Status of Women in India (henceforth referred to as RCSW) has noted similar trends to those described in this chapter:

> 'Amongst the well-to-do also, the spheres of men and women are well-defined and separate. With domestic help, the burden of drudgery does not fall on the woman, but she is still expected to run the home and bring up the children ... Home-making is raised to a fine art, and trifling details assume exaggerated importance.'
>
> (Government of India 1974: 85)

What the committee failed to see, however, is that such details are far from trifling; they are part of the vital task of the female householder whose role in domestic labour, child-rearing and socialization, marriage negotiations, extra-family relationships, ritual, and membership of voluntary associations is crucial not only in the maintenance of the structure of family and kinship, but also in the perpetuation, reproduction, and formation of life-styles or cultures associated with class. To define class according to males' occupations and incomes alone is to ignore the vast and complex process of culture formation, which is primarily carried out by women.

5
Women as paid workers

In Chapter 4 I considered examples of the vast majority of women of the urban upper middle and upper classes who do not work for pay outside the home, and whose time and energies are primarily consumed by their reproductive role. These women's relationship to the class structure is a complex one – although they may be assigned a class position on the basis of the occupations and incomes of their husbands or fathers, as I sought to show in the previous chapter, they themselves play an active role in creating class culture through reproduction.

This chapter considers the minority of women of this class level who do work outside the home, primarily as professionals. Such women have, in certain senses, a more direct relationship to the class structure, since they are productive workers. Yet for many of them, namely those who are married, their reproductive activities also remain exceedingly important.

Through looking at the constraints that operate upon women of this class level – first in obtaining suitable qualifications, then in finding a job, and finally in balancing their productive with reproductive activities or else abandoning the latter for the former by remaining unmarried – it is possible to see why so few of them undertake paid work.

Women as paid workers in India

There is a large literature on women and work in India.[1] Here it suffices to note a few important points, particularly with regard to the urban areas. First, only a small minority of women are classified as productive workers, and the figures have shown a persistent decline in the proportion of women working from the turn of this century. In Madras, for example, the 1901 census classified 11.6 per cent of women as workers, but by 1971 this had dropped steadily to 5.05 per cent, a figure that rose slightly in 1981, possibly because of the broadening of the definition of 'worker'. Second, there is a curvilinear relationship between education and likelihood of work participation. Illiterate women and highly educated women are most likely to work, although even here, the latter constitute a small minority of such women (V. S. D'Souza 1980).

Recently, absolute *numbers* of women working for pay have increased in the urban areas, with new job demands coming from middle-class women, educated to the level of matriculation or above, seeking white collar employment as teachers or clerical workers. However, with the slowing down of expansion in these areas, there is a rising tide of educated female unemployment in the cities. Finally, educated women workers tend to be clustered in occupations like teaching, clerical work, and medicine;[2] even within these sectors, they are grossly over-represented at the lower end of the pay scale.

Attitudes to work

For women from the upper middle and upper classes, employment at any level other than professional is almost unthinkable. For most women, employment outside the home is not considered at all desirable. Although the present generation of such women almost invariably goes to college and completes a degree, marriage takes place immediately afterwards and is seen as the most important part of a girl's life. Most women who are now housewives in their thirties and forties have never worked, and never really contemplated doing so.

'My husband doesn't want me to work, and there is no economic necessity.'

'I would have liked to work, to pass the time and get some money. But I am not qualified and there are no jobs.'

'My husband would never agree. I would have liked to teach, both to pass the time and earn money. But we have never seriously discussed it.'

'In my community we never allow our women to work, except in case of dire economic necessity.'

These are all comments from middle-class housewives. A few however genuinely regretted their lack of training, and were determined to see that things were different for their daughters. One woman with six children, who had raised her family on a relatively low government servant's salary, had ensured that all of them, both boys and girls, received the best possible education, and had encouraged the girls to work: 'We suffered so much on my husband's salary ... [If they work] they will be better off.' But other women had different reasons for wishing that they had jobs. A wealthy woman told me: 'I wish I had been educated and working – but I had no college education. If I had been working, I wouldn't have got sick [depressed] – I wouldn't have had time. My daughter must finish her studies and work. She must be independent and stand on her own feet.'

Several commented that girls must have training, 'even if they don't use it after marriage'. But other parents are opposed to girls doing anything other than the conventional Arts or Home Science degree. One woman with a daughter reading psychology told me, 'She wants to do medicine but I am opposed. It is a strain to be a housewife and a doctor. We want to settle her [i.e. get her married] early, and some people don't like doctor wives.' Other girls manage to get round their parents, like one whose father refused her permission to do medicine, but did allow her to do an MSc after she had finished her first degree. She did so brilliantly that according to her mother, 'We couldn't stop her continuing and taking her PhD' even though both parents felt that 'running a family is more important than being a career girl'.

There are then a number of reasons why women at this class level undertake paid work. One is if a girl shows herself both brilliant and determined to pursue a career, but in this she needs the support of her parents; they will have to support her economically through her studies, and be willing either to defer her marriage or else to ensure that they choose for her a husband who will agree to her studies and career continuing. The second reason for undertaking paid work is 'economic necessity', to support either the woman's natal family (particularly on the death, illness, or unemployment of the father), or else her own children if she is widowed. At this class level it is much less likely to be for support of the family if she is married, for most husbands will be earning good salaries. In other words, it is only for a small minority of women, who have either exceptional abilities or who suffer economic misfortune, that it is considered legitimate to work.

Women who fit into either of these categories before marriage may well find that their careers effectively preclude marriage. Their natal families are financially dependent on them, or else their very professional success and high education make it difficult to find a suitable husband. For this reason, some remain unmarried.

The sample of professional women

As already stated, four associations of professional women were studied, one by participant observation and the remainder by use of questionnaires. Two of the associations were 'service' clubs, akin to Rotary, with membership restricted to limited numbers of particular professional categories,[3] one was a graduates' association, and the last was for women in a particular profession. The associations are small, and the total number of women in the sample is sixty-six, slightly less than their total membership. Almost all were in their forties and fifties in 1974–75.

In terms of occupation, these women are clustered into a relatively small area. The largest single category in the sample are teachers (24.24 per cent), all working at a senior level as headmistresses or subject heads of department; most of them are in the private sector of education. The next largest category are lawyers (21.21 per cent of the sample); their proportion is high because one association consists of women lawyers only, although overall women form a tiny proportion (1.2 per cent) of the legal profession. There is a much higher proportion of women in the medical profession (20,000 women doctors in India) but a relatively small proportion (18.18 per cent) of the sample fall into this category; they do however form the largest single category of the Women's Professional Association, which was the organization studied in greatest detail. Other women in the sample are in business (usually family businesses since very few are employed in senior positions in private industry), government service, social work, or banking. In almost all cases these women are senior in their profession, drawing high salaries of between Rs 1,000 and 5,000 per month (1974–75 figures: £55–£277).

All these women professionals are highly educated, virtually all have first degrees, and many have postgraduate qualifications. Most of their fathers are graduates, although their mothers are not – many indeed had not even matriculated. Thus these women are in many senses trend-setters in their families. Their mothers did not work outside the family, but their fathers were involved in a variety of occupations – government service, law, medicine, teaching, business. On the whole, there is little difference between the occupations of the professional women's fathers and those of the fathers of the women who do not work outside the home.

MARRIED WOMEN

Only half the professional women are or have been married – and this is one of the most striking differences between them and the housewives discussed in Chapter 4. The professional women mostly had married much later than women who did not work, had frequently chosen their own partners, and some had married across boundaries of caste, religion, and language. The association studied in detail contained a Christian woman married to a Brahmin, a south Indian Brahmin married to a north Indian non-Brahmin, and two Nair women from Kerala married to Brahmins.

The husbands of the married women are all in prestigious highly paid jobs, and very few of the wives need to work for economic reasons. Almost half the husbands are at senior management level in (mostly private) companies. A further quarter have their own businesses. The remainder are high ranking army or police officers, senior government servants, lawyers, doctors, and college professors.

Women who are married or who have been married (a few women are widowed, and one is separated; none is divorced) have very small numbers of children. They average only 1.5 per woman, and since most women have passed the age of forty, they are unlikely to enlarge their family size.

The majority of married women are living in nuclear family households. A small minority live in joint families. The remainder live with a varying combination of other relatives; only two (both widows) live alone.

WIDOWS

Women who are widows generally show quite a different pattern of life from women currently married. The widows in this sample had mostly lost their husbands when they were quite young, often with young children to raise. At the time they had not been working, nor even necessarily trained for any career. Widowhood is however the 'dire economic necessity' that obliges a woman to find a job,[4] and is a situation in which she will not be criticized for doing so, even in the most orthodox of families.

One of the women in my sample had married young into a very orthodox Brahmin family. Her husband died when she was in her early twenties and had two young daughters. She had very little education, but her late husband's mother took her to Sister Subbalakshmi, a Brahmin woman who pioneered education for young Brahmin widows (cf. Chapter 6) and she was helped to get a job. Meanwhile, both her husband's father and brother tutored her at home so that she could take her degree externally. Later she trained as a social worker, and worked for the state government for many years. She herself paid for the education of her two daughters to college level, arranged their marriages, and saved enough to build herself a house; during most of her working life she has continued however to live with her husband's family.

Another widow described how when her husband, a government servant, died, she was offered a job in his department since she had a degree and was thus at least formally qualified. In this way she managed to raise her children.

SINGLE WOMEN

There are very few women who remain unmarried in Indian society, and single women may thus be seen as highly deviant in this respect. There appears to be a clear correlation between their single status and their careers. One medical specialist told me 'I just never thought about getting married – I was simply too busy.'

Other women take up a career and start earning – perhaps because of exceptional ability or in order to help their natal families – and may then find it difficult to get a suitable husband, as the following quotation shows:

> 'Most single women who are doctors, or members of other professions, are eldest children. After all, one can leave a doctor unmarried, and people won't criticize. They are wage-earners, and the family becomes dependent upon them, and subsequently reluctant for them to marry as they will lose this source of income (to the husband and his family). I have a colleague of thirty-eight who has been in love with her cousin for five years, but her mother doesn't want her to marry. And I know other younger women doctors who would like to get married, but they can't broach the subject to their parents. They tell me bitterly that their youth is passing, their siblings are getting married, and what about *them*.'
>
> (Medical college professor)

In any case, after working independently for some years, 'You don't feel like having a marriage arranged for you by your parents' as one doctor who had chosen her own husband in her thirties put it. Such a late marriage was an unusual case, for by the time a woman reaches her late twenties there are very few eligible men left for her to marry. Even at the professional level it is considered essential for a husband to be his wife's senior both in age and earning capacity – so women's age and career status make it difficult to find husbands.

Another reason why some women now middle-aged did not marry was because they were among the first in their communities (sub-castes) to get an education. One lawyer told me,

> 'Ours is a business community, and it wasn't thought necessary to send children for education like the Brahmins did. But my parents, especially my father, were progressive, and so I got sent to an English-medium school, then I went and did a law degree. However, there just weren't any suitable young men of my sub-caste who could match me in education at that time. Now it's different. So I stayed single.'

In short, the three main reasons for remaining unmarried seem to have been personal choice, need to support the natal family, and lack of suitable men. The patterns of living for single women are somewhat different than for their married sisters. Some, just under one-third, do live alone, but this is a very rare phenomenon in Indian society. It is considered extremely improper for a woman to set up an independent household, and indeed, such a woman may find it difficult to live with the censure of neighbours, as well as family. Where there is no family, the suitable solution is seen to be hostel living. Some of these women are living, or had lived, in hostels either built specially for working women or else attached to hospitals, colleges, or other places of work. Women who have families living in the place where they work invariably live with them, and some even take their parents with them when they are posted away from the city. Thus a third of the unmarried women are living with their natal families, and form part of either a nuclear household (parents and possibly some unmarried siblings) or a joint household (parents and married brothers, their wives and children). The remainder live with relatives, often a mother or a sister.

Professional women and their problems

Problems that all professional women share are: first, getting a job; second, possible discrimination in promotion; and third, relations with male colleagues.

The incidence of registered unemployment is consistently higher for females than males regardless of educational qualifications (Prasad 1979: 885). For a professional woman this is not usually insurmountable, yet even doctors find fierce competition in the job market. Many women doctors go into private general practice, even though such a tactic means there are no promotion prospects. Women who would like promotion are of course often seen as a threat by male colleagues, and many women commented that 'You have to be at least twice as good as a man' before getting a higher position.

Relations with male colleagues can be difficult. Those of equal seniority may be jealous of women if they appear successful and therefore might threaten their position. Junior colleagues who might resent having a woman tell them what to do are also a source of difficulty. One senior government servant told me she always

made a point of being extremely firm with new male juniors, so
that they realized immediately that she was in fact in charge; once
this point was established, and accepted, then she could relax more.

Another woman who works at a senior level in a bank related
the following incident.

'The other day we were very busy in the office because some
high-ups were coming on an inspection tour. Most of the
men in the office were wanting to get away to go and see
a Test cricket match, and one of them asked me to do a
certain thing. As it happened, I was already in the process of
doing it, although he hadn't checked first to see, but I
resented being asked to do it. I said to him "Why don't *you*
do it? You think because I'm a woman I should be the one
to do it. Do you think I've nothing else to do? And don't I
know that the reason you are so busy is that you are trying
to get away to the Test match?" The man was very much
surprised and embarrassed at my reaction, although he is very
much junior to me. Later my boss asked me why I'd got
angry and I told him I don't have to do what people who
arrived yesterday tell me. Of course, they think I am an
aggressive woman, and they don't like it when I speak my
mind in that way.'

The problem with male colleagues that is seen by society as of
paramount importance concerns the possibility of sexual relations
developing.[5] Women who work outside the home are often
thought to be 'immoral' for this reason. While older and more
mature women can cope with such innuendoes, it can be a real
problem for younger women. One young woman lawyer
described her plight graphically: initially, she had problems at law
college, for she was one of 22 women to 800 men. The women
could not speak to the men without getting nasty comments; this
applied equally to talking to male lecturers. Once qualified, she
had to become the junior of an established male lawyer. This might
mean going to his house to prepare and discuss cases, which could
occasion gossip. She had been invited to the cinema by her senior,
but her mother refused her permission to go and since then her
senior had been angry with her, and she felt that her career chances
were being jeopardized. Further problems arise over the courts –
several women lawyers said their families had refused to allow

them to do criminal law, because of the types of courts they would have to go to and the clients they would have to represent. Therefore most of them remained as civil lawyers. But even so, they have various practical problems. One is where to eat, since women are not supposed to eat in hotels or cafes alone, yet courts do not provide canteens. Another concerns cases that involve sexual matters. An unmarried lawyer in her forties said it was very difficult in such cases 'For I am not supposed to know anything about sex', and she added quickly 'And of course I don't, except what I've read in books.' It is thus not surprising that most women settle for jobs in virtually all-female spheres: teaching in all-girl schools or all-women colleges and the obstetric and gynaecological branches of medicine.

Another further problem for some concerns transport. Those in extremely well-paid jobs can afford to run a car. But others dependent upon public transport suffer not only from its relative paucity in Madras, but also from the length of time needed for travelling by public as opposed to private transport. A further and very important problem to urban women workers of all classes in India travelling in buses and trains is that they are frequently subject to verbal (and occasionally physical) harassment from men. For this reason, most trains have separate all-women compartments and there are 'women-only' buses;[6] these however are not sufficient in numbers to alleviate the difficulties. This is not however a problem that affects many women at this level, for the majority of them do have cars. Most can get to work in half an hour or less, and the majority are also in the happy position of being able to adjust their hours to some extent.

MARRIED WOMEN'S PROBLEMS

In some respects it would appear that middle-class employed women in India are better off than their western counterparts. There is still an abundance of cheap domestic labour, and any household with middle-class pretensions employs at least a part-time servant who comes in daily to clean the house, wash the clothes, and help with kitchen work for very little pay.

On the other hand, marriage is considered the most important sphere of a woman's life and a married woman must please her husband, her children, and frequently her husband's parents too.

Furthermore, at this class level, while a married woman may have relatively little to do in the way of domestic labour in the narrow sense, her 'status production' work-load is a large one, as was shown in Chapter 4. She must ensure that her children go to the 'right' schools and colleges, that they study conscientiously (she takes responsibility for employing a tutor if she does not coach them herself), and that they engage in the expected extra-curricular activities (sports for boys, music or dance for girls). In addition, she must participate in the social life that is expected of couples in this position − giving and attending dinner parties of colleagues and friends, for example, as well as taking care not to offend extended family members by neglecting invitations to weddings and other functions.

A married working woman must not only put her home and family first, she must be seen to do so.[7] One department head told me that she had noticed that in the first year of their marriage young women had a high absentee rate. She attributed this to sensitivity to their in-laws' opinion. A medical specialist told me, 'My husband doesn't mind me working − in fact he's proud of me. But he hates it if I'm not home when he gets home. And I always ask him before taking on extra duties, especially at night.'

In spite of the ready availability of servants, a woman's domestic duties cannot always be delegated. For example, although ayahs can be employed to care for young children, they are generally regarded as untrustworthy, unhygienic, and possessing other undesirable traits. An article on childcare for working parents quotes the following statement:

> 'My husband and I realized that the constant company of the ayah had its impact on the child. He picked up dirty words, ate the wrong food, and was dirty too. My husband told me one day "Let us not miss the woods for the trees." The child is more important than the few hundreds I bring in each month. So I resigned the job and am happy now I did. Everything is normal now and we have domestic peace.'
> (*Hindu*, 16 August 1981)

In other words, this woman is making it clear that it is not possible to delegate her maternal functions to a paid servant. The reasons are not hard to seek; given the enormous gulf between the working and middle classes in India it is simply not possible for a member of the former class effectively to socialize a child to be an appropriate member of the latter class. In Britain in the nineteenth century this problem was overcome by having specially trained nannies and governesses (often poor gentry) who were able to teach their charges the manners and customs of the latter's own class level. This has not happened in India, so the only solution, apart from the drastic one adopted by the woman quoted, is to seek someone else to 'supervise' the ayah, usually a relative.[8]

For women living in a joint family the problem of childcare is solved to some extent. Even here, there may be conflicts about the way in which a mother thinks her children should be brought up and the way that grandparents treat them. One doctor told me that she had resigned her interesting and well-paid post to take up a boring and routine family planning job so that she could be nearer home and work shorter hours, and thus keep a closer eye on her children: 'They pay no attention to what their grandparents say; they just run wild' she remarked.

Such women also suffer from their own guilt feelings. In the last few decades the Indian middle classes have enthusiastically adopted much of the ideology current in the west regarding the need for children to be with their mothers constantly. This is reinforced both by traditional Indian ideas on child-rearing, which de-emphasize independence, and by the need, already discussed, for children to receive extra 'coaching' in academic subjects, which it is expected that mothers will give.

Women tend to attribute any problems in their children – failure to do well at school, misbehaviour, or even sickness – to themselves for 'not spending enough time'. This is, of course, not peculiar to these particular working women. Kirkpatrick's study of professional women in Bangladesh reports women saying '*I have to worry if my children get sick, it is my fault in the eyes of my husband and society*' (1978: 161). Chakrabortty's working-woman informants in Calcutta went even further and attributed their children's sickness to 'maternal deprivation' (1978). In the study by the Madras School of Social Work, 'About one-sixth of working mothers and one-third of their husbands feel that mothers' employment affects children's studies adversely. There is a significantly direct association between [the] age of children and anxiety in this regard' (1970: 73).

Husbands rarely assume any responsibility for any aspect of

domestic labour,[9] even though they may give moral support. Indeed, many of these women are quite shocked at the idea that they might do so. One professional woman commented, 'He doesn't even know how to light the gas [her husband was an engineer!], so *of course* he couldn't make his own coffee, much less cook.'

A final factor in the situation is the widespread and often reiterated view that married women who work outside the home are 'taking away jobs from the men'. I frequently heard this view from housewives, as well as reading it in newspapers and magazines. It was, however, most forcefully and succinctly expressed in a paper presented to a conference organized by professional women in 1975 as follows:

> 'In the case of married women, they are engaged in the creative productivity of the Nation's highest wealth – the manpower of the country. A married woman's primary concern is to her home. A child needs the constant care and vigil of its mother ... [Thus] it is the bounden duty of every mother to maximise the quality of this national wealth without sacrificing it for a monetary benefit for herself.
>
> Moreover as women we feel more for an unemployed father, brother, husband or son than for ourselves ... When our country is facing the grim problem of educated unemployed, women should not rush into a professional career unless it is financially necessary to do so.'

This paper led to a major debate at the seminar, which was attended only by professional women, all currently employed. To my surprise, this viewpoint received a fair amount of support from many women present.

Only women blessed with an abundance of health and energy can cope successfully with this kind of load[10] and these sorts of pressures – in short, 'superwomen' – and the majority of married professional women whom I know fit this label very well. It is perhaps for this reason that many of them refuse to acknowledge that they suffer from problems, discrimination, or prejudice; their attitude is 'I've done it, so why can't others? Women *can* have careers if they want to, but not all want to. That's why women are in the minority in professions.' Thus the majority of professional married women do not challenge the status quo in the way they organize their own lives and, even more strikingly, in the way they bring up their own children, particularly their daughters. Women who have themselves deviated considerably from the norm in carving out a successful career still raise their daughters to think of marriage and family as the most important aspect of their lives. Perhaps, as Maria Mies (1975) has suggested, it is precisely because such women never overtly challenge the ideals regarding womanhood that they are in fact able to deviate so considerably from them.

SINGLE WOMEN'S PROBLEMS

The problems of single women are somewhat different. Rarely do they have to cope with what in the west has come to be termed 'the double shift'. Most of them continue to live with relatives, particularly their own mothers, who take responsibility for household chores. The majority said that they spent almost no time on housework.

However, relatives are not always available, and those that are do not live for ever. It may well be the unenviable lot of a single middle-aged woman to find herself alone and lonely in spite of a successful career. Loneliness arises for a number of reasons. First, most Indians are not socialized to live alone and it is considered, as already stated, not quite respectable for a single woman to do so, even when she is middle-aged. Second, much of Indian social life takes place within the context of the family – initially the natal family, later the family of procreation. For single women, as the members of the former die off, there is none of the latter to replace them. Furthermore, single women are an anomaly in situations where interaction is mainly by couples; they may miss out on social invitations for this reason.

One woman, a childless widow in her forties, told me that after her husband died some time ago, she had decided to live alone, even though her husband's family offered her a home. She did not regret that decision although it meant making certain compromises: 'I can't go off to the cinema on my own.' She also commented that she had left the political party to which she and her husband had been committed members 'Because of the way the men behaved after he died' (in other words, their expectation that she was now 'available'). For many such women the professional women's association is important to them for the sake of the friendship that it brings; spending time with relatively large numbers of other single women is a means of coping with one's deviant status.

None the less, in spite of problems, the majority of single women cope very well. Many of them have nephews and nieces in whom they take an interest, most have close friends, and also have outside activities and hobbies apart from their job. They belong to a strikingly large number of associations, as well as the one under consideration. In fact these women have the highest rate of 'joining' of any, averaging three or four each. One lively woman lawyer, who belonged to a large number of associations and enjoyed going out, had solved her transport problem by having a long-standing arrangement with a particular cycle-rickshaw man who always took her out in the evenings and waited to take her home afterwards.

Single women also have to contend with their own feelings about whether or not they should have married. One woman who worked in publishing said she had noticed that married women look down on spinsters 'as if they had achieved something and we had not', and she noticed this attitude frequently reflected in literature. In fact, since marriage is most usually arranged in Indian society women do not 'achieve' marriage in the same way as women are thought to do in the west. Women who do not marry are not pitied because they were not able to 'catch a husband' or because 'no one would have her'; staying single is the fault of circumstances, or perhaps the fault of parents, but it is not thought to be a woman's fault. Her self-esteem suffers less than it might otherwise do.

Even so, in a society where girls hear constantly '*When* [not 'if'] you are married' from their earliest years, to be unmarried and over the age of twenty-five is an anomaly. Only a minority of women achieve a recognition that marriage is not the be-all and end-all, like a middle-aged doctor who decried it as a form of 'licensed prostitution – a total humiliation for women'. A friend of hers, also a doctor, said, 'I shock my extended family by telling all the girls not to worry about getting a bridegroom, but to get a *job*. The major solution for women is *not* marriage, but economic independence.'

Conclusion: why few women are paid workers

The purpose of this chapter has been to show the reasons why only a very small minority of upper-middle and upper-class women undertake paid work outside the home. In sum, these are the lack of economic necessity, a relative lack of jobs, competition in the job market from men, an education that does not prepare them for the labour market, and the importance of their reproductive role. Such women tend to be married to men who have a relatively high income, who may well be highly mobile because of the nature of their work, and whose need is not primarily for another income earner, but for a wife and mother of their children who can devote her energies full-time to reproductive tasks.

All these factors are backed by an extremely strong ideology, drawn in part from 'traditional' Indian sources on the 'proper' role of women, and reinforced by such western ideas as the 'feminine mystique', the manufacture of housework, and 'maternal deprivation'. These all combine to ensure that the place of women, at this class level is in the home.

Or is it? There is in fact in India a public arena in which women play a very important part, albeit unpaid, and that is the field of social welfare. The women who engage in voluntary social work are primarily the non-employed women of the upper middle and upper classes, and it is to a consideration of their role in this sphere that the remainder of this book is devoted.

Notes

1 Some of the more important sources are Ahmad 1979; ARTEP 1981; Gadgil 1965; Gulati 1975; Mitra 1979a; Mitra, Srimany, and Pathak 1979; Nath 1965; Ranade and Ramachandran 1970; Sengupta 1960; the Decennial Censuses and the Report of the Committee on the Status of Women (Government of India 1974) are also useful.

2 By the 1880s, more than twenty women were studying medicine in India; and the proportion of women doctors in India was much higher than in the west until recently. For the past several decades, the proportion of Indian medical graduates who are female has ranged between 20 and 25 per cent of the total.

3 In practice the amount of sub-categorization allowed for in the

regulations meant that virtually unlimited numbers of women of the same broad professional category could join.

4 Sen's (1960) study of Calcutta found that more than *half* of the women who were working at that time were widows.

5 Rama Mehta's study of divorced working women notes that 'They were vulnerable and could be exploited by men, especially their superiors. The women reported that they were threatened that if they did not do as they were told, their confidential reports would be spoiled, or they would be demoted or even thrown out of their jobs . . . by exploitation they meant "anything and everything" ' (1975: 56).

6 In the latter part of 1981 there was a long-running debate in the correspondence pages of the local English-language press about this practice. Many men wrote to protest that seat reservations and 'women only' buses were unfair to them. Eventually a man took out a court case, claiming discrimination, but the court ruled in favour of the reservations for women continuing (cf. *Hindu*, 14 November 1981).

7 This is true of other parts of the Indian sub-continent. Kirkpatrick's study of educated Bangladeshi women reveals much the same trend:

'That the family looms large in their scale of values is especially apparent when they discuss their roles as mothers . . . Visits by in-laws or own kin often require a woman to take leave for a week or so in order properly to care for them. She cannot do any professional work at this time, as "they would not understand, they would feel hurt", or "it would not look nice, they would think me disrespectful".'

(Kirkpatrick 1978: 142–43)

8 The study by the Madras School of Social Work found that 'a greater proportion of families of working mothers have both relatives and servants for supportive services; a greater proportion of families of non-working mothers have servants (only) or no support services at all' (1970: 74).

9 My findings in this respect are consistent with other studies. The Madras School of Social Work study (1970) reported that very few husbands of white collar working women helped their wives.

Another Madras study, this time of factory workers, stated that 'a majority of women workers in the present sample indicated that they could hardly get any help from the menfolk in their domestic work' (Kalanidhi 1973: 287). Similarly Chakraborthy's study (1978) of working women in Calcutta reported very little help from husbands.

10 The study by the Madras School of Social Work (which looked at women white-collar workers) found that 'There is no significant difference between working and non-working mothers regarding

the amount of time they spend daily in household work; nor does the presence or absence of supportive relatives and number of children make any significant differences in this regard' (1970: 74). Although the study found that a majority of husbands 'share' household tasks with their wives, this was primarily confined to shopping and some childcare (1970: 59).

PART THREE

THE WOMEN'S ORGANIZATIONS

6

The growth of women's organizations in India

In this chapter I consider the development of women's organizations in India over the last century in order to provide some historical background to the case studies of the organizations in Chapters 8 and 9. There now exist several excellent studies of the women's movement in India, notably Maclay (1969), Everett (1979), various articles by Forbes (1979a/b/c, 1980, 1981, 1982), and others.[1] These have all helped to remedy the previous situation in which Indian history scarcely took any account of women.[2] Even so, much of the history of women's organizations in India is of necessity somewhat selective, for not only are women rarely included in most of the official records, but those records that are available pertain primarily to organizations which were led by upper-class women and which were allied with the Congress Party, such as the Women's Indian Association (WIA) and the All-India Women's Conference (AIWC). For such 'elite' organizations, there exist reasonably detailed and available records, many of which have been used by the historians mentioned above. For the more politically radical and/or mass-based organizations, there are few records: they were either never kept or else destroyed (Forbes 1980: vii). Thus the information on Communist women's organizations is relatively sparse (although Chakravarthy's book (1980) does help to fill the gap). The same is true of rural movements like Tebhaga and Telegana in which women have been active; although recently a number of scholars have been researching them.[3]

None the less, the following account is largely of the 'establish-ment' women's organizations, for they are the precursors of the organizations I studied in Madras city in 1974–75 and 1981–82. In order to comprehend the workings of these organizations today, it is important to look at their history. As will be shown, the direction in which they moved has been shaped by their past, parti-cularly their relationship to the nationalist struggle; by the nature of their membership, which was and is largely upper middle and upper class; and by their ideology, which has never been a very radical one.

The period under review may be conveniently divided into three phases: the nineteenth century, when a number of male reformers raised the issue of 'social evils' which affected women; the early twentieth century, when women themselves began to form organizations; and the post-independence period.

The nineteenth century: male reformers

Much of the debate on the 'woman question' in the nineteenth century arose from the questioning of Indian values and institu-tions by such reformist movements as the Brahmo Samaj, Prarthna Samaj, and Arya Samaj,[4] each of which had women's wings and worked, *inter alia*, for widow re-marriage, the raising of the age of marriage for women, and the abolition of child marriage.

Many of the men who supported the suppression of these 'social evils' were themselves western-educated Hindus; they felt either threatened or shamed by the activities of Christian missionaries, who not only were succeeding in converting large numbers of Hindus, especially those of low caste, but who also actively engaged in social service. While admiring much of the techno-logical progress of the west, many of these reformers towards the latter part of the nineteenth century were becoming conscious of the stirrings of an Indian nationalism, and were among those who helped to found the Indian National Congress in 1885. The follow-ing year its first resolution was on female education: on the need for women teachers, for training schools for teachers, adult classes for married women, religious instruction, and text books 'suitable to the requirements of female schools', training in needlework, cooking, domestic economy and childcare (Singh 1968: 175). Sub-sequently however, it was decided that Congress should not concern itself with social reform matters. Indeed, Congress often tended to show a reluctance to support reformist moves.

What characterizes the nineteenth-century period is that there were very few women organizing for women; men organized on their behalf. All the major reforms of this period, from the Abolition of Sati in 1829, the Widow Remarriage Enabling Act of 1856, the Marriage Act of 1872, to the Age of Consent Act in 1891 were primarily due to the efforts of men, mostly those involved in the reformist movement and/or the embryonic nationalist movements. The few women who became active towards the latter part of the nineteenth century were themselves mostly from reformist families and were encouraged by their fathers or husbands.

Not all modern scholars would agree that it was the influence of the west that produced new social movements and attitudes, but rather that the social changes which were coming about – greater urbanization for example – meant that alterations in many spheres would inevitably follow. Mazumdar (1976) contends that two of the major campaigns of the social reformers – education for women and widow re-marriage – were brought about primarily because, with the growth in cities and the employment of males in government service, new demands were made on women.

An examination of the history of women's education would seem to support her conclusions. Sita Ram Singh's (1968) excellent study of nationalism and social reform in the late nineteenth and early twentieth centuries shows that by the turn of the century almost all shades of opinion – reformers, revivalists, even the orthodox – were in favour of women's education. It is clear that the education that such men envisaged women receiving was not to enable them to become independent earners, but rather to enable them to be 'better wives and mothers'. The Leonards quote a not untypical statement from an 1885 article in a Madras newspaper:

> '[India's] need is to devise such a system of education for Hindu females as will make her an agreeable companion, a good mother, an intelligent and loving wife, and an excellent housewife. We want her to possess those mental accomplishments which enable the wife to serve as a solace to her husband in his bright and dark moments, the mother to undertake, or at least to superintend, the early instruction of

her child, and the lady of the house to provide those sweet social comforts idealized in the English word – Home.'
(Quoted in Leonard and Leonard 1981: 33)

This ideal of womanhood might be construed as an attempt to maintain the status quo, but as Mazumdar has pointed out, the domestic roles which women were being taught through the new educational system were roles required by a modernizing family in changing circumstances, particularly in the urban areas; women had in certain respects to take over a wider range of domestic jobs as men spent more time away from home in government or other jobs (1976: 63).

To put it another way, because of the increasing gap between the life experience, including education, of women and men of this class, women could not continue to fulfil their roles as reproducers, especially as socializers of children, unless some suitable form of education was devised for them. Hence the apparent contradiction that the 'progressive' cause of education for women was actually seen as contributing to the maintenance of existing values: 'Education would not turn the women away from their traditional familial roles, but improve their efficiency as wives and mothers, and strengthen the hold of traditional values on society, since women were far better carriers of these values' (Mazumdar 1976: 50).

It is thus scarcely surprising that the concerns of the male reformers were focused very much on the 'problems' or 'social evils' which affected their own womenfolk, and which they saw as hampering this process of 'modernization'.

On another level, the issues men chose to highlight have been said by a number of historians to reflect a dialogue which they conducted with Christian missionaries on the one hand, and their British rulers on the other. In both contexts the 'status of women' was a key symbol, loaded with many significata. Both Indians and British took it as axiomatic that a 'civilization' can be measured by the status of its women. Thus it can be argued that in this situation, as in others, Indian women were seen as important symbols, not only of 'Indian civilization' but, more importantly, of the fittedness of Indians to rule themselves (Everett 1979: 101, 105; Minault 1981: 7–8).

The early twentieth century: women begin to organize

The period between the turn of the century and the coming of independence in 1947 is characterized, as far as the Indian women's movement is concerned, by the founding of numerous women's organizations and their activities in the fields of the franchise[5] and struggles for the growth of women's education, as well as the involvement of many women in the nationalist movement. In this section, I shall concentrate largely upon happenings in Madras city and Madras Presidency, partly because that is the focus of this book, but also because Madras occupied an important place during this period.

Education for women continued to grow slowly. For example, Subbalakshmi Ammal, a Brahmin widow who was the first woman of her community to be trained as a teacher, founded a widows' home in 1913 which later became a teachers' training college (cf. Felton 1966). Although more educational establishments like this were founded, it continued to be stressed that education for women should fit them to be better wives and mothers. The *Indian Ladies Magazine*, for instance, founded in 1901 by Kamala Sattianadhan, wife of a Christian social reformer, often took up the theme of women and education:

'We do not want our women to become literary luminaries and scientific prodigies, so as to enable them to question the superiority of man, and claim equal rights with him, as the enlightened ladies do in England by what is known as the "Woman Suffragist Movement". It is enough if besides being loving and sweet-spoken as they are, they become helpful companions to their husbands in passing through life's wilderness. We have men enough and to spare for sterner works of toil and thought and therefore we do not need that our finer sex should have to trouble their heads with complex problems for which they are naturally unfit.'
(*Indian Ladies Magazine*, VIII: 150 (1909),
quoted in Singh 1968: 172–73)

None the less, women were gradually drawn into political life, especially during the Swadeshi Movement (1904–11).[6] In Madras a group of women formed the Women's Swadeshi League. Its primary aim was to encourage hand-spinning and weaving. Later, however, many of the members became trained volunteers in the demonstrations which were a part of the nationalist struggle; they acted as stewards on demonstrations and led the singing, and helped those who were injured in *lathi* (baton) charges by the police. The members of the League were also active in picketing foreign cloth shops. One account states that their presence was so successful that not only did many customers refrain from entering these shops, but that the salespeople would not sell goods while the picket was on. Women pickets were frequently arrested, and this only helped their cause further.

'The spectators became very annoyed when the non-violent volunteers were arrested. They shouted slogans against the police and would try to garland the women volunteers in appreciation of their bravery in facing the police. But when the police prevented the people from doing so, they would shower the rose petals from the garlands on to the police van.'

(Rau, n.d.)

Many commentators have pointed out that the use of women in such demonstrations was peculiarly effective; the police appeared even more brutal when they *lathi*-charged or roughly handled women. Pearson suggests that in this way women provided an important cohesive force for the nationalist movement; womanhood seemed to transcend caste or class, and helped the Congress leaders to present the movement as one which represented all social groups (1981: 176).

In Madras, foreign women active in the Theosophical Society, notably Annie Besant, Margaret Cousins, and Dorothy Jinarajadasa[7] were responsible for founding the Women's Indian Association in 1917. The following year the Montagu-Chelmsford Commission was sent by the British government to suggest changes in the franchise in India, and Margaret Cousins organized a deputation of women to give evidence to the Commission. Initially, the idea had been to make demands regarding improvement in women's education, but they were told that this fell outside the terms of reference of the Commission. They thus demanded that when the franchise be reformed, women be recognized as 'people' and thus included in the right to vote. The deputation was led by Sarojini Naidu, a Telegu woman who wrote poetry in English (cf. Baig 1974), but it included the three European women Theosophists already mentioned, and other WIA members, as well as a number of women from elsewhere in India (AIWC 1970: 16–18; Muthulakshmi Reddy 1956: 4–7).

Subsequently, the WIA grew rapidly. It was supposed to be an all-India association, but in fact its impact was largely confined to Madras Presidency. Even so, by 1922 it had forty-three branches with 2,300 members, and five years later this had increased to eighty branches and 4,000 members. The Association was supposed to be non-political, but it rapidly became caught up in the growing nationalist movement, particularly when its founder, Annie Besant, was imprisoned by the British for her nationalist activism, whereupon WIA members petitioned for her release. (When she was freed after a few months, she was elected the President of the Indian National Congress, the first woman to hold such office.) Apart from acting as a political pressure group, the WIA also wanted other social reforms. The members were active in the movement to close brothels and open 'rescue homes', in the abolition of the traditional south Indian temple dancers (*devadasis*) who often acted as sacred prostitutes, and in the raising of the age of marriage (Muthulakshmi Reddy 1930). But during the 1920s, much of their energy was taken up with the franchise.

The recommendations of the Montagu-Chelmsford Commission were that women's suffrage be deemed 'a domestic matter', i.e. each of the provinces should decide for itself. Madras Presidency was among the first to give women the right to vote on the same conditions as men, although these were highly restrictive in terms of education and property holding. None the less, it was thought significant by women in the associations that this principle had been conceded by the men without much opposition, whereas in 1918 women in England had only finally been given the vote after years of struggle, and even then it was only initially granted to women over thirty years of age.

Although as the 1920s progressed, more women were entitled to vote as the franchise was widened, very few women were chosen as candidates, and those who were selected were all Congress stalwarts, not veterans of the women's associations. Women who tried to stand for other parties or as independents usually found themselves defeated.

In 1927, when the WIA compiled a list of women in public life, most held office by virtue of nomination not election, and were members of organizations that had submitted their names. In Madras, for example, Dr Muthulakshmi, a WIA activist, was co-opted to the Legislative Council and was chosen as its Vice-President. This was hailed as a great triumph by the WIA. Most members of the women's organizations strongly opposed the British proposal to extend the franchise to women on the basis of wife-hood. As Dr Muthulakshmi put it, 'We do not think woman's rights as a citizen should depend upon her marriage which in the majority of cases in India at present is not entirely under her control' and 'We women wish to be citizens in our own right, independent of any male relations' (Muthulakshmi Reddy 1964: 99). For the next several years, the WIA members petitioned to have all provinces grant the franchise to women on the same terms as men, and this was finally achieved in 1929 when Bihar, the last province to do so, finally gave women the vote.

In the meantime, Margaret Cousins founded in 1926 the All-India Women's Conference (AIWC) in order to press for improved educational facilities for women. For some time, the WIA and AIWC co-existed relatively independently, but in 1935, the WIA became the Madras constituent branch of the AIWC (WIA 1967).

The AIWC was soon widely recognized as the most important women's organization in India. From the 58 delegates representing 5,000 women at the first conference in 1926, the numbers had grown by the 1930s to 126 elected delegates, and 36 constituent organizations, although there were by that time as many as 137 AIWC branches in India. The area of activity had also broadened from the early centring on education to take in social service, personal law, suffrage, employment, and health.

The AIWC leadership used various strategies to gain its end: they presented their views to government officials; they formed committees of investigation on a variety of topics; and they demanded that women be selected to sit on official bodies. In addition, they engaged in fund-raising and setting up adult educa-tion classes, rescue homes, and the like.

In the same years as the founding of the AIWC, Sarojini Naidu, a WIA leader, became President of Congress which further strengthened the links between the nationalist and women's move-ments. As a result of this, the women's movement tended to adopt the official Congress ideology that feminism meant a 'sex war' which would detract from the main struggle (Forbes 1981:60).

The women's organizations accommodated many of the unchanged rules governing relations between women and men – for example, they never challenged purdah, instead seeking to ameliorate it by organizing such institutions as 'purdah parks' and separate compartments for women in trains and trams. To attack such institutions was thought to risk alienating both women and men, and also being branded as 'pro-western', and thus, implicitly, collaborators with the British. In return for women's support, Congress rewarded some women with important tasks. For example, Dr Muthulakshmi was selected in 1928 to go to the first Round Table Conference in London.

The year 1930 saw the start of the Non-Cooperation Movement, headed by Gandhi. It was initiated by the Salt Satyagraha, a march to the coast where, in defiance of the law, participants proceeded to make salt. Gandhi and many other activists on the march, including Sarojini Naidu, were arrested. Dr Muthulakshmi resigned from the Madras Legislative Council in protest.

Gandhi and women

It is important at this point to consider Gandhi and the impact he had upon the women's movement. It is frequently said in India today that it was because of Gandhi that large numbers of Indian women came out of their homes to participate in the nationalist struggle, and thus were able to become emancipated. The picture, however, is somewhat more complex. Some see Gandhi as a progressive force in the women's cause, others have labelled him reactionary.[8] His own writings on the subject are somewhat contradictory. On the one hand, he castigated many of the customs that he saw as holding women down – early marriage and enforced widowhood for example. He also maintained that there should be equality between the sexes:

'Woman is the companion of man, gifted with equal mental capacities. She has the right to participate in the minutest details of the activities of man, and has the same right to freedom and liberty as he ... By sheer force of a vicious custom, even the most ignorant and worthless men have been enjoying a superiority over women which they do not deserve and ought not to have.'

(*Young India*, 26 February 1918)

He professed himself entirely in favour of women's participation in the nationalist struggle: 'To me the female sex is not the weaker sex. It is the nobler of the two; for it is, even today, the embodiment of sacrifice, silent suffering, humility, faith and knowledge' (1942: 12). For this reason, Gandhi was anxious that women join the struggle: 'I would love to find that my future army contained a vast preponderance of women over men. If the fight came, I should then approach it with much greater confidence than if men predominated. I would dread the latter's violence. Women would be my guarantee against such an outbreak' (1942: 167). Also, 'Since resistance in *satyagraha* is offered through self-suffering, it is a weapon open pre-eminently to women ... She can become the leader in *satyagraha* which does not require the learning that books give, but does require the stout heart that comes from suffering and faith' (1942: 187).

Some commentators have stated that Gandhi co-opted a growing women's movement, and channelled its energies into the struggle which he led (Omvedt 1973). For this he has been hailed for his perspicacity in realizing that in the women of India there lay a vast untapped source of energy (Mazumdar 1976). And yet, he has also been accused of de-radicalizing the women's movement by emphasizing woman's 'nobler nature' which stems from her capacity to give birth, and what he saw as her 'natural qualities' as a mother (Mies 1975). Gandhi stated several times that he saw women's and men's roles as complementary: 'Equality of the sexes does not mean equality of occupations ... Nature has created [the] sexes as complements of each other. Their functions are defined as are their forms' (1942: 236); and 'I do not envisage the wife, as a rule, following a vocation independent of her husband. The care of the children and the upkeep of the household are quite enough to fully engage her energy (Gandhi 1942: 21).

While several western feminist scholars, such as Mies and Omvedt, have been critical of statements such as these, and indeed negative in their appraisal of Gandhi's effect on women, Indian scholars have usually been kinder in their judgements. Vina Mazumdar, for example, sees Gandhi as having broken away from the reformist tradition by preaching absolute equality between men and women, and by enrolling women in the nationalist struggle which would be the precursor of the abolition of all kinds of inequality (1979: xii). Renu Chakravarthy, long an activist in the Communist movement, makes much the same point (1980: 221) and so does the Report of the Committee on the Status of Women in India (Government of India 1974: 285). Forbes (1981) has also pointed out that only a few people, like Gandhi, were actually able to understand that the 'separate worlds' concept so prevalent in Indian society is related to deep-seated notions about female sexuality.

Gandhi wrote and spoke over a long lifetime and although his ideas changed, as he himself was the first cheerfully to admit, some of his statements placed side by side do sound contradictory. As Mazumdar has said, 'Gandhi was the only one who went beyond customs and individuals, and sought a new social and moral role for women, outside sex relationships. But even he could not free himself altogether from the familial images and the language of the reformers' (1976: 66). Thus Gandhi's ideas about women were a mixture of traditional Hinduism, with his extolling of Sita (heroine of the Ramayana) as the ideal chaste and loyal wife, and the Victorian 'angel in the house' (Mies 1975: 58).

The name of Gandhi today can be invoked to justify quite radical feminism, as well as more traditional ideas about women's role and nature. Gandhi's relations with the women's organizations were also somewhat equivocal. He did not support legal reform, regarding it as a palliative to the problems of upper-caste, upper-class, urban women. In reply to a letter from Dr Muthu-lakshmi Reddy, which urged his support for the eradication of 'social evils', he wrote in *Young India* that they should realize that in the villages, there was neither child marriage nor prohibition on widow re-marriage. They (i.e. the women's associations) were concentrating on problems that affected only a minority of middle-class urban dwellers.

> 'Before, therefore, reform on a large scale takes place, the mentality of the educated class has to undergo transformation. And may I suggest to Dr Muthulakshmi that the few educated women that we have in India will have to descend from their Western heights and come down to India's plains?'
> (Muthulakshmi Reddy 1964: 114)

In many respects this dialogue is intrinsic to many political struggles: which is paramount, women's emancipation or the freedom struggle? Gender or class? Those who believe the latter is can relegate women's problems to the background by labelling them as 'elitist' or 'western', as did Gandhi, and later Nehru. The latter condemned many of the demands of the women's movement as 'superficial' because he said they did not enquire into root causes. But Kamaldevi Chattopadhyay replied to this by maintaining that the fight which women were conducting against society and its rigid codes was far harder than any political struggle (quoted in Forbes 1982).

None the less, Nehru had a point in emphasizing the economic content of women's problems, which most of the women's organizations failed to do. Addressing women in Bombay in 1936, he said, 'Freedom depends on economic conditions even more than political, and if a woman is not economically free and self-earning, she will have to depend on her husband or someone else, and dependants are never free' (Nehru 1972: 235–36).

The women's organizations were not, however, concerned with viewing women as productive workers. On the contrary, they played an active part in getting the government to pass protective legislation to debar women from working in coal mines; once this was passed (and hailed by the AIWC as a great victory), large numbers of working-class women found themselves jobless.[9]

The women's organizations, composed as they were of wealthy, urban upper-caste and class women, still thought they could represent 'Indian womanhood'. As Dr Muthulakshmi said 'only a few educated women of the land can speak, on behalf of our sex, who have been denied for ages the freedom and opportunities to develop their full moral, intellectual and physical height' (1964: 47). Thus the women's movement continued by and large to voice a largely conservative view of women's role. In 1932, the AIWC took what Kamaldevi Chattopadhyay described as the 'very wise and commendable step in setting up a college of Home Science, Lady Irwin College [named after the Viceroy's wife] in Delhi . . . [which] became in [the] course of time a great landmark in women's education' (1975: 30). Education for what she does not say, but plainly such a place would primarily turn out home-makers who would be capable of fulfilling their productive functions in a modernizing and urbanizing society.

The ideology of the women's organizations

It is tempting to adopt the view taken by various commentators on this period that most members of women's organizations were extremely careful not to alienate male support, and thus chose their arguments to fit the occasion. The kind of arguments put forward in support of their case by women had to be in a language both the nationalists and the British could understand. This was not too difficult, because in many ways they had rather similar ideas regarding women. Both believed that women had a special function and nature because of their family roles, and that women should be well treated because of their importance in the family; both believed that the index of a civilization was the position of women. Similarly, both Indians and British had a respect for 'modern science'.

Thus campaigners could justify women's separate education and health facilities, and the training of women teachers and doctors in terms of women's 'special needs and qualities'. They also turned to history and the sacred scriptures in an attempt to show that their activities neither challenged orthodoxy, nor were without precedent. Muthulakshmi Reddy for example, made a speech to the International Congress of Women in Paris in which she quoted women in Indian history

> 'who had distinguished themselves in every sphere of life, i.e. in art, philosophy, literature and in the art of government, such as the famous Padmini of Rajputana ... Chandibibi, Warrior Queen of the Deccan, Alahalyabai of Malwa who fought on the battle-field with her husband Dasaratha, and the famous Avvai of the Tamil country who sat in the Tamil Sangam and whose immortal verses will live as long as the world lasts.'
>
> (Muthulakshmi Reddy 1964: 42)

Women campaigners also maintained that in the early Vedic period in India there was no child marriage, that both boys and girls were educated, that girls had a coming of age ceremony just as boys did, and that there was free marriage choice. Only later accretions to pristine Hinduism and particularly the Muslim invasions had resulted in such 'social evils' detrimental to women as purdah, child marriage, and so on.

While such arguments proved tactically useful on many occasions, and were often reinforced by judicious reference to 'modern science' as well, they were of course limited in their impact. As Everett points out 'The use of religious ideals to legitimize their activities would make it difficult for women leaders to attack Hindu law, Islamic law, or the caste system – each of which were significant obstacles to improving the status of Indian women' (1979: 67).

By and large, the language in which women presented their case was one of caution, almost apology, never confrontation. A good example is the text of a petition for the removal of the disqualification of women to vote in Bihar, the last province to grant the franchise to women in the 1920s.

'This present disqualification is a purely modern and western importation out of keeping with the religious attitude of India towards womanhood and it is urgent that it be removed at the beginning of a new era in self-government ...

Women consider it is giving them an inferior and degrading status for them to be classed with lunatics, criminals and children, as these are the only disqualifications for voting ...

We confidently appeal to you to vote for this Resolution because:

It is only a permissive, not a compulsory opportunity.

It will affect only one woman as compared with every twenty men in Bihar province.

It cannot interfere with the home duties of this small number of qualified women as voting takes place only once every three years ...

It will not interfere with purdah customs ...

It will not admit women to sit in the Council ...

It will show that Bihar men honour their women folk as highly as do the Madras and Bombay men, and as highly as do the men of Western countries.'

(Muthulakshmi Reddy 1956: 36–8)

Here appeals are made to the past glories of India, when the country was free of foreign rule and women were also free, to the veneration for women as mothers, and implicitly, to Bihar men to show themselves as progressive as men in other parts of India, as well as in the west. And yet the tone is apologetic, hastening to point out that giving women the vote will not really make any difference to anything – and certainly not to women's domestic role. Similarly, an examination of the stated goals of organizations like the WIA and the AIWC shows this pre-occupation with women as mothers. Among the WIA objectives are:

'1 to establish equality of rights and opportunities between men and women . . .
2 to help women to realise that the future of India lies largely in their hands, for as wives and mothers they have the task of training, guiding and forming the characters of the future rulers of India.'

(Muthulakshmi Reddy 1964: 160)

One area that was never attacked or even discussed by the women's associations was women's reproductive role. It was assumed that it was 'natural', 'noble', and that it should be 'improved' by education. The rights of women to be independent wage-earners, or for their burden of housework to be shared, is never heard. Occasionally there are glimpses that there must have been some discussion on the value of domestic labour:

'Home-keeping women are waking up to the fact that their hard work is at least half the labour for which their man is being handed certain money which he incorrectly calls "his" pay . . . There are many signs pointing to a new recognition by law that the wife is entitled to the honourable status of the technical term "worker", and as such entitled to a proportion of the "pay" of which the present economic system gives full control to the man.'

(Cousins 1947: 181)

Cousins suggested that the government guarantee housewives a proportion of their husband's income (Everett 1979: 97), but such proposals never appear to have been taken up seriously.

In 1937, a National Planning Committee was instituted, and one of its sub-committees was charged with examining the role of women in a planned economy. The best they could offer to reduce women's domestic burden was a recommendation 'That adequate leisure for women may be ensured with regard to the timings of meals at a fixed hour so that the housewife could be released for a while from the duties of the kitchen' (Shah 1947).

Conclusion

It is of course easy in retrospect to dismiss much of the women's movement as bourgeois, elitist, and basically conservative, not to say politically naïve. However, the conditions from which it emerged must be borne in mind, in other words, its progress must be judged by its baseline. As Nehru put it:

'Our women came to the forefront and took charge of the struggle. Women had always been there of course but now there was an avalanche of them which took not only the British Government but their own men folk by surprise. There were these women, women of the upper or middle class, leading sheltered lives in their homes, peasant women, working-class women, rich women – pouring out in their tens of thousands in defiance of government orders and police lathis. It was not only the display of courage and daring but what was even more surprising was the organisational power they showed.'

(Nehru 1972: 3)

It can thus be argued that the women's movement had to compromise, and had to adopt a language and devise goals and aims which would not alienate male support. There was therefore no attack on the patriarchal bases of Indian culture. This might have been unlikely in any case, for the majority of women's leaders, who were themselves drawn from the upper castes and classes, shared with men of their background a concept of complementary sex roles. There is little in their own writings to suggest that their private views were different from those they put forward in public (cf. also Everett 1979: 65).

It may be debated whether or not the history of the growth and activities of women's organizations in India constitutes the history of a 'women's movement'. In many respects, it was not a completely autonomous movement. It began with the reformist movements of the nineteenth century, which were all led by men. During the pre-independence period of the twentieth century, when women's organizations existed, they had to compromise on many issues because of their relationship with the nationalist movement, which again was largely led by males. Women were unwilling or unable to alienate male support by appearing too radical. In any case, most of the organizations I have been considering in this chapter were drawn from the upper classes and castes, and would scarcely be likely to espouse a radical ideology.

Throughout this period it is important to view the organizations and their members in wider context. They must be viewed historically, for they were the products of a specific constellation of factors at a particular time. As society was changing, new roles for women, particularly in the reproductive sphere, were needed, and new jobs created to teach those roles. Women were needed in the nationalist struggle, partly as a universal symbol, partly because they were good at the kind of tactics being used by Gandhi and his followers, and partly because so many men were imprisoned. The wider society viewed women as an 'index of civilization', as well as 'upholders of Indian tradition'.

Most members of the women's organizations genuinely believed that with independence and the passing of the legal reforms for which they had campaigned,[10] they had gone a long way on the road towards emancipation. But by not challenging patriarchy in the form of religious norms and values, or their assignment to reproductive roles, women never really examined the reasons for their own oppression. Their ideology contained many contradictions, which were reflected in their aims and tactics. In the post-independence era, as I shall show in Chapter 7, the women's organizations have virtually ceased to act as campaigning pressure groups. They have turned their attention instead to social welfare, a field which may well be viewed as an extension of women's domestic role.

Notes

1 Other useful works are Basu 1976; Chakravarthy 1980; Cousins 1947; Kaur 1968; Leonard and Leonard 1981; Luthra 1976; Mazumdar 1976; Minault 1981; Pearson 1981; Singh 1968.
2 This is true even of the work of many modern scholars writing recently on the nationalist movement, as Pearson (1981: 188) has pointed out.
3 For information on peasant movements and women's roles in them see Baghuna 1980; Mies 1975; Omvedt 1975a, 1978.

4 The Brahmo Samaj was founded by Ram Mohan Roy in 1825 to oppose the dogmatic structure of religious Hindu tradition. Its members advocated the abolition of child marriage, seclusion of women, and polygamy, and emphasized the need for women's education. They also sought to bring untouchables into the Hindu fold and advocated inter-caste marriages. It was active mainly in Bengal and north India, but was also influential in parts of south India, particularly Andhra Pradesh.

The Prarthna Samaj was founded in 1867, with similar ideals. Some of its members were active in campaigning for reforms concerned with women, particularly Ranade, who also founded the National Social Conference. Two leading Prarthna Samajists were Vice-Chancellors of the women's university started by Karve. The Samaj was confined mainly to western India.

The Arya Samaj, founded in 1875 by Dayanand Saraswati, was a religious, rather than a reformist, movement. It sought a return to the purity of the *Vedas* and rejected the rigidity of the caste system, while not seeking its abolition. The Arya Samaj set up many educational institutions for women.

5 The best sources on this campaign are Everett 1979 (Chapter VII) and Minattur 1980; Chaudhary 1961 is also useful.

6 The Swadeshi (literally 'own country') movement was a campaign to persuade Indians to stop using imported European goods and, so far as possible, to use locally made products. This applied particularly conspicuously to cloth, and the use of handspun cloth became an important political symbol.

7 Annie Besant had been active in England as a suffragist and in campaigns for birth control. She then became a Theosophist, and went to India in 1893. She later settled in Madras, where she was active as a Theosophist (President of the Theosophical Society for many years), in the women's movement (helping to found the WIA) and in the Indian National Congress, of which she was elected President in 1918 (cf. Aiyar 1963; Besant 1894; Nethercot 1960, 1963).

Margaret Cousins was also a Theosophist and educationalist who, like Annie Besant, was from an Irish and suffragist background. For accounts of her life see Cousins and Cousins 1950 and Muthulakshmi Reddy 1956.

There is very little information available about Dorothy Jinarajadasa, other than that she was a European married to a Singhalese who was President of the Theosophical Society, and that she was active in the WIA.

8 Among those who have called Gandhi a progressive in terms of his attitudes to women are Basu 1976; Forbes 1981; Mazumdar 1976;

Muthulakshmi Reddy 1964. Those who are more critical of his role include Everett 1979; Jayaraman 1981; Mies 1975; Minault 1981; Omvedt 1975b; Pearson 1981.

9 A booklet published by the AIWC in 1973 states that:

'Long before there was any concern on the part of the authorities regarding the position of women working in plantations and mines, the AIWC set up its own Investigation Committee. Its report influenced the tenure (*sic*) of reforms that came subsequently. When the ban on women working underground in mines was withdrawn by the then Government in war years, the representative of the AIWC and other National Women's Organisations in the Central Assembly sponsored a resolution which was accepted with the help of the Congress and (Muslim) League benches. The resultant effect was that the ban was reimposed.

'Even after independence ... the AIWC and its branches were vigilant on behalf of the working classes with special emphasis on women labour.'

(Lam 1973: 3)

10 The best sources on this campaign are Chaudhary 1961; Everett 1979 (Chapter VII); Minattur 1980. The Acts are:

1 *Special Marriage Act* (1954) allowed civil marriage to all Indians, divorce by mutual consent, and raised the age of marriage to eighteen for females and twenty-one for males.
2 *Hindu Marriage Act* (1955) legalized inter-caste marriage, directed monogamy, and allowed for divorce in Hindu marriage.
3 *Hindu Succession Act* (1955) gave females absolute estate in property, and allowed widows, daughters, mothers, and sons to get equal shares.
4 *Hindu Minority and Guardianship Act* (1956) gave custody of a child under three to the mother. Appointed as the children's 'natural guardian' first the father and then the mother.
5 *Hindu Adoptions and Maintenance Act* (1956) allowed for adoption of daughters.

7
Women's organizations and social welfare in India

Prior to independence, the women's organizations had two main functions, as was shown in the last chapter. One was to act as a pressure group in bringing about changes in the laws which affected women – the vote, inheritance, marriage, and so on. The other was to press for better educational and health facilities for women and, in many instances, to set up and run such facilities themselves.

In the immediate post-independence period, many women's organizations began to lay greater stress on social welfare activities, which they saw as a contribution to the sort of 'constructive work' Gandhi had preached. At the same time, the state (i.e. the Union government) had also declared itself ready to try and ensure the existence of social services for all citizens and began programmes of building schools and colleges, hospitals and dispensaries. While committing itself to the ultimate objective of a 'welfare state', there was realization on the part of the government that resources were grossly inadequate and, accordingly, it was decided to utilize as far as possible the voluntary sector, comprised to a large extent of women's associations.

This chapter examines the role of the women's organizations in the field of social welfare, and the relationship between the state, at both local and national levels, and the voluntary welfare sector.

Social welfare, the state, and the voluntary sector

An important distinction has grown up in India between *social services* on the one hand, and *social welfare* on the other. The First Five Year Plan (1951–56) gave social welfare a comprehensive definition.

'The object of social welfare is the attainment of social health which implies the realisation of such objectives as adequate living standards, the assurance of social justice, opportunities for cultural development through individual and group expression, and readjustment of human relations leading to social harmony.'

But it also saw social welfare programmes essentially as promoting the welfare of 'under-privileged groups, neglected areas, the vulnerable section of the community, and those who are labouring under physical or moral handicaps' (Government of India, Planning Commission 1953: 226). This latter, narrower definition of social welfare as being primarily for 'weaker' or vulnerable sections has now become standard,[1] as has the identification of women and children as the main recipients of social welfare.

Social services, on the other hand, are seen as 'an investment in the betterment of human resources in general' (Government of India, Planning Commission 1968: 403) such as health, housing, and education. Between 12 per cent and 21 per cent of total Plan allocation[2] is given to social services. By contrast social welfare has never had an allocation higher than 0.3 per cent (Patil 1978: 66).

The social services, particularly education and health, are seen as a form of social investment, whereas social welfare, as it has come to be defined, is largely viewed as a social expense, being particularly concerned with those who are unemployed. The state itself makes very little provision for the latter category, instead it concentrates its resources on controlling agencies, such as the police. Social welfare has been largely left to the voluntary sector, but the state has intervened in a number of important ways, as I shall show in this chapter.

Because voluntary social welfare agencies tend to be run by women's associations and thus to concentrate their welfare programmes upon women and children, social welfare has been viewed very much as their province, both by the organizations themselves and by the state. From the beginning of the post-independence era, the state has stressed the role of the voluntary agencies in social welfare activities. As the First Plan put it:

> 'It is envisaged that, within the limitations, the Central and State governments and the local authorities will strive to undertake more direct responsibility in respect of social welfare than hitherto. But the voluntary agencies will have to share the major burden in this field, and their role in social welfare is emphasized in the plan.'
>
> (Government of India, Planning Commission 1953: 239)

The government did not leave the voluntary agencies to their own devices, but proposed to set up a Central Social Welfare Board (CWSB) to act as a co-ordinating and grant-giving body for them. This idea was largely the brainchild of Dr Durgabai Desmukh,[3] a member of the Planning Commission, whose husband was the Finance Minister, and who herself became the first Chairman of the Board.[4]

The reason for deciding to use voluntary agencies was a combination of expediency (that they were already in existence, had a pool of voluntary labour, and could generate some of their own funds) and ideology (that they are thought to be less bureaucratic and more democratic); in many respects, this view has not changed in the twenty-five years since the Board's inception.[5] The Draft Five Year Plan for the Sixth period for example directs that: 'State intervention has to be kept at a minimum and voluntary action has to be promoted to a large extent' (Government of India, Planning Commission 1978: 250–51).

Even so, there have been considerable shifts in the relations between the state and voluntary sectors and in the position of the Central Board itself *vis-à-vis* both Union and state governments. What is important to note at this point is that social welfare is seen as an area in which women and children are the main beneficiaries, which is primarily the concern of the voluntary sector (particularly the women's organizations), and that although the government gives funds to the voluntary sector, it does not do so in large amounts.

The Central Social Welfare Board (CSWB)

The CSWB was set up in 1953, with the objectives of studying needs and requirements and evaluating programmes in social welfare, and also of promoting social welfare through setting up new voluntary organizations where these were needed. Its main activity in fact has largely consisted of giving grants-in-aid to voluntary institutions carrying out welfare work. During the first twenty-five years of its existence it disbursed Rs 610 million (CSWB 1978b: 613).

The Board is composed of a mixture of voluntary 'social workers',[6] who are invariably women, and one of whom is the Chairman (*sic*), and representatives of government. Out of a current membership of forty-five, around two-thirds are likely to be women voluntary social workers.[7] Membership is an honorary post, except that travel and other expenses are paid, and in recent years the Chairman has been allocated a salary. It is laid down that members should be educated, familiar with English, experienced in social work, have sufficient time and be sufficiently free of domestic commitments to be able to attend their duties and travel when needed; they should also be 'non-political' but have wide contacts with both state governments and legislatures, and social welfare agencies (CSWB 1978b).

In 1954, Boards were set up in each of the States of the Union; these are likewise composed largely of female voluntary social workers with similar qualifications to the Central Board members. Half the State Board members are nominated by the Central Board and half by the state government. The Chairmanship is fixed by mutual agreement between the state government, which makes the nomination, and the Central Board, which must approve it. Chairmanship of a State Board is almost a full-time job, since not less than 4–5 hours of office-work per day are required (Chowdhry 1971: 196). The functions of the State Board are broadly to assist and advise the Central Board. All grant applications come in the first instance to the State Boards, where they are scrutinized and passed on with recommendations to the Central Board.

Since the setting up of the Central Board in 1953, voluntary agencies have become increasingly dependent upon it, as well as upon other government sources for grants. This was inevitable, given the terms of reference of the Board to encourage the setting up of agencies in areas where these did not already exist. In the years immediately following the Board's inception, a plethora of new organizations was founded, more than at any time before or since (cf. Chowdhry 1971: 43).

Initially, after the inception of the State and Central Boards, women voluntary social workers were chiefly responsible for administering most of the state's funds allocated to social welfare through their voluntary agencies. Quite a number of such women who had been engaged in social welfare at the time of independence found themselves recruited into the bureaucracy, and some became members of state legislatures, or even cabinets at Union or state level (cf. Chowdhry 1971: 34). For women, then, social work at this period provided an avenue to politics (cf. also Wolkowitz 1983). However, any interest in such matters always had to be circumspect, otherwise a social worker might be accused of working for ulterior motives, as indeed some were (cf. Nanvathy 1968: 92–3), or or using social welfare work as a stepping stone to a political career (Malkani 1968: 409).

Gradually, however, the relative political and economic power of the Central and State Boards has decreased because of a number of policy decisions. The state, both at Union and local level, has increasingly intervened directly in the field of social welfare in two ways: first by lessening the autonomy of the CSWB, and second by involving itself directly in more social welfare programmes, including acting as a direct granting agency. I discuss each of these in turn.

The status of the CSWB has always been somewhat anomalous. When it was established in 1953, it had no rival in the field. Subsequently, a Ministry of Social Welfare was established in 1960, although relations between the Ministry and the Board were never clearly defined or demarcated. The Ministry itself initially had a somewhat chequered career, beginning its life in the Ministry of Education, being shifted to Law in 1964, to Planning the following year, and then back again to Education, where it resides currently. With the creation of a Department of Social Welfare at the Union level (part of the Ministry), the autonomy of the Board was further reduced. Furthermore, over time the Ministry and the Department have been given far more money than the Board has received.

Areas that were originally under the purview of the Board have passed to the central or state government. For example, the Family and Child welfare projects, which the Board initiated, have been transferred to the state governments, leading to a decline of the activities of the Board in the rural areas (CSWB 1978b: 13). The Board itself is unable to counter such moves, since it is dependent upon the state governments for its finances. At one time, the Board had a member in the Planning Commission and therefore was in a position to assist in policy-making, but this is no longer the case.

The decline in the relative power and autonomy of the CSWB and similarly of the SSWB, has not, however, necessarily meant a decline in the importance of the voluntary sector. The state itself may deal directly with the voluntary organizations rather than through the medium of the Central and State Social Welfare Boards.

Certain services previously provided by the voluntary sector have come to be defined as 'statutory services' (which by law must be provided by the state). For example, in 1956, the Prevention of Immoral Traffic in Women and Girls Act was passed, by which the state itself is obliged to provide 'rescue homes' for women 'in moral danger'. In such instances, the state may choose to act through existing voluntary agencies (or be obliged to do so by financial stringency) (cf. Kulkarni 1981: 60) but it may also decide to set up its own institutions. Since the former seems to have been the more popular option, the voluntary sector may actually benefit financially from such changes in the law. According to Chowdhry (1971), the proportion of income which the voluntary agencies received from statutory sources increased from just over 30 per cent in 1953 to nearly 40 per cent in 1961.

The state may give grants directly to existing voluntary bodies even in areas that are non-statutory. This also appears to have become an increasingly important source of funding, particularly at the local state level, from where in 1971, nearly a quarter of the voluntary agencies' income came (Chowdhry 1971: 63).

Thus, while in the early years after the founding of the CSWB the voluntary agencies became increasingly dependent upon it for funds, latterly, they have also become dependent upon state funds given directly (cf. Kulkarni 1981: 61). Other money comes from fund raising, donations, subscriptions, and the services of volunteers which can be given a nominal cash value for the purpose of raising the 'matching' part of grants.

None the less, in spite of its economic dependence, the voluntary sector has played an important role in formulating policy, especially during the early years. Indeed, it still has greater importance than the state sector in terms of the number of its beneficiaries. In this sense, it is possible to agree with Chowdhry that 'The bulk of social welfare services in the country is organized by voluntary agencies' (1971: 171), even if much of the funding comes from the state.

Voluntary and paid social workers

Studies that mention voluntary social workers all seem to be in agreement on the kind of person who engages in this activity. Most are women, they come from wealthy families, are well-educated (many to graduate level), and usually are aged between forty and sixty (Chowdhry 1971; Government of India, Planning Commission 1971; Mehta 1968). Most of them classify themselves as either 'housewives' or 'social workers' (Chowdhry 1971: 200).

Within a voluntary organization the office bearers and committee members tend to have the longest experience (usually more than ten years) in social welfare. Most of those who are allocated to the category of 'social worker' are doing supervisory or executive work, rather than grass-roots work (Chowdhry 1971: 295). N. V. Lalitha's study of what she terms 'operational' volunteers (i.e. as opposed to 'administrative' volunteers, who are the committee members, and the ones usually designated as 'voluntary social workers') found a wider range of occupations and incomes in this category. Even so, she describes most of the women as middle or upper middle class, and 65 per cent of her volunteers had an independent income (Lalitha 1975: 54).

Much lip service is paid by the voluntary sector to the need for social work training, and indeed, many of the schools of social work that have been founded in India since independence came into being because of the efforts of the voluntary sector. None the less, there is considerable tension between professional and voluntary workers.

Professional workers are graduates who have undergone postgraduate training in social work. On a formal level, they are better educated than most voluntary workers, relatively few of whom hold postgraduate degrees. They tend however to come from a somewhat lower class background than voluntary workers; Desai describes them as essentially an 'upwardly mobile social group and likely to have considerable achievement-orientation and aspirations regarding jobs, security and salaries' (1981: 222).

While the approach of voluntary social workers to their clients is very much that of 'philanthrophy' or 'charity' (sometimes described as 'paternalistic' (*sic*); it is discussed in greater detail in Chapter 10), the approach of professional social workers is somewhat different. Social work training in India is heavily influenced by American methods and techniques, which tend to utilize an individual case work approach, attributing clients' problems to individual pathology, and seeing solutions in terms of therapy (cf. Midgley 1981). This approach was criticized in India even twenty-five years ago (e.g. Khinduka 1965) and has been more forcibly criticized in a volume edited by Nair (1981; see particularly the articles by Desai; Gangrade and Varma; and Singh). Many of the contributors point out that training in social work is oriented to relief, to system maintenance, and not at all to social change, much less to social justice:

> 'They [professional social workers] aim at helping people adjust . . . social work was established to help the deviants of the system to adjust to it and to provide remedial services . . . the emphasis is on social and individual problems of pathology rather than the problems of the individual and the society in the context of development.'
>
> (Desai 1981: 212)

In other words, professional social work has always been a means of propping up the system, rather than trying to change it. One of the ways in which it does this is to label as 'deviants' people who are poor and handicapped, particularly if they are female. There is however a marked reluctance to change social work training, partly because of its middle-class biases, partly because of the strong resistance of the managing bodies of many schools of social work (which are often composed of voluntary social workers), and partly because of the students' anxiety over employment prospects (Nair 1981).[8]

None the less, large numbers of professional social workers are being trained, many of them men, and many of them do seek work in the social welfare sector. Numerous studies indicate that professional social workers who are employed in social welfare agencies suffer poor pay and working conditions (cf. Government of India, Planning Commission 1971; Nair 1978; Rama 1974),[9] which rarely include pension rights or maternity leave. In addition their skills and training are infrequently recognized. Most decision-making is in the hands of the voluntary social workers, and professionals may have little say in formulating policies (Ranade 1968: 45). Indeed, the atmosphere in such agencies may be quite unfavourable to professionals, as Basu (1971: 93) points out, for 'practising social workers even today come across numerous people for whom a "social worker" is a person with charitable leanings' (Gangrade and Varma 1981).

A study by Nair (1978) in Tamilnadu found that most agencies either do not employ professional social workers at all, or, if they do, offer them very low wages, rather poor service conditions, and little access to decision-making. The vast majority (70 per cent) of paid workers do not have any job security, and more than half of those interviewed by Nair's team had never ever been informed of their terms and conditions of service. Most paid executives in voluntary organizations are men, usually well educated, while the majority of voluntary workers are women. Most agencies are reluctant to employ professional social workers, or even trained workers of any kind, if they can make do with the services of voluntary or untrained people. The major reason cited is of course, cost, but some agencies also say that 'paid workers lack dedication, and that to serve should be its own reward' (Nair 1978: 248). There is increasing pressure from the state, however, that a 'scientific' approach to social welfare is necessary, and that trained workers should be employed as much as possible.

Women voluntary social workers feel themselves threatened by professionally trained social workers who are from a lower class background, often male, and who may try to propose different methods and solutions to their own. Attacks are made on such workers in such terms as the following:

'There was a time when we used to get workers who never asked for a single pie to organise the work. Now our educated women are using their education and degrees to build up their own careers. I am very sorry to say this. They may be

angry with me, but the dedicated workers from among the educated are not coming forth. What is necessary today is a dedicated, spirited and intelligent Voluntary Social Worker.'
(Speech by Durgabai Desmukh on the occasion
of the CSWB Silver Jubilee, CSWB 1978b: 33)

In the years since the founding of the CSWB, there has been something of a decline in the power of the Board, which has meant that women no longer have quite the same 'sphere of their own', or avenue to the wider political sphere; in addition, there has been a growth in the number of professional social workers available. Furthermore, there has been a shift in the order of priorities of the CSWB in the periods between the First and Fifth plans. By and large, they have moved towards giving more money and assisting more programmes for children and families, and less for women's programmes.[10]

Programmes run by voluntary agencies

NON-INSTITUTIONAL

At present, the order of priorities in allocating resources of the CSWB is as follows: children, women, handicapped, medical welfare, youth, aged, and infirm. In practice, most of the money goes to the first two categories, leaving only a token amount to the rest. The two major kinds of provision for women are 'socio-economic' and 'educational'. The latter programmes include basic literacy, especially in rural areas, and a shortened (or 'condensed') course leading to the Secondary School Leaving Certificate (SSLC) for adult women who have not completed their schooling. By socio-economic programmes it is meant classes in some skill, such as tailoring, embroidery or handicrafts, which should enable the students to generate income (Lalitha 1975: 40). Some agencies also run their own production unit which markets the finished goods. Grants are available from the CSWB for such programmes.

'Destitute women and women from low income groups have largely benefited by the rehabilitational programmes sponsored by the CSWB ... By the end of March, 1975, the socio-economic programmes of the CSWB had benefited about 5,300 women through 218 centres and 75,369 women through 3,232 craft centres ... Not only are the women benefited *per se*, but their families also benefit, mainly through the work and wages scheme. Women from the low income group have been able to earn during their leisure time and supplement the family income, and thereby maintain or improve the level of living.'

(Patil 1978: 77)

In the context of the millions of women in India living on or below the poverty line, help for a few thousand over a twenty-five-year period is somewhat inadequate. Furthermore, while in theory such programmes might sound like a good idea, in practice there are frequently problems.[11] Chowdhry (1971: 233) criticizes them for neither providing proper training nor giving real employment opportunities. Women, once trained, may not have the capital equipment (such as a sewing machine) to start up on their own, or they have not been taught marketing techniques and thus do not know what to do with the finished goods. Where they are in production units run by voluntary agencies, they often work for pitifully low wages,[12] and the same is true of women who, after learning a skill, practise it at home as 'out-workers'.[13] Or they may find themselves in competition with others; for example women trained in tailoring are relatively disadvantaged in a country where traditionally this has been a caste-specific occupation practised mainly by males who have done it since their childhood.

Thus most of the socio-economic programmes for women impart skills which do not earn much money and which have only recently come to be defined as 'feminine' in Indian society.[14] The reason for this is that women's earning is regarded as a 'supplement' to that of the main bread-winner, her husband. The basic premise of the voluntary agencies, the CSWB, and both Union and state governments is not that women are autonomous individuals who need to work and support themselves, but that they are a part of a family with a male head and chief earner (often referred to as a woman's 'guardian' or 'protector'). Official publications are replete with this view of women's proper place being in the family, and thus of her earning needs being both secondary to those of her husband and also to her own domestic duties:

'Work and Wage is the great need of all those who are economically backward, physically handicapped, and socially maladjusted. The socio-economic programme of the CSWB endeavours to provide destitute women, widows, deserted wives, and the physically handicapped opportunities for engaging themselves in ... employment ... to *supplement* their meagre family income. They can either obtain their wage *while working at home* or at a *nearby place without dislocating their domestic life.*' (my italics)

(CSWB n.d.: 17)

The Board also describes its family and child welfare projects as providing 'training to young mothers in home craft, mother craft, education and personal hygiene, health, sanitation, nutrition, family planning etc.' (CSWB n.d.: Appendix 6). In its Silver Jubilee programme in 1978, it was suggested that a new departure for the CSWB should be to embark on 'family counselling centres to keep the family united and to prevent disintegration of the families' (1978b: 9). Social scientists themselves are not free of this bias; Chowdhry for instance advocates: 'With the advancement of social science and stresses of urbanisation and industrialisation, it has become necessary to maintain [the] integrity of the family. Hence family welfare services have been added to the list of welfare programmes for *women*' (my italics) (1971: 136).

Educational programmes likewise tend to emphasize skills which better enable women to carry out their roles of wife and mother. For example, the functional (basic) literacy programmes combine reading and writing with childcare. The *mahila mandal* programmes, which were set up by the CSWB, are a prime example of such an emphasis on domesticity, while at the same time being almost entirely irrelevant to the real needs of the rural women for whom they are intended. In 1961, it was decided that their activities should include: 'Talks and demonstration ... on [a] balanced diet, family planning, training in domestic chores, use of spare time to improve the economic condition of the family, social education, knowledge of agriculture and animal husbandry ... and baby shows' (Jain and Krishnamurthy Reddy 1979: 2). The *mahila mandal* programme, like most non-institutional programmes, views women essentially as members of families. It seeks to 'educate' them to play their roles better, or to impart a skill which enables them to 'supplement the family income' and thereby raise its standard of living (cf. Sharma 1983).

The RCSW was highly critical of these tendencies in social welfare. It points out that the plans have all along emphasized women's role in the family; family welfare services are seen as *women's* welfare services; women are the ones thought to need protection from injurious work and creches for children (measures which have resulted in the unemployment of thousands of women); 'training' for women frequently means training in housewifery; emphasis on women's health is often synonymous with family planning, and family planning is seen as a programme essentially for women (Government of India 1974: 329).

INSTITUTIONAL SERVICES

Institutional or residential services are designed for women and children who are either not in families or in families that cannot support them and who thus are thought to be in need of 'care and protection' and 'rehabilitation'. A large proportion of agencies (Chowdhry's 1971 study quotes over 70 per cent) run residential services, particularly orphanages and homes for destitute women. Indeed, institutionalization is seen very largely as the appropriate solution to such problems. The state has concurred in this view by both giving grants to set up such places and then by contributing to the upkeep of their 'inmates'.

In spite of criticisms from some quarters and suggestions that institutionalization is not a satisfactory solution to problems of poverty, they continue to flourish. Destitute women are likely to be put into 'service homes', particularly if they are thought to be in 'moral danger' and thus can be apprehended under the Prevention of Immoral Traffic Act (cf. Gupta, Haksar, and Sivadas 1982). Similarly, children of very poor families, particularly where no father is present, are often placed in orphanages, where their numbers usually exceed those of children who have no parents. Suggestions that the state should either help support such families so they can keep their children or institute a foster care scheme have met with little response, in spite of the arguments that they are actually cheaper to run, and less psychologically damaging to children.

Although successive DMK and ADMK governments in Tamil-nadu have spent relatively lavishly on the social services (e.g. slum clearance; see Wiebe 1981) and on social welfare, they do not differ greatly from the voluntary sector in the way solutions to problems are perceived. Institutionalization is seen as one way of coping with destitution. During the DMK period for instance, it was announced that the government intended to set up numerous orphanages ('Homes of Pity') in the state. The press soon reported that in order to fill these institutions in time for their official inaugurations, some children were virtually kidnapped from their families for the occasion. Only among some professional social workers is there an awareness that large-scale institutionalization might not be an ideal solution to problems of poor children.[15] In fact, most of these orphanages subsequently closed down.

When the ADMK government came to power in 1977, it likewise announced a similar grandiose scheme of opening several orphanages, each of which would house a thousand children. As had happened on the previous occasion, there were protests against this 'mass institutionalization', and finally four orphanages were opened with 'only' 250 children in each. The government meanwhile turned down a proposal for a larger-scale foster care scheme for children, preferring that there should be more orphanages. It does appear now to be encouraging what is known as the 'cottage' system (i.e. small groups of children living with a house-mother rather than in large impersonal institutions).

By choosing large-scale schemes, the state government has sought to project itself as concerned about the 'weaker sections', and to be tackling problems directly. However, the state government has also been willing to utilize voluntary agencies. For example, it set up guidance bureaux for the welfare of widows and destitute women 'To assist the children of poor widows in getting admission through [to] Voluntary Welfare Institutions for [their] shelter, maintenance, and education' (Government of Tamilnadu n.d.: 33). In addition, the government runs five 'service homes' 'for the benefit of poor widows, deserted wives and destitute women' (Government of Tamilnadu n.d.: 22).

The aim of institutionalization is said to be 'rehabilitation' and the main ways in which this can be achieved are thought to be training, especially for boys, and marriage for girls. Another possibility for girls is placement in domestic service (another form of 'protection', and one singularly ill-paid). Several of these institutions or 'service homes' run domestic service courses. Many more girls than boys are placed in orphanages, probably because they are thought to be in greater need of protection (Chowdhry 1971: 110). Destitute women who are taken into service homes (also, interestingly, often referred to as 'orphanages for women') are supposed to be taught some skill. The RCSW is sceptical of their efficacy: 'We visited some of these protective homes (for "rescued" women) . . . efforts are made to rehabilitate the inmates by providing training in sewing and embroidery. There is no formal procedure for marketing of these products, nor are the inmates given any training either to organise production or marketing' (Government of India 1974: 337). Nor may all women wish to be 'rescued' in this way: 'A frank talk with prostitutes in back alleys however revealed that they lived in dread of social workers who wanted to rescue them and put them into impersonal institutions . . . One young girl who was about 17 said that she hated embroidery' (Balse 1976: 88).

Even women who are educated and have jobs are, if they are not living within a family structure, thought to be 'vulnerable'. Again the solution is a modified form of institutionalization in the form of working women's hostels which often have extremely strict rules (cf. Tharu and Melkote 1981). Both the Union and state governments as well as the CSWB have encouraged the growth of such hostels in the last few years by giving relatively lavish grants to voluntary agencies to build them.

In sum, women and children who are not part of a family unit with a male head are stigmatized; they are thought to be in need of care and protection, otherwise they may be in moral danger.

In Tamilnadu, as elsewhere in India, a major solution to the problems of poor women and young girls is seen to be marriage or re-marriage. In 1975, the DMK government instituted the 'Social Welfare Scheme for Destitute Women' by which, if a widow re-married, the couple was given a government bond which matured at an attractive rate of interest after seven years, and the husband was given special preference for government employment (Patil 1978: 34). It is hoped in this way that men will be induced to marry poor women, and thus 'rehabilitate' them. A more recent scheme has been to pay the costs of the gold needed for a *tali* to enable the daughters of poor widows to marry; in 1982, this was commuted to a cash grant of Rs 1,000 (*Indian Express*, 9 March 1982).

Social welfare and politics: the case of Tamilnadu

The political situation in Tamilnadu State has had important repercussions in the field of social welfare. The state has not had a Congress government since 1967, although Congress has been consistently in power at the Centre, apart from the brief period of Janata rule following the Emergency. Social welfare is defined in India as a 'concurrent subject' which means that it is the responsibility of both the Centre and the state governments. The latter functions through the State Ministry of Social Welfare and the Directorate of Social Welfare, but the main avenue of the Centre is through the apparatus of the Central and State Social Welfare Boards.

For this reason, changes in government at either the Centre or local state level are likely to bring about changes in the composition of the SSWB (since half the members are nominated by the Centre and half by the state), and particularly in the person of the Chairman, who is nominated by the Chief Minister (i.e. the government of the state) but who must be acceptable to the Centre also.

When the DMK came to power in Tamilnadu in 1967, the Chairman of the SSWB and many of the members, most of whom were associated with Congress, resigned. Some felt they could no longer serve, while others were under some pressure to go from the new government, which naturally wished to see its own supporters in such positions. Accordingly, a number of women from DMK families were appointed to the State Board. However, this was said not to have worked very well because, as one informant put it,

> 'It's a problem to find suitable DMK (and now ADMK) people. They are not so rich or forward or educated as the others [i.e. Congress supporters] were. Such women do not run institutions. At first, when the DMK government came to power, it wanted to get rid of the Congress women from the SSWB, and also make life difficult for voluntary social workers (most of whom had a Congress background). But very soon it realised that it had no choice but to work through them and their voluntary agencies even though they

were set up by Brahmins and Congress. Many of the women who had lost their SSWB posts were soon asked to return.'

When the ADMK government came to power in 1977, at which time Janata was ruling at the Centre, there were again changes in the composition of the Board. In 1980, when Mrs Gandhi and the Congress Party regained power at the Centre, the chairmanship of the Board was due for renewal. The Centre refused to renew the appointment of the (ADMK supported) Chairman, and later turned down a subsequent nomination by the Chief Minister of Tamilnadu. The post of Chairman of the State Board remained vacant for more than a year, until a candidate acceptable to both parties was found. In the end, the new appointee had in fact a Congress background (her husband had earlier served as a state governor under Mrs Gandhi's previous government) but since she herself was said to be 'not very political' (and since also perhaps by this time the ADMK was seeking an alliance with Mrs Gandhi), it was felt that she could serve.

The vagaries of electoral alliances apart, both the DMK and ADMK governments have rapidly realized in turn that it is preferable to utilize the voluntary agencies, even if they are dominated by 'Brahmins and Congress supporters'. First, the agencies are relatively cheap to run, given their large number of voluntary workers and the fact that many agencies do raise substantial portions of their own funds. Second, while the state is putting funds into the voluntary agencies, it can exercise some control over them. There is even an acknowledgement on the part of the government that voluntary agencies are less likely to be corrupt than state agencies. Thus in 1982 it was announced that a massive (Rs 100 crore – nearly £$\frac{3}{4}$m – per annum) midday meals scheme for all poor children in the state would be instituted. This was to be effected by voluntary agencies, and was headlined in the chief English-language daily as 'Women to implement free meal scheme'. The article went on to quote the Chief Minister as stating that the project 'will be implemented entirely by women and their organisations, utilising their knowledge, experience and spirit of service' (*Hindu*, 3 June 1982).

Conclusion

The major activity of women's voluntary organizations since independence has become social welfare, and they are largely responsible for running most social welfare programmes in the country. However, through social welfare women are marginalized in several important ways. First, social welfare is *not* seen as a part of development, which is after all the main goal of planners in India. Development has until very recently been thought about in terms of, and has largely affected, males. Women, who have lost out in the development process in many instances, especially in the rural areas, have been allocated social welfare. Social welfare is also separate from basic social services such as education and health which the state seeks to provide, and which also differentially benefit women and men (see Chapter 1). Social welfare itself in any case is not a priority area of government policy or financing, although the state has played an increasingly active role in it, initially through the CSWB, and later by giving money directly to the voluntary agencies.

Women, particularly poor ones, are categorized as 'social problems' along with the handicapped, and allocated special programmes under 'social welfare'. At the same time, the programmes that are organized in the social welfare field reveal certain fundamental assumptions on the part of their organizers – that women and children are, or should be, part of a family with a male head. Women and children who are not living in such a unit are thought to be in need of substitute 'protection', hence the widespread use of institutionalization as a solution to their problems, and the frequent goal of marriage or re-marriage for poor women and girls as a means of 'rehabilitation'. In welfare programmes women are taught skills that are primarily meant to improve their abilities as wives and mothers. Even when they are taught skills to enable them to earn, these are seen only as 'supplements' to the income of the (male) bread-winner, and a way of improving the standard of living of the family.

Women of the upper classes have been equally marginalized by being given social welfare as a 'sphere of their own', a kind of extended house-keeping which is seen as peculiarly suitable for them. The rhetoric of social welfare (discussed in greater detail in Chapter 10), emphasizes 'service' and, either directly or by implication, denigrates professionalism. It thus contributes to the attitude, already widely prevalent in Indian middle and upper-class society (as shown in Chapter 5), that it is inappropriate for women to work for pay.

Recently, the situation has deteriorated in certain respects both for voluntary workers and for clients. With the diminishing of the importance of the CSWB, women have lost an avenue which previously gave them a political ladder and access to policy-making. Only in certain states, such as in Tamilnadu where a non-Congress government is in power, is the composition of the SSWB considered important enough for the Centre to worry about. In terms of beneficiaries, women are now seen as less important than children and/or families; this was always implicit in the programmes, but now it has been made explicit.

Social welfare in India is highly elaborated, both ideologically (as discussed in Chapter 10) and organizationally, both through the CSWB and other bodies, and through the voluntary organizations. In its premises, programmes, and methods of operating it contributes in no small measure to the reinforcement of the basic attitudes towards women which have already been discussed – that they are, and should be, dependent.[16]

Notes

1 Social services means 'investment in the betterment of human resources in general' whereas social welfare services are 'meant for the underprivileged sections in the community' (Ray 1968: 403). Rao also defines social welfare as 'rendering assistance for the weaker sections of society' contrasting it with social reform movements which had sought to change society (Rao, personal communication). Patil likewise sees social welfare as applying only to a particular category: 'Social welfare services are the enabling services for those who cannot take advantage of the social services [which] constitute an investment in the betterment of human resources, they are designed to enable the underprivileged and handicapped sections to raise themselves as close to the level of the community as possible' (1978: 65).

2 The budget allocation for the whole of the social services was highest in the First Plan (21 per cent of the total outlay), but in subsequent plans it has declined to 15.5 per cent in the Second Plan, to 15.1 per cent in the Third, 12.7 per cent in the Fourth, and 14.2 per cent in the Fifth (Jagannadham 1978: 47).

3 Dr Durgabai Desmukh had been involved in the nationalist movement and spent some time in prison. She later founded an organization in Madras called the Andhra Mahila Sabha which developed into
an important orthopaedic centre and hospital.

4 As she herself acknowledges, it was largely because of the fact that
her husband was the Union Finance Minister for a long period after
independence that the CSWB was able to obtain money for its activities: 'As the Union Finance Minister he was kind enough to give me
assistance on a liberal scale' (CSWB 1978a: 34).

5 According to the Planning Commission: 'Voluntary organisations
are said to be democratic bodies organised to meet the welfare needs
of the community without any profit motive. Adaptability to changing conditions, the human touch in the services offered, community
support, and mobilisation of local resources are said to be their forte'
(Government of India, Planning Commission 1971: 3: 1).

   Gore (1965) characterizes voluntary agencies as having the following advantages over government services: they are pioneering,
independent of politics, flexible and non-bureaucratic, cheap, and
provide training grounds for leadership.

6 In India the term 'social worker' means a volunteer, usually well-to-
do, who engages in charitable or welfare work.

7 The composition of the CSWB is as follows: Chairman, preferably
'a woman social worker of standing' nominated by the government;
1 woman representative from each state and Union Territory (total
25); 2 social scientists; 3 social welfare administrators; 5 prominent
'social workers' (i.e. voluntary) nominated by the government; 1
representative from each of the six ministries mainly concerned with
social welfare (Finance, Health, Community Development, Education, Social Welfare, and the Planning Commission); 2 representatives
from the Lok Sabha (lower House of Parliament); 1 from the Rajya
Sabha (Upper House); and a Secretary (later re-designated Executive
Director) who is a senior civil servant.

8 Most parts of the organized sector of industry employing more than
a very small number of people require the appointment of labour
welfare officers; in the private sector these are usually quite well paid.
Because of the demand for such courses, labour welfare is given the
greatest prominence of any aspect of social work training, both in the
curriculum of the schools and also in the numbers of articles published
in the journals. This is one of the major contradictions in social work
training, for while the profession of social work is supposed to help
the underprivileged, personnel management has quite a different
aim.

9 The Planning Commission study of 1971 noted that while supervisory and managerial staff were paid an average of Rs 354 per

month, teachers employed by voluntary organizations got much less, and unskilled workers were paid only Rs 109 on average. Chowdhry (1971; most of his figures refer to a slightly earlier period) found the salary scales even lower – 55 per cent were earning less than Rs 50 per month, and only 5 per cent got more than Rs 150. Rama (1974) quotes a monthly salary of *Rs 10* in 1974 for an organizer of a *mahila mandal* (rural women's association set up by the CSWB) in Tamilnadu, while the most recent study by Nair (1978) states that 6 out of 7 professionally trained social workers who are in voluntary agencies in Tamilnadu are paid less than Rs 1,000 per month.

10 For example, the number of *mahila mandals* has declined from 624 institutions and 1,629 centres in the First Plan to 406 institutions and 1,498 centres in the Fifth Plan (CSWB 1980).

11 A recent study conducted by Devaki Jain (Institute of Social Studies 1981) aimed to compile a catalogue of around a hundred agencies which would meet the following criteria: they should be working for women's development, reaching the poorest sections, helping a minimum of fifty women, and achieving self-reliance. She comments that after studying the CSWB directories of each state (listing a total of 6,000 organizations in India), after visiting many states and their respective SSWB, and after making field visits, it proved difficult to find such organizations.

> 'Scrutiny of several women's organisations working in the field revealed that most of them were reaching very small numbers of women who had been handicapped, socially or economically; they were reaching them with some welfare services more in the form of charity or relief rather than with the intention of developing the women into a force for social change or with the intention of making them self-reliant.'
>
> (Institute of Social Studies: 1981: xvii)

12 Workers in production units run by voluntary social welfare institutions are, like paid workers, not covered by the relevant industrial acts which govern minimum wages and conditions of work in the organized sector of industry. At a meeting I attended between a Director of Social Welfare and the representatives of a women's association, the former suggested setting up a production unit in the association, as 'it would not be covered by the labour laws'.

A recent article in the CSWB's journal *Social Welfare* on employment for needy women and the disabled notes approvingly that some socio-economic units in voluntary organizations are actually linked to organized industry, while others use out-workers; the author claims that these generate a 'handsome income' for those thus employed, but gives no figures (Chari 1982).

13 In a recent article that looks at the export garment industry in Madras it is shown that the majority of the 32,000 workers employed in this area in the city are non-factory (i.e. home-workers). Most are women. Their rates of pay are generally very low. Whereas the factory sector has had some success in unionization, this is obviously much more difficult for home-workers (Kalpagam 1981).

14 In many respects, this sex stereotyping of skills owes more to western than to traditional Indian norms, particularly in terms of sewing as a female activity; perhaps this dates back to the nineteenth century and the missionaries' introduction of such subjects into the curricula of their schools for girls.

15 The Director of the Madras School of Social Work wrote to the press as follows: 'Experience and research all over the world have shown beyond doubt the ill-effects of institutionalisation ... Foster family care, children's villages and other family-centred child welfare measures are given high priority in all societies. But in India, indiscriminate institutionalisation continues to be the prominent child care programme' (*Hindu*, 19 May 1975).

16 This is not, of course, a situation peculiar to India, as Barbara Rogers has shown in her book on women and development (1980). She examines the 1978–80 Plan for Bangladesh and quotes the comments of two economists on it: 'The Plan document, by dubbing women's programmes as "welfare programmes" and relegating them to one of the two sub-sectors of the social welfare sector, has faithfully mirrored a male-dominated society's attitude towards women ... they have been treated on a par with marginal groups' (Rogers 1980: 80).

8
Five organizations and their activities

In this chapter I describe in some detail the five organizations which were studied in depth. I begin with a brief description of each and its formal structure, and then consider the members, particularly from the point of view of caste and class background. Next follows a description of the different activities of the organizations – recreational, educational, and philanthropic. Funding is discussed in the final section, with a consideration of how money is both raised and spent.

The five organizations

The largest and oldest of these organizations is the *Institute for Women*, with a membership of 125 women, and a founding date which coincides with India's independence in 1947. It was started by a woman from a prominent south Indian Brahmin family who had worked with Gandhi, and who donated part of her share of the family's Madras land to build an institution for helping women. Many of the members have been involved with it for a long time.

The *Housewives' Association* was founded only in 1970. Its founder President at one time was a committee member of the Institute for Women and had decided to form an association whose members would meet monthly and each donate a few rupees towards a particular charity, as well as enjoying talks, outings, and demonstrations. During the first year of field-work, this association doubled its membership, and subsequently grew even larger; it also embarked on much more ambitious activities in the field of social welfare.

The *Neighbourhood Club* began in 1971 in a suburb of south Madras consisting of around 130 houses built by the Tamilnadu Housing Board. I have given this area the pseudonym of Kamalapuram. Because the President of the club, the wife of a senior civil servant, had contacts with the Tamilnadu Housing Board, the club was able to raise a large loan and put up a building for its activities, which was opened just before my arrival in 1974. At that time, around half of the households in the suburb had a member in the club.

The *Wives' Auxiliary Association* is the counterpart to a branch of a men's international 'service' association (henceforth referred to as the *Men's Service Organization*), one of many which flourish in India (e.g. Rotary, Lions, Round Table, and Jaycees). All these organizations admit male members only, although some, such as Rotary, have auxiliary associations for wives. The aim of these associations is friendship between members and 'service' to others, which generally takes the form of raising money for charity. To the former end, membership is restricted to a maximum of thirty persons in any one branch, and organizational format demands a heavy degree of participation on the part of all members.

The Men's Service Organization connected with the Wives' Auxiliary being studied had 31 branches in India at the time of field-work, although there were only 14 counterpart branches for wives. In Madras, there existed 3 men's branches, and 2 Wives' Auxiliaries. The one I studied had been inaugurated in 1969, although the men's branch had been in existence since 1960. In the interim the wives had helped their husbands in their fund-raising, and participated in some joint social activities.

The fifth organization is the *Professional Women's Association*; this is a branch of an international women's service organization, one of several founded originally by American professional women, largely as a response to their exclusion from men's associations like Rotary. Most of these women's associations very closely resemble those of the men in their aims, objectives, and structure. The Professional Women's Association was originally begun in the USA sixty years ago, and its headquarters remains there; the first branch was founded in India in 1963, and the following year a

Table 3 *Chart summarizing the salient features of the five organizations*

	Institute for Women	Housewives' Association	Neighbour-hood Club	Wives' Auxiliary Association	Professional Women's Association
members					
no. of members	125	100	60	15	17
average age	50	37	39	32	48
class	upper	upper middle	upper middle	upper	upper
% Brahmin	83	75	58	none	30
activities					
(a) *recreation*					
national festivals	x	x	x	–	–
religious festivals	x	x	x	–	–
outings	x	x	x	x	x
sports	x	x	x	–	–
demonstra-tions	–	x	x	x	–
dinners	x	x	x	x	x
picnics	x	x	x	x	x
(b) *education*	sewing music drawing painting Hindi	paper flowers hair-dressing cooking crochet embroidery seminars	sewing music cooking bhajans Hindi English public speaking	none	seminars
(c) *social welfare*	balwadi clinic tailoring printing secretarial course	residential institution book bank feasting children stipends to students and handi-capped	balwadi clinic tailoring	fund-raising visiting orphanage	balwadi clinic
funds	souvenirs donations charity shows CSWB TN government Lions SSWB	collections donations advertising in papers	CSWB charity shows fetes SSWB	charity shows sales plays donations from abroad	donations Lions Rotary TN government donations from abroad charity shows
paid workers	12	4	5	–	3

branch was also inaugurated in Madras. At the time of field-work only three Indian cities had branches, but another three have been started since that time.

Formal structure

The formal structure of all the associations is highly bureaucratic and hierarchical. All five associations are registered societies under the Societies Act of 1860 and, more recently, the Tamilnadu Societies Registration Act 1975. There is provision in each constitution for regular elections, although in fact selection for office is usually by consensus rather than election. Each organization has a chief officer, referred to either as a President or Chairman. In two cases (the Institute for Women and the Housewives' Association), the Founder Presidents hold office for life. In addition, there are usually one or more Vice-Presidents (the Institute for Women has three, while the others have one each); the holding of this office is a formal honour often conferred on people who have previously served the association as Treasurer or Secretary, or else who have made generous donations to its activities. All the associations likewise have honorary secretaries and treasurers. The two international organizations also have officers who are responsible for liaison with other branches of the organizations.

There is a striking contrast between the two international organizations and the remainder in the turn-over of office-bearers; both in the former category have rules that ensure that office-bearers change regularly (every second year in the case of the Professional Women's Association, and annually in the case of the Wives' Auxiliary). In the other associations the same people tend to hold office for relatively long periods.

All the organizations' constitutions provide for an annual meeting of the general body of members, at which reports are read, accounts approved, and any change in office-bearers takes place. In addition, all the organizations hold regular committee and/or general body meetings. Only two organizations actually distinguish between the committee and general body − in the remainder, business is transacted at meetings which all are free to attend.

In addition to office-bearers and ordinary members, there are two other categories of members: *patrons*, who have usually given an exceptionally large donation to the institution and/or are eminent people whose name is useful; and *life members*, who pay a large once-and-for-all subscription.

With the exception of the Housewives' Association, all the clubs have formal links with other organizations. Two (the Neighbourhood Club and the Institute for Women) are members of the Women's Indian Association (see Chapter 6), and one is also linked to another city-wide women's welfare organization, which sponsors its *balwadi*. The two international organizations have links with other branches of the same organization, both in other cities in India and abroad.

Most of the organizations are focused on particular individuals, namely the Founder Presidents, two of whom are still in office (Institute for Women and Housewives' Association) and a third (in the Professional Women's Association) continues to play a leading role and is very much respected.

The tendency for organizations to be 'one-woman' shows is in fact very pronounced in many of the organizations I surveyed. The organizations which work most efficiently are the ones headed by a strong leader who is able to command both the allegiance of the membership and also the respect of the wider society. Where this is lacking, there will generally be problems, for there is little experience in Indian society of running an organization any other way. However, the two international organizations have lengthy rule-books, while the Institute for Women and the Housewives' Association have evolved a set of standard procedures during the years of their existence which enable them to function relatively smoothly.

Members: caste and class

To a large extent, members have already been discussed in Chapter 2, but here it is appropriate to make certain distinctions between the organizations in terms of class background. The majority of the members of the Institute for Women, the Wives' Auxiliary, and the Professional Women's Association belong to the upper classes, whereas those of the Housewives' Association and the Neighbourhood Club may be characterized as upper middle class. Members of the former category are married to men who (or in the case of the Professional Women they themselves) were earning over Rs 2,000 per month in 1974–75, and are engaged in high status occupations; the husbands of many of the members of the Institute for Women and the Wives' Auxiliary in particular own their own companies. In addition, many of the women in the former organization or their husbands own land, either rural lands from which they receive rent and/or grain, or urban land or houses, which again is rented out.

Indeed, ownership of one's own company, or else being a senior executive or director in industry or commerce is the largest occupational grouping of the husbands of these women, although their fathers and husbands' fathers would have been more likely to be in government service. This does perhaps provide an additional reason for social welfare activities. Industry does not carry the same prestige as government service does – a legacy partly of British ideas that 'trade' and 'commerce' were not suitable occupations for gentlemen, and partly because of the Brahminical ideal that a man should earn his living through some form of 'service' whether this be in the priesthood or government service. Thus giving to charity, whether on an individual or company level, is a way of mitigating what is otherwise apparently naked profit-making (cf. also Madan 1970); equally, for the wife of such a man to be involved in voluntary social welfare work raises the family's prestige considerably.

In terms of caste background, there is a heavy domination by Brahmins of all organizations except the Wives' Auxiliary. They constitute 83 per cent of the membership of the Institute for Women, 75 per cent of the Housewives' Association, and 58 per cent of the Neighbourhood Club; they are also the largest single caste grouping in the Professional Women's Association, constituting nearly a third of members. In view of the prominence of Brahmins in the nationalist movement and the founding of women's associations in Tamilnadu, this is perhaps not surprising. Brahmins, as already stated, are disproportionately represented in the higher class levels in Madras and Tamilnadu generally; the women have been receiving an education for a long time, and thus are equipped to deal with the world of voluntary associations. None the less, the continuing dominance of Brahmins in this area does have to be seen perhaps in the context of their eclipse in the political arena in the state. Like other minority groups unable to organize formally, they have chosen to organize informally in order to retain some of their political and economic power; women's associations, especially their voluntary social welfare activities, provide one such arena.

Homogeneity in caste membership can of course be an advantage to the smooth running of an organization, for it reduces the likelihood of factionalism along such lines. Heterogeneity in caste membership seems to have contributed to the problems faced by the Neighbourhood Club.

At the time of field-work, Brahmins constituted an absolute majority with just under 60 per cent of the membership. By the time I returned in 1981, club membership had halved, although Brahmins still remained the dominant group with 19 members out of 34. Non-Brahmins sometimes voiced their resentment against what they perceive as the Brahmins' assumption of leadership; the contest for presidency between two IAS officers' wives, one a Brahmin, one a non-Brahmin, was sometimes viewed in these terms.

Resentment is also expressed about the supposed unwillingness of Brahmins to recognize how much things have changed in Tamilnadu over the past several decades. Thus, for instance, a Brahmin woman who had recently moved into Kamalapuram was invited to the *balwadi* Parents' Day to give out prizes. The Secretary, a Tamilian non-Brahmin, was extremely embarrassed that the Brahmin used the lowest grade honorific speech form to address the parents: 'These Brahmins think they can still talk down to people', she remarked.

However, in many respects, the club has successfully projected itself as encompassing all castes and religions in the neighbourhood. On important occasions, care is always taken that the minority communities like Christians and Muslims should be seen to participate. The core active group that has persisted over the years is very mixed, composed of three Brahmins, two Tamilian non-Brahmins (a Mudaliar and a Kallar), a Muslim, and a Christian. Several of these are extremely close friends, and regularly visit each other's houses.

Such neighbourhood ties can however raise other problems, for boys and girls who grow up as neighbours sometimes form romantic attachments across caste boundaries. Usually these are firmly discouraged. It is for this reason that the Youth Club, whose foundation was encouraged by the Neighbourhood Club members, consists only of boys. On one occasion, when these boys wanted to use the club to hold a discotheque, the club members vetoed the idea as it would involve boys and girls mixing together in a way which they thought was quite improper.

None of these problems is likely to arise in the Institute for Women or the Housewives' Association. Indeed, in these, information on marriages and 'prospective alliances' is a frequent topic of conversation and a source of useful information.

The Wives' Auxiliary membership is very different from that of the other organizations, for all of them are north Indians – mainly Punjabis, Bengalis, and Sindhis. From a perusal of the directories of members of all the branches of both the men's organization and the Wives' Auxiliary in south India, this appears largely typical. In many respects this association has strong elements of 'ethnicity' about it, for instance, conversation is as likely to be in Hindi as in English (Tamil is never used). At the same time the life-style of these women differs considerably from that of the members of the other organizations. Although they are still young (in their late twenties or early thirties) most are wealthy, with husbands owning their own business, working in a family firm, or already at senior management level in large companies. Most tend to live in large and expensive rented flats, and their homes are much more 'western' in appearance than the somewhat more spartanly furnished homes of even wealthy south Indians, being replete with carpets, curtains, pictures, and other luxurious features. They spend a great deal of time, money, and energy on their personal appearance, visiting beauty parlours and hairdressers, and utilizing make-up; they frequently wear western dress as well as saris or *salwar-kamiz*. This is in great contrast to south Indian women, who, although they are likely to own costly saris and expensive jewellery, always dress very demurely and conventionally.

Their life-style also differs in many respects from that of well-to-do south Indians. Marriages are 'companionable', with many activities carried out jointly by husbands and wives. Life-style is also based on conspicuous consumption with every occasion involving careful dressing and grooming; this does not mean 'formal' dress, but often an ability to dress informally, yet with chic, knowing the right thing to wear on each occasion. It involves a great deal of expenditure on food (a mixture of Indian and western) and drink; all accounts of men's meetings in particular contain references to 'the bar' or being offered drinks. It involves having the right sort of home to which friends can be invited, knowing what to serve and how to serve it. In India and elsewhere it is generally the case that the higher the class level, the greater the likelihood not only of joining a voluntary association but of being a 'multiple-joiner'. The Wives' Auxiliary does not fit this pattern largely because the organization demands such a total commitment in time and energy, absorbing almost all the members' social life outside their families. Members of the other two 'upper-class' organizations – the Institute for Women and the Professional Women – on the other hand, are multiple-joiners, averaging membership of two or three other associations. In many instances members belong to the same set of other organizations. Members of the Housewives' Association and the Neighbourhood Club, however, tend not to be multiple-joiners, and average only one other organization each.

Activities of organizations

Organization members tended to give three reasons for joining: to make new friends, 'learn new things', and do social welfare. Broadly speaking, these correlate with three categories of activity: recreational, educational, and philanthropic.

RECREATION: 'MAKING FRIENDS'

In all the associations, making friends was undoubtedly an important aspect of belonging, in some more so than others. For example, the women who belonged to the Professional Women's Association were in many ways different from most women of a similar class background. All had jobs, and many were unmarried. It was scarcely surprising that they should seek out other women like themselves, even if this was admitted as a reason for joining the organization less often than that of 'doing social service' (cf. P. Caplan 1977). Similarly, women who belonged to the Wives' Auxiliary were isolated in certain respects from south Indian society by their north Indian origins, their lack of Tamil, and their mobility, which meant that many of them moved frequently from one part of India to another.

Women in the Neighbourhood Club, on the other hand, were already neighbours, but they too tended to be fairly geographically mobile, or else came from families that had left the more crowded central areas of the city. Such women were likely to be relatively isolated from kin, and furthermore, to spend much of the day alone as husbands and children were at work and school. Friendship patterns formed through the club cut across caste and even religious or language barriers.

All the associations have recreational activities for the members – these range from outings to temples, beauty spots, or other places of interest, to film shows and dinners. The Neighbourhood Club has held occasional dinners, particularly for farewells to departing members who are leaving the area, and the Professional Women dine together formally after their Annual General Meeting. Dinners are a particularly important feature of the Wives' Auxiliary, which meets together with the men's branch once a month at the house of one of the couple members; after completing their respective business meetings, the men and women join together for dinner, which is usually followed by games or dancing.

Such activities would be unthinkable to most south Indians, whose life-style, even if they are upper class, tends to be much less sophisticated and cosmopolitan. (Members of the Wives' Auxiliary may perhaps be termed 'spiralists', while the remainder are 'burgesses'; cf. Watson 1964.) The leisure and social lives of the Wives' Auxiliary and the Men's Service Organization are centred on the organization in a way that is not true of any of the other groups. One member who kept a diary for me for a fortnight recorded *three* official meetings during that period, and *four* other encounters with various members, including a dinner, a children's tea-party, an afternoon tea, and a game of mahjong with other members; in addition, she had numerous contacts by telephone with fellow members.

Given the high degree of geographical mobility of these women, who move around India and even abroad when their husbands are transferred, promoted, or go to set up new branches of their companies, it is scarcely surprising that they should belong to such an organization. They can always find new friends through the association when they move or travel. An article in the magazine of the men's association defined 'fellowship' as follows: 'You arrive in a town, flip open your organisation directory, announce your arrival, and the rest is "fellowship".' This can range from invitations to dinners and meetings, to help in making business contacts, or in finding accommodation, schooling for children, advice on which clubs to join, and so on. In this organization, links are not only important between members, but also between branches both in India and abroad. With their sophisticated life-style, such men and women can 'fit in' almost anywhere in the world with people of the same class background.

EDUCATIONAL ACTIVITIES:
'LEARNING NEW THINGS'

As can be seen from *Table 3* (p. 148), several organizations run a number of classes for their own members and sometimes for other women of the neighbourhood. The classes organized by the House-wives' Association and the Neighbourhood Club emphasize largely domestic accomplishments. One of these is handicrafts, such as paper flower-making, crocheting, tatting, doll-making, and a multitude of other skills which produce objects used to decorate the home, but which are never sold outside for cash. Another popular class is cookery – western baking, jam and juice-making have now been added to the traditional south Indian cooking skills. A third type of class which is frequently well attended is English conversation, for most of these women feel that an ability to converse fluently in that language is essential, so they can com-municate with their husband's foreign colleagues and their wives.

All these accomplishments reflect the changes in women's domestic roles already discussed in Chapter 4. Women are now required to be an asset to their husbands in terms of their ability to cook western food, converse in English, and beautify the home with their handiwork. In the process of doing this, they are, of course, contributing in an important way to the formation of a particular class culture.

The Institute for Women, on the other hand, does not hold these types of classes for its members. It is rather more likely to hold them in religious-based activities, such as learning *bhajans*, classical music, or listening to religious discourses. There are two reasons for this. As already pointed out, the age of the members of this association is higher, and most of the women are at a stage in the life cycle when they have become mothers-in-law and grand-mothers. In many cases their daughters-in-law are responsible for most of the major domestic responsibilities, leaving them free to spend more time on religious activities, which is in accordance with the Hindu view of the proper way to spend one's declining years. In any case, women of upper-class background have little need of domestic accomplishments – they can afford to hire cooks, or to buy handicrafts if they want them. The Professional Women, in contrast, do not define themselves in terms of a domestic role at all. They tend to look elsewhere for skills they wish to acquire – such as one doctor who had taken a course in mountaineering.

SOCIAL WELFARE ACTIVITIES: 'DOING SOCIAL SERVICE'

The main *raison d'être* of all the associations is said to be social welfare, and all engage in some philanthropic activity on some scale. Those who join social welfare organizations genuinely feel that they are helping to alleviate some of the problems they see around them: 'As an individual, I can't do any charity, but as a group we can achieve something. We'd like to eradicate poverty, but it is not possible' (member of Housewives' Association). 'Why did I join? Because together we can help people somewhat. I really wanted to do something. We have the time and some money' (member of Housewives' Association). In other words, their personal motivations are often compassion and a desire to fulfil their religious duty. Many say that to do social service 'sincerely', it should not be motivated by any desire for personal gain of any nature:

> 'Only when religion and social service go hand in hand, can some good be achieved. Society will deteriorate if we forget our religious duties and traditions ... For an organisation to be stable, its members should serve mankind along with religion and should not be on the look-out for executive posts. One should work with purity of heart and self-disci-plined ideas ... forgetting oneself, one should do social service; such service is the best of all.'
>
> (Article by Chairman of the SSWB
> in Neighbourhood Club *Souvenir*)

Three organizations run *balwadis* for children of the neighbourhood; two have large numbers of children, ranging from 60 to 100, while the third, which restricts intake to the children of women who are working for pay, has a smaller number. The children spend the day on the premises, being cared for and receive a midday meal. They are supposed to be taught songs and rhymes, and the older ones their alphabet.

Two associations also run dispensaries for poor people of their localities. Each has the services of a doctor, who visits once or twice a week, and one also has a regular nurse and a volunteer dispenser, and offers family planning advice. In addition, the Neighbour-hood Club arranges occasional check-ups of its *balwadi* children, and also offers mass vaccinations to poor children of the area. At the time of my first visit, a third organization was also running a clinic but had afterwards closed it down on the grounds that it was being used by people who could afford to pay for medical treat-ment, and also that it was located in an area where there were several government hospitals.

The Housewives' Association, which for the first several years of its existence only raised money for charity, now has its own residential institution. Another long-term venture of this associa-tion has been the purchase of a large number of college text-books to form a 'book bank' for poorer college students who can borrow the books for a year at a time. In addition, this organization regularly financially sponsors a number of students and physically handicapped children and makes occasional donations to orphanages or to voluntary clinics. Its members, individually or collectively, also 'feast' the children of an orphanage or a *balwadi* on some special day, such as a religious festival or a rite of passage in their own family.

A favourite form of charity with some organizations is the provision of a gold marriage chain (*tali* or *thirumangalyam*) to 'poor deserving brides'. One association holds large sums of money in trust for such purposes.

The Institute for Women, which has by far the largest pro-gramme of social welfare activities, also conducts vocational courses for women. At the time of field-work it ran a short matriculation course for adult women; this has now been discon-tinued in favour of a secretarial course. In addition, it has for some years run classes in tailoring. It also has a printing press, which is supposed to generate money for the institution and to train young women as printers and binders. The Neighbourhood Club has also on occasion run classes in tailoring, and conducted adult literacy classes open to both men and women of the area.

Generally speaking, the *balwadis* and clinics are meant for 'poor' people (i.e. members of the working class), whereas classes in tailoring or typing are meant for women of the lower middle classes, from whose ranks women are now beginning to enter the job market in large numbers.

In addition to all these formal activities, the organizations, either through individual members or collectively, try to help individuals in distress who come to them. For example, one girl was enabled to get a college place through the influence of a member of the Housewives' Association, and some destitute children were admitted to an orphanage run by a woman known to the President.

The only organization that does not engage directly in social welfare in terms of running its own programmes is the Wives' Auxiliary. At the time of field-work, these women were helping to collect money and raise funds for an orphanage in the city, which they also visited from time to time and to which they sponsored the visits of a doctor. However, by the time I returned in 1981, this had stopped, and the women were only helping their husbands with their project of endowing scholarships for students.

Competing priorities: recreation or welfare?

Which of the categories of activities carried out by women's associations are, then, given the highest priority? Most would claim that social welfare is their chief *raison d'être*, yet in fact this is not always the case, and there are shifts over time.

In a relatively brief period of existence the Housewives' Association has changed quite considerably its aims and objectives, as well as its methods. In 1973, for example, the Secretary's report stated that 'We do not expect to do fantastic things' and stressed that 'We do not interfere in the household chores of members, or cause them to neglect their duties at home towards the children and family.' A booklet issued the following year stated firmly that the prime duty of members was their role as housewives, and another booklet that came out in 1975 also stressed that charitable work was done by the club members 'Without neglecting children, husband and homes'. The emphasis during this early period was not only on collecting for charity, but also on educational and recreational activities for members such as handicraft classes and outings.

However, although these themes continued to be stressed, the charitable work became more important. The President told me, 'I want them to know about suffering, not just going for picnics and recreation.' For this reason, she often arranged visits to other institutions – a rescue home, an orphanage, and so on. In 1975, she made a speech in which she said: 'The association has a very good name now, and many people are asking us to come and do things. If you are a member you should be a credit to the club, and an example to others.' The following year she wrote that 'Public opinion about the association is quite high, and we are able to carry on more work.' As the programmes supported by the association grew in size, the format of the giving also changed; from donations being simply handed over to beneficiaries, full-scale ceremonies were organized, with important chief guests such as the State Governor or Ministers of State, and by the time their residential institution was ready to be opened, the association was actually in a position to invite and receive an acceptance from the President of India.

In contrast, the Neighbourhood Club has seen a diminution in its level of activity between 1975 and 1981. The club has a multiplicity of functions, but there is some disagreement among the membership about priorities. During the first year of field-work, the club tried to run a great many activities, an average of five events a month. However, quite often events were postponed, cancelled at short notice, or only a few people turned up. A major reason for this is that women in the suburb have heavy domestic commitments and simply do not have time either to help in organizing events or to attend all the planned happenings. For the majority of women, classes which enable them, as they see it, to be better housewives have proved popular – cookery is the prime example – and so have classes such as English conversation or public speaking. Activities connected with religion are also felt to be a justified way of spending time, thus observance of special festivals, talks on religion, or special *pujas* to mark a club anniversary are usually well attended.

There is no such consensus about social welfare activities, how-ever. Several of the active committee members would like to make this the main focus of the club's activities, and so enable it to 'earn a good name'. But many members are not interested in this aspect, since they have neither the time, nor the money, nor the social contacts and know-how to get involved. The social welfare side has become increasingly dependent upon grants, and upon the efforts of a very small number of committee members. 'People around here are just not interested enough, and they don't come for events, they don't co-operate with us' was the constant refrain of the active committee members, who also claimed that the suburb's residents were not 'service-minded'. Several felt that the reason for this was the relative paucity of 'people of the right calibre', particularly IAS officers' wives, to whom they tended to attribute natural leadership qualities. They made unfavourable comparisons between their own club and the flourishing one in a neighbouring suburb: 'They are able to get things done through their husbands because so many of them are IAS officers' it was commonly said.

Thus there can be disagreement about priorities for association activities, although it is rare to hear anyone publicly disagree that social welfare should be the most important activity. However, an examination of how funds are raised and, even more impor-tantly, spent, does suggest that ideal and reality are not always in harmony.

Funding

HOW MONEY IS RAISED

There are three sources of funding: donations, grants, and fund-raising efforts. Two of the associations rely heavily on donations from both individuals and groups. One gets a large donation (over £1,000) each year from a large south Indian industrial firm, receives regular donations from wealthy individuals on such occasions as the annual festival of Deepavalli, and also gets money from patrons and members, particularly committee members. The other began by collecting donations, initially only from its own members but later it began to attract money from outsiders. In the last few years it has been in a position to solicit quite large sums from charitable trusts and has also very successfully tapped indivi-duals who are working abroad (particularly in the Gulf countries) who are anxious to retain ties with their homeland. In addition, this association has on occasion advertised in the newspapers for donations for specific projects, usually quite successfully. Both the international organizations have also been in receipt of funds from abroad through other branches in the west, although not in very large amounts. Two other sources of donations must also be mentioned. One is men's 'service' clubs in the city, such as Lions or Rotary, which raise money and donate it to voluntary social welfare organizations. Two of the five have been able to solicit money from such sources in recent years, and indeed, one Lions Club has 'adopted' the *balwadi* of one organization, and recently rebuilt its kitchen.

Most donations are received from individuals or other associations with which members have personal links; thus those who have the widest-ranging links with wealthy individuals or with large companies are most successful in raising money in this way. Many Indian companies regularly make donations to charity for a number of reasons. First, they do not pay tax on charitable donations. (In this respect, Indian tax laws resemble more closely those of the USA, rather than Britain.) Second, companies give for reasons of prestige and status, as indeed do individuals; as already mentioned, industry is still not considered as prestigious an occupation in India as government service or the professons, and one way of buying a 'good name' is through donations to charity, which are almost always publicly given (as I show in Chapter 10). A third reason is a complex ideological one, also discussed at the end of this chapter, concerning Hindu ideas of earning merit.

Several organizations produce what is termed a 'souvenir', a sort of occasional magazine containing articles of general interest, photographs, reports on activities, and a lot of advertising. It is the last which produces the income – generally the 'advertisement' says little more than 'Best wishes to the organization from x company'. One association produces a souvenir each year, and raises around Rs 6,000 (about £350).

Another major source of funds is through the holding of a charity film show, variety concert, or play. The upper-class organizations can do this annually and raise large amounts, for the tickets are sold at very high prices. This is not so easy for other organizations. One middle-class organization which used a film premiere to make money at its inception found that in subsequent years it was not easy to sell high-priced tickets; people are willing to buy once, but not every year. They tend to use other methods of making money, such as holding a fete or sale, or a similar event. Apart from donations or money raised by direct efforts, the third major source of funds is grants. Two organizations receive grants from the CSWB to support their *balwadis*, and one, which has good connections with the CSWB (since one of its ex-secretaries was Chairman of the Tamilnadu State Board), also receives funds for a vocational course and clinic. The other major source of grants is the Tamilnadu government, which has encouraged organizers of *balwadis* to carry out feeding schemes; grants of 15 *paisa* per child per day are available, although all agencies claim that it is impossible to produce a meal for that amount of money. None the less, all three of the *balwadis* run by these organizations do get some money from this source.

To what extent then do the organizations depend upon fund-raising, donations, and grants? The Institute for Women, for example, costs nearly Rs 50,000 (around £3,000) per year to run (1981 figures). It receives grants totalling Rs 23,000, and a large donation from a company of Rs 20,000. It usually raises Rs 6,000 from its souvenir, giving a total of Rs 49,000. In addition dona-tions of varying sizes are given at Deepavalli by both members and non-members, totalling around Rs 1,000. Another few thousand rupees are raised every two to three years by putting on a play. Basically, this Institute depends upon grants and donations (both of cash and of 'advertising' in the souvenir) rather than on fund-raising efforts. Although it makes enough money to cover its expenses, there are not large amounts left over, a factor which can raise problems when maintenance work needs to be done. How-ever, like most institutions, it is not anxious to have large unspent bank balances, as these might create tax problems.

The Housewives' Association has to find a similar amount in order to run its institution; it receives very little in the way of grants, largely because it is a new organization, although it has applied to the CSWB. Most of the money needed comes from the association's own funds (from regular collections and donations) and from other donations given direct to the home. It has successfully launched a number of sponsoring schemes whereby donations of varying sizes can be used to feed the inmates for a day, or for one day every year (in commemoration of a special event in the family for instance). It has also been among the first organizations in Madras to utilize 'sponsored walks' by schoolchildren and students as a way of raising funds. Like many other social welfare agencies, it takes care to give good publicity to donors: in this case, their names are inscribed on a board in the home for all to see. The Neighourhood Club has to raise Rs 5,000 each year to repay the loan on its building. This the members normally do by holding a sale, a fete, or a film show. Most of the money for their *balwadi*, on the other hand, now comes in the form of grants. The Wives' Auxiliary has no set amount to raise, since it is not running its own project. However, its annual film show usually makes a large amount (around Rs 7,000) and about half as much again is received in donations from abroad. The Professional Women's *balwadi* also gets some money from sister organizations abroad and from men's service clubs, and it gets a grant from the Tamilnadu government; the members rarely engage in fund-raising.

What is of very minimal importance in all cases is fees paid by clients. Most agencies do make a nominal charge for services like *balwadis* or clinics, but it does not cover costs. Most voluntary workers maintain, however, that some charge is necessary 'Because otherwise people wouldn't value the service'.

In short, while grants from the CSWB or the state government are important, they constitute much less than half the funds needed in any agency; ability to solicit donations is much more important. Here obviously the most successful are those with members who have wide contacts with wealthy and important people. It is likely, however, that grants, particularly from the state government, will become more important. At the end of 1981, the Tamilnadu government announced that it would give 90 per cent grants to cover running costs of *balwadis*, in order to encourage voluntary agencies to set them up, and a few months later it announced the aforementioned comprehensive feeding scheme for children (see Chapter 7) which would be implemented through women's voluntary associations.

HOW MONEY IS SPENT

Since most associations have more than one activity, it is worth considering the allocation of funding within the association. Generally speaking, more tends to be spent per head upon what is termed 'social education' (i.e. classes for members and others) than on welfare activities. Contrasts are sometimes glaring; in one set of minutes, Rs 100 was sanctioned from the general account to give a lunch to a visiting member from another branch, while at the same time the same amount was sanctioned from the charity account to give a party to all the children (over a hundred) of the orphanage which the branch sponsored.

Similarly, another association at one time received a visit from its International President and organized a lavish round of entertainment for her costing a great deal of money, while a party given for the *balwadi* children a short while before had been done 'very economically' for just over Rs 200. A third organization likewise frequently organizes Annual Day dinners for members at expensive hotels, while the Annual Day for beneficiaries takes place at the institution. However, much of the money spent on recreation does not pass through the associations' accounts, because it is spent by members individually; for instance, dinners in hotels may well be paid for by individuals, rather than coming out of association funds.

The Wives' Auxiliary provides a good example of the way in which membership may involve spending a great deal more money than the very modest level of subscriptions would suggest. One couple who had been members of the Men's Service Organization and the Wives' Auxiliary told me that they left because they could no longer afford to belong when the husband lost his job after an illness. He reckoned that even in 1970 it cost him an average minimum of Rs 100 per month and his wife another Rs 60 on dinners, rounds of drinks, and so on. If this kind of money is included, then obviously much more is spent on socializing than 'service', although the members might argue that they do raise a good deal of money for charity in their fund-raising activities. It can, of course, also be suggested that at this class level members would in any case spend a lot of money on entertaining, whether or not they belong to voluntary organizations.

However, money spent on social activities is often spent willingly and is not carefully counted by members, whereas money spent by them as individuals on charity is carefully budgeted. For instance, members of one organization who meet each other regularly even though they live scattered all over the city for informal activities such as playing mahjong, going to the cinema, or having tea-parties, complained that they could no longer afford to take it in turns to take the honorary doctor to the orphanage they sponsored to check the children's health 'because petrol is so expensive now'.

An account of a recent All-India Annual General Meeting of both the Men's Service Organization and the Wives' Auxiliary includes the following description of the entertainment following the meeting:

> 'The culmination of that glorious day was the steamer trip on the river. Two large steamers tied together, brightly lit and decorated and on board a roaring crowd of male and female members. Old friends were hailed, new friends were made, and all of us went slightly crazy! The barbecue was literally mobbed, and the dance floor jam packed. The bar overflowed. It was just great.'

Obviously such a lavish style of entertainment over a period of several days costs a good deal of money, and at that particular AGM, a motion was put forward to 'place emphasis on simplicity and austerity, avoiding all unnecessary expenses'. This motion, after some debate, was defeated, with one of the opposers stating that 'Let's face it, we're all here to have a good time in addition to business. What's the point in depriving ourselves of life's good things?' In an article in the men's magazine describing the annual conference, one member wrote 'It is time for us to realise that we are in an association for fellowship and at today's market rate, fellowship costs money.'

Another factor in the willingness to part with money is class level, and thus the availability of money. Members of upper-class organizations can make regular donations, and can also help out if the organization has financial problems. But members of middle-class associations are not usually in a position to be so lavish with money. Indeed, one such association held a fete to raise funds and it was decided that members should run a sweet stall. At the planning meeting, many women indicated their readiness to participate, but later many of them came privately to the Treasurer and asked for a reimbursement for the materials, on the grounds that the cost of sugar (which had just gone up enormously) was too great for their housekeeping budgets to bear.

In short, organization membership involves a good deal more

than a list of the formal activities would suggest. This is reflected in the way in which money is spent by members, with rather more being spent on 'social' or 'recreational' activities than might appear from a reading of the annual budget, where it would seem that most of the funds are devoted to charity.

Conclusion

The kind of activities fostered by the women's associations does then make important symbolic statements. First, it denotes a particular class status to have the leisure and money to engage in such activities. Differences in emphasis between the associations reflect in part their difference in class level. Those of the upper classes define their membership in terms of social welfare. Although those of the upper middle class may also see this as a reason for joining, in addition they demand classes which will give them the skills to operate in a rapidly changing situation. Associations that consist primarily of south Indians may also strive to pass on 'traditional' skills which define them as culturally specific, for example Carnatic music or the drawing of *kolams*. But most organizations de-emphasize activities of this type and concentrate on areas that transcend differences of language, caste, region, or religion. Rather, they choose activities that help create the culture specific to a particular class, and for this reason baking a cake, learning to conduct a conversation in English, or giving to and organizing charity are important symbolic statements about class.

9

The politics of women's organizations: gender, class, and caste

In this chapter I consider further the areas of gender, class, and caste. In the first part, the role of men in women's organizations – as husbands, beneficiaries, and others – is examined, and it is shown that men are frequent and important participants in their affairs, even though they may never be present at meetings. In the second part, I consider another category who are rarely present at meetings, but form the *raison d'être* of the organizations' existence – the beneficiaries of social welfare programmes. Finally, there is a discussion of the political role played by women's organizations in the wider public arena, particularly in terms of the Brahmin–non-Brahmin split in Tamilnadu, and also the relations between the Union and Tamilnadu governments.

In all these areas, the surface appearance is somewhat deceptive – the organizations are supposed to be run by women, their programmes are supposed to be for the poor, regardless of caste, and they are also supposed to be non-political. As we shall see, the picture is not quite so simple.

Gender

THE ROLE OF MEN IN WOMEN'S ORGANIZATIONS

All the organizations under consideration, although they consist of women members only, have important relations with men and men's organizations. On the most basic level, almost all the members themselves have husbands, and the way in which the women are able to interact with the organizations depends to some extent on the husbands' attitudes.

Thus for example, the husbands of women who belong to the Institute for Women are usually supportive: 'My husband is proud of my being an office-bearer in this association. He always makes it a point to tell colleagues and guests who come home' said one member. Similarly, as the Housewives' Association grew in size and importance, the President told the members, 'Your husband should be as proud of you for belonging to this association which does such good work, as you would be of him if he is a member of Rotary or any other good service club.'

None the less, it is apparent that in many instances husbands are ambivalent about their wives' activities. The Housewives' Association, even in 1981, was always careful to limit the time and financial commitment of its members, and to state frequently that their prime duties were to husband and children. At the same time, they had by this time formed an 'advisory committee' composed largely of the husbands of office-bearers, ostensibly on the grounds that 'We need some male guidance now that we are involved in such big things'; but there is also little doubt that for a husband to be invited to participate in such a committee helped deflect any potential criticism of his wife for her commitment to the organization.

Members of the Neighbourhood Club have been much less successful in this regard. Husbands frequently grumble about the amount of time and money their wives spend at the club, particularly if the activities cannot be justified in terms of either improvement in the members' skills as home-makers or performance of religious duties. It is probably for this reason, among others, that club membership has declined, and it also explains why members find it difficult to commit money to the club.

Members of the Wives' Auxiliary too find an ambivalent attitude towards their activities on the part of husbands. The men's organization, as I have already said, existed for a number of years before the Wives' Auxiliary was set up, largely on the initiative of some of the men in the organization. At first I had thought therefore that wives of male members were under pressure to join the Wives' Auxiliary, but later came to realize that in fact the men have mixed feelings about the existence or otherwise of a formally constituted women's branch. If there are disputes between women members, the men are likely to complain that 'The girls are scrapping again' and this endangers their own good 'fellowship'. In many respects it is of course advantageous to the men for there to be a formally constituted wives' branch. This means that they get regular help with their fund-raising, and that extra social events can be arranged by the women's auxiliary. On the other hand, they are careful to try and limit the activities of the women's auxiliary; this is not always easy as it sometimes tries to act independently. The group with which I worked records in its minutes that there was a dispute with the men's branch, which had held a fund-raising fete. The Wives' Auxiliary group ran a food stall and expected that they and their project would receive the profits for this. But the chairman of the men's group wanted to give them only a fixed sum which annoyed the women very much. On another occasion, at the annual conference of all branches in India, the Wives' Auxiliary organization wanted to hold their formal dinner along with that of the men. They proposed that they too should contribute to the dinner and make it a joint event, but this was refused by the men.

In fact, on my return, I found that the project of the women's auxiliary group had more or less folded, and it was decided that they would no longer run their own project but concentrate on 'helping our husbands'. This seems to be a not uncommon experience, since a recent issue of the all-India magazine records that one branch decided to do likewise: 'It was suggested that we would work together as a team and share the profits. Needless to say everyone jumped at the idea, because working together is so much more fun and exciting.'

On occasion, the 'service' work of the men's organization may actually be carried out by the wives. For example, in one issue of the magazine it is recorded that a particular men's club member is helping an orphanage by himself paying for lunch for all the children on one day of each week; 'Not only a cheque book charity is this, for his wife visits the school each week and personally supervises the project.'

It can even be the case that the Wives' Auxiliary does 'too' well in its projects, as was reported in a branch newsletter. The women's group had made Rs 12,000 (over £700) profit on a film show: '"How come you girls did such a good job without our help? Why don't you organise our fund-raising too?" is the general refrain.'

The attitude of husbands towards their wives's organizational activities is thus a complex one, and is really determined to a large extent by the benefits which the men themselves get out of it. Husbands of the members of the Institute for Women, who are mostly from the upper class, encourage their wives to 'do good works' and 'make a name', for this adds to the family's status. Besides, there is no conflict with such activities and domestic duties in households wealthy enough to afford enough servants, particularly a cook.

The husbands of the Housewives' Association members are also encouraged by their wives to think along the same lines, although limits in time and money are always strictly drawn. Potential problems have perhaps been averted by co-opting husbands on to an advisory committee.

As far as the husbands of the Neighbourhood Club women are concerned, on the other hand, there is little benefit to them if their wives participate actively, except in so far as they may acquire such skills as baking or improving their English. The focus of the men's lives does not lie in the suburb – it lies in their place of work, and for some, in their membership of recreational clubs in the city. If they are anxious to raise the family's prestige, it is not in the arena of a middle-class suburb, but elsewhere. Those men resident in the suburb who are interested in forming relationships with neighbours can do so by joining the Kamalapuram Residents' Association, discussed below. Thus most husbands of Neighbourhood Club members simply do not see the benefits of their wives' membership of the club, and are likely to be hostile if they think that too much time and money which should be spent on the household are being spent on the club.

For the Wives' Auxiliary, which exists by definition to complement the activities of the men's service club, the situation is also complicated. On the one hand, a man does gain prestige from having a wife who is successful in terms of the Wives' Auxiliary. But on the other hand, most men are anxious that the women's organization should be, and should be seen to be, subsidiary to their own. Any attempt at equalization is put down firmly.

Men do not only play a role, whether direct or indirect, in the women's organizations *qua* husbands, but in other ways too. The Neighbourhood Club has a number of informal links with the only other association in the suburb, the Kamalapuram Residents'

Association, composed almost entirely of men. Interestingly, very few of the husbands of women involved in the Neighbourhood Club belong to this. The Residents' Association has been in existence for a decade longer than the women's club, but has not yet acquired a proper building. Its activities consist largely of celebrating national holidays and putting on occasional film shows. In many respects it was, during the time of field-work, less active than the women's club. This is scarcely surprising, given that most men are away from the area for much of the day and thus have little time to organize it. The men are aware of this, and have sugested at various times that there should be a merger between the two clubs. The women, however, are afraid that the main inducement to this suggestion is their fine building and that once merged, the men would make all the decisions and the women do all the work. They have thus declined, claiming that decorum is better served by two clubs for the two sexes.

None the less, the women's club members are sometimes uneasily aware that the Residents' Association members have more experience of administration than they do, and will sometimes call on them for help or advice. For example when they conducted their elections during the period of field-work, they asked one of its officers to be the Election Officer. The reverse situation never occurred, and would be highly unlikely.

Several organizations frequently invite men to be guest speakers at their meetings on the grounds that they are important politicians or religious leaders. The Institute for Women also organizes many of its 'functions' to coincide with the anniversaries of 'great men'. Even the Professional Women's Association will invite males as its Chief Guests on the occasion of the Annual dinner or other important functions; during the year of field-work this was the Governor of Rotary, and in seeking a format for the investiture of officers, a Rotary model was used.

Another way in which men are involved is as recipients of charity. Although the majority of social service projects are aimed at benefiting women and/or children, some also benefit males: for example, students helped by the Housewives' Association in the form of grants and the book bank, or people who needed help with medical bills. Similarly the scheme in which the Wives' Auxiliary had joined together with their husbands' service club was to provide scholarships; it was apparent these would primarily benefit males. There is little feeling among members of any organization except perhaps the Institute for Women that their energies should be devoted solely towards helping other women.

DISCUSSION

Just as the early women's associations in India had to tread a careful path in order to try and deflect male opposition from their aims, so too are the organizations under consideration at pains to try and balance their members' domestic roles with their public ones as participants in women's organizations. It is possible to argue that women themselves have perhaps internalized the view that much of what they do has to be validated by reference to males, whether these be husbands, important guests, or members of men's associations. On the other hand, it might well be difficult for women to participate in such activities in the teeth of opposition from their husbands, and in order to be publicly effective women's activities have to seek co-operation from the world in which most power, and certainly most economic resources, are controlled by males.

None the less, women themselves *are* playing a significant political role in running such organizations, as is seen in an examination of who is helped and why, and in the relationship of women's welfare programmes to state policies. These topics are discussed in the following sections.

The beneficiaries of social welfare: caste and class

An important feature of the women's organizations' social welfare programmes is the public giving of gifts to beneficiaries, by either the members of the organizations (the 'social workers') or else their guests: 'National and religious festivals and celebrations to commemorate the memory of great men [*sic*] are observed with splendour [in the association]. During these days there is poor feeding and distribution of sweets and clothes' (Institute for Women, Annual Report). Gifts are almost always in kind (sweets, food, clothes), rarely in cash. And they are not simply handed over, but 'distributed', that is, they are publicly presented by the donor to the recipient(s) on an occasion where many witnesses of the same social status as the donor are present.

It is always the officers of the association rather than the recipients who give thanks for the gifts. The recipients do not speak on such occasions, although they may do a reverential *namaste* with folded hands and bowed head. Nor of course, do the recipients on any occasion make counter-gifts. If then, as many anthropologists have suggested (cf. Mauss 1967; Sahlins 1974), gifts must be returned in equal value in order for giver and receiver to maintain an egalitarian relationship, what is being witnessed here is a totally asymmetrical relationship between donor and recipient, for the latter would appear to have nothing to offer in return, not even thanks.

And yet this view might be countered by an examination of the Hindu philosophy behind giving to charity. As Moorthy has pointed out: 'Even the giver of help is really helping himself' (1981: 29), for by giving and helping one acquires religious merit which enables both self-realization (*swarupa*) in this life, and hope of a better reincarnation or even total release (*moksha*) in a future life. Some of these ideas were elaborated by Gandhi into his trusteeship theory; by this he meant that those who have greater advantages (whether of position, power, or possessions) have a moral duty in relation to the less advantaged. The able should help the less able or disabled, and the wealthy should use their money for the betterment of the poor (Moorthy 1981: 49).

At its most revolutionary, this concept involves giving up all one has in order to serve others. More often, however, it is interpreted as meaning that if one gives charity, then one can continue to enjoy the remainder of one's wealth (or power or abilities) (cf. also Madan 1970: 316). At a more mundane level, the giver of course obtains other advantages. These include a 'good name' and the recognition and respect of one's peers. This is manifested in the sort of rituals I have been describing and even more particularly in ceremonies held specifically to 'felicitate' or 'honour' someone for their work: 'On the occasion of X organisation's 25th anniversary, mementoes were presented to distinguished social workers' (*Hindu*, 4 March 1975).

During the International Year of the Child (1979), the Union government set up a new annual award for the best institutions and workers in the field of child welfare. In addition, well known social workers receive press publicity, and may also get awards such as the Padma Shri or Padma Bhushan, which are announced by the President of India on Republic Day each year.

In short, then, giving to charity is not without its considerable benefits at many levels to the donor.   However, it may be argued that none of these benefits comes directly from the recipient – fellow social workers conduct ceremonies during the course of which 'distinguished workers' are honoured; the press gives publicity; the government gives tax relief on charitable donations, and also confers awards; ultimately, only God confers merit. To obtain all these blessings, it is necessary for a class of those in need of social welfare to exist; by being there, by accepting charity, they enable all the foregoing to happen. None the less, their status *vis-à-vis* the givers remains intrinsically unchanged.

Social welfare activities thus appear to be very much about defining class relations – a class of givers and one of receivers. Caste is never mentioned as a consideration, and all the organizations define themselves as 'secular'. Yet caste has already been shown to be highly significant. Two organizations consist largely of Brahmins, and in a third, cleavages are likely to be on Brahmin–non-Brahmin lines. Does class, then, encompass caste in this context?

During my first period of field-work (1974–75), and in subsequent publications (e.g. Caplan 1978), I was convinced that caste had relatively little significance within the organizations. However, when I returned to Madras in 1981, I decided to interview as many of the beneficiaries of the social welfare programmes of these women's organizations as possible. I was very surprised by my findings on two counts. The first was that frequently beneficiaries shared the same caste status as donors (i.e. many of them were Brahmins). The second was that many recipients were not the poorest of the poor   indeed, it was rather ambitious members of the working class or lower middle class who often availed themselves of such opportunities.

I interviewed several sets of beneficiaries: parents of children in all three *balwadis*, parents of children in a creche, women taking vocational training courses at two associations, and the residents of the institution run by the Housewives' Association, as well as some of their individual recipients of charity.

BALWADI CHILDREN

Interviews with the parents (mostly mothers) of children in the *balwadis* run by two associations reveal great similarities in background. The occupations of the fathers of these children are mainly skilled workers – drivers, masons, tailors, smiths – with a minority of unskilled workers such as peons, watchmen, and, in the case of the Neighbourhood Club, of caste-specific jobs (tailor or washerman). Their monthly income in 1981 was in the range of Rs 150–400 per month. Most of the mothers do not have jobs outside the household, except for a handful who work as part-time housemaids for between Rs 25 and Rs 50 per month. Almost all parents have had some schooling, although the fathers were usually better educated than the mothers. Most households live on the husband's income, usually in rented accommodation – a hut or a room – for which they pay between Rs 30 and Rs 75 per month.

The caste background of these beneficiaries is varied, although only a small minority interviewed admitted to being an Adi-Dravida (untouchable); the rest are middle-range castes such as Mudaliar, Naidu, Chettiar, Pillai, and Naicker.

These then are not the poorest of the poor. Almost all the fathers have jobs, albeit low-paid, and most of them are skilled workers. Their reason for sending the children to the *balwadi* is not so that mothers can take paid work, but because parents see it as a good educational beginning: 'They look after them very well, and they learn things'; 'It's better for them to learn than to be playing around at home.' The free midday meal is much appreciated, as is the fact that only nominal fees are charged. The children are given a certificate at the end of their time in the *balwadi* and parents feel that this helps when they take them to get admission to the primary school at the age of five.

Most of these parents have thought about the future education of their children currently attending the *balwadi* and can name the school to which they intend to send them. While many will go to the corporation (public) school, a significant number are to go to schools maintained by voluntary organizations, which are considered to have a higher standard than the public schools. A few parents even stated that they intended to put their children in one of the many small, private, fee-paying 'English-medium' schools which are found in most neighbourhoods.

Such schools are of course far removed from the private schools to which the upper middle and upper classes send their children; the fees of the former schools are low – around Rs 10–20 per month. But the fact that even quite poor parents are willing to spend this money (plus the cost of uniforms) is indicative of the extent to which English is still important, in spite of half a century of Tamil nationalism.

These parents, then, are members of the 'respectable' working class, with some hopes of upward mobility for their children; their reasons for using the *balwadi* are educational rather than economic, believing that it makes the child more receptive to learning in the primary school.

The background of the children in the *balwadi* run by the Professional Women's Association, on the other hand, is different in certain respects. Children are only admitted if their mothers are employed and a certificate from the employer is produced. Women who stop working are asked to remove their children because it is not thought necessary for them to have such facilities 'just so that they can attend to their household duties'; members feel that only the children of 'really working mothers who need our help' should be given places.

The majority of women whose children are in this creche are employed as housemaids, and their pay ranges from Rs 20 to Rs 75 per month. There are also a handful of women who work in government concerns and earn considerably more – between Rs 300 and Rs 500 per month. Several women are separated from their husbands, usually deserted by them. Most of the resident husbands are extremely badly paid and a higher proportion of them are unskilled than those of the fathers of the children in the other two creches. The educational level of the parents is also lower than for the parents of the other *balwadi* children – only just over half the fathers and mothers have had any schooling at all.

It is perhaps not coincidental that there are also far more Adi-Dravidas in this sample than in the other two. Adi-Dravida males are less likely to be skilled workers, thus they earn less; Adi-Dravida women take on jobs as housemaids out of sheer economic necessity, and also because they are perhaps more willing than members of other castes to do such defiling work as cleaning bathrooms. Thus the household income of most of the children in this *balwadi* is lower than that of the two others, in spite of the fact that all the mothers are in paid employment. All the mothers interviewed stated that their main reason for sending their children to the creche was the need for them to work.

THE CRECHE FOR WHITE COLLAR WOMEN
WORKERS

The creche for clerical workers was originally set up by the members of the Professional Women's Association, which later handed its running over to the Department of Social Welfare. Twenty-six women were interviewed, all white collar workers in a large complex of government offices.

These women are not highly paid; they earn only between Rs 150 and Rs 600 per month, with the majority between Rs 300 and Rs 400. All are Tamilians and the majority (fifteen) are Brahmins. More than half have received some form of higher education, four being graduates, and another eleven having done either intermediate or pre-university courses. Most of their fathers were government servants at a fairly low level, others worked in shops, or as teachers. Almost all are married (twenty-three) and the occupations of their husbands are also at white collar level, the majority (twelve) being government servants (clerks, etc.) or else in industry. The educational level of husbands and wives is fairly similar, but the husbands tend to earn more money than their wives, mostly between Rs 500 and Rs 600. When asked what their major problems were, most of the women mentioned the double burden of paid work and household work.

All the women stated that they work for economic reasons. Most of their pay goes directly into the household budget – only four women keep a personal allowance for themselves, and only six have a bank account in their own name. Most said that they and their husbands decided jointly how the household income should be spent. Their incomes added to those of their husbands brought the total monthly income up to around Rs 1,000 per month, effectively lifting the family into the middle ranges of the middle class. It is at this level that the standard of living has been eroded considerably by inflation in the last decade or so. Without the wife's contribution, it would have proved extremely difficult to continue such middle-class standards as employing a part-time servant, and, most importantly, being able to afford some sort of 'decent' private education for their children. For such families, then, the economic contribution of the woman is absolutely crucial to their maintenance of class position and their aspirations for mobility for their children. Although they may be seen, and see themselves, as 'supplementing' the family income, none the less, without their contribution the family's life-style would be very different.

VOCATIONAL TRAINING STUDENTS

Tailoring classes are held regularly twice a week at the Institute for Women for around half a dozen women. Their class background is wide, ranging from the wives of a college lecturer and an accountant, to a widow working as a housemaid. The women of high socio-economic status said that they wanted to learn tailoring 'for interest' and 'to make clothes for my children', whereas the poorer women hoped that their training would enable them to earn some money afterwards.

Another type of class run by the same organization is a secretarial course, which involves several months of study for five mornings per week. About thirty young women are admitted at a time to learn typing, shorthand, English, and simple accountancy. Most of these women are aged between sixteen and twenty, are unmarried, and living with their parents. Since the organization, in conjunction with the SSWB, not only gives them free tuition but also pays them a monthly stipend of Rs 15, the course attracts people from quite a distance – several were prepared to travel for more than an hour by bus or train in order to attend.

The socio-economic background of these young women is either skilled working class or lower middle class. Their fathers work as clerks, teachers, and drivers, and earn between Rs 200 and Rs 700, although most get between Rs 300 and Rs 500 per month. Only one has a mother who works outside the home, but all the students intend to look for a job after finishing the course. They are thus the first women in their families to contemplate taking up paid employment, and many said frankly that it was for purely economic reasons 'to help support the family', 'to help my brothers' education', and 'to save for my dowry'. All said that their parents were agreeable (albeit sometimes reluctantly) to their taking a paid job. These young women are, like the mothers who use the creche previously described, part of the growing number of females in white collar service jobs whose earnings are a vital part of maintaining their family's standards of living.

More than half of the class are Brahmins, and there are two

possible reasons for this. One is that recruitment to this course is frequently by word of mouth, and the Brahmin network, often through kin, tends to pass on information to other Brahmins. The other is that just as the Brahmins were the first Hindu community in Madras to send their daughters for education, so they are among the first to have women participating in paid employment. The pattern also fits in with the findings from the interviews conducted with white collar government employees, discussed in the prevous section.

INDIVIDUAL RECIPIENTS OF CHARITY

Only one organization gives help of various kinds on an individual level to students to pay their fees and lend them books, to handicapped children who need calipers, and to people who are sick and cannot afford the costs of an operation. Some of the beneficiaries of this organization are males, for the aims of the organization are 'charity', and there is no specific emphasis on helping women. Thus a large number of the school and college students who get bursaries are boys, although there are some girls who receive aid too. However, many more girls are assisted by the organization to get married rather than to study; they are given the basic necessities essential to marriage – a *tali* and a new sari.

There are a number of routes by which people apply to the organization for help. Some hear about it from friends. Others see mention of the organization and its activities in newspapers and magazines. But a large proportion come through personal contacts and, as such people are likely to be fellow caste members and even kin of organization members, it is scarcely surprising to find that most are also Brahmins.

THE RESIDENTIAL INSTITUTION

The thirty residents in this institution come from a wide socio-economic spectrum, although in order to be admitted they must be destitute or nearly so. Some have previously worked as servants, but others have known more prosperous times, like two women whose husbands had been college lecturers, another whose husband had been a film producer, and a fourth whose husband had been an accountant. Sometimes such people fell into poverty when their husbands retired, or after the death of their husbands. Very few of the women in this institution have children, although a handful have had children who pre-deceased them, or else they have children who are living but with whom they have lost contact. A few residents still have contact with kin but these are unable to support them.

The institution admits women 'without distinction of caste or creed', and it is made clear to residents that strict orthodoxy in such matters as eating cannot possibly prevail. They must accept to eat with everyone regardless of their background. However, the majority of residents are Brahmins and most of the remainder are higher caste Hindus, such as Chettiars and Naidus, or else non-Hindus (three Christians and one Muslim). The reason why there is such a preponderance of Brahmins is again undoubtedly not due to discriminatory policies on the part of the management committee, but to the fact that so many come through personal contacts with members of the organization, most of whom, as already stated, are Brahmins.

DISCUSSION

Several striking facts emerge out of an examination of the background of the beneficiaries. The first is that their class background is mixed. Most of those who send their children to the *balwadis* are members of the working class, although they are rarely the poorest of the poor (such as unemployed, beggars, etc.), but are the children of skilled or semi-skilled workers. Those who come for vocational training or other educational help, on the other hand, are primarily of middle-class background, being the children of lower grade white collar workers.

Second, these class distinctions are clearly recognized by the members of the voluntary associations. For instance, one organization holds three annual sports days – one for the members, one for the vocational training students, and another for the *balwadi* children and their parents. The minutes of the same organization record that:

'It is proposed to start the following activities:
(1) tailoring, lace-making and needlework for *extra* earning of the girls and women of *middle-class lower income group* [i.e. what might be termed middle middle class];

(2) preparation of *appalams* and *vadams* [cooked snacks] to benefit destitute women of the *lower middle-class group*, work to be done in their own homes and sold by the association for wages fixed by the association;
(3) preparation of leaf plates and leaf cups [used as disposable tableware in south India] by the women of the *working class* in their own homes.'

Class differences are also reflected in use of space. In two organizations, the educational activities for the lower middle classes take place inside the main building, whereas in all cases, the *balwadis* are separately housed in a building at the back, in a lean-to at the side, or in a separate annexe.

The third fact that deserves some consideration is the extent to which beneficiaries (except in the case of *balwadi* children) share the caste background of the members of the association. In other words, a large proportion of them are Brahmins – half of the secretarial course students, most of the mothers using the creche for government servants, the majority of the inmates of the residential institution, and not a few of the recipients of individual charity. In part, as I have said, this is not a conscious policy of discrimination. Beneficiaries are recruited by word of mouth, and caste and kin networks are important in this respect. However, there is also a strong feeling on the part of many members of the voluntary organizations that the government policy of helping Scheduled Castes and Tribes in India as a whole and Backward Classes in Tamilnadu has gone much too far. All experience problems in getting places in college for their children, because they are members of Forward Communities, and they feel sympathetic towards poorer and less advantaged members of their own caste whose problems are compounded by poverty. They frequently say that the people who are best suited and qualified to do such courses are from the Forward and not the Backward communities, for the latter do not have the same tradition of acquiring education and skills, especially the women. Thus all these factors operate, often at an unconscious level, to produce a situation in which a large amount of help extended by the voluntary agencies, particularly those dominated by Brahmins, goes to people who are fellow caste members, albeit of a different class level.

Why then, given its importance, is caste never mentioned publicly? Why, on the contrary, does the rhetoric, as seen in the next chapter, stress the language of class? We can discern a complex process at work here. Members of women's organizations can help fellow caste members by giving them charity. At the same time, the very act of giving and receiving charity defines classes, and thus cuts across caste links. In many instances women help members of their own caste, yet by so doing, they define themselves as members of a class that can afford to dispense charity to one that needs to receive it. There is thus no real contradiction in the operation of caste and class in this process.

One may, however, ask whether there is a conflict of interest between state welfare policies and those of the women's organizations. I consider this point in the next section.

The political role of the women's organizations

On the day on which the State of Emergency was declared in 1975, one of the Vice-Presidents of the Institute for Women had made a radio broadcast in which she gave support to Mrs Gandhi, declaring that the charges against her (of misuse of electoral funds) were trivial. She reflected the views of most members of this organization (although she broadcast as an individual, not as an association member), who largely support the Congress Party, as did most members of the other associations.

The Union government is, in turn, particularly interested in giving support to the women's organizations in Tamilnadu, because (as was shown in Chapter 7) through them, and particularly through the SSWB, it has some access to the politics of a state which has not had a Congress government since 1967. This support is evidenced by the readiness of the Union government to send its local representatives – the state governor or his wife – to functions organized by the women's association and, not infrequently, of Union Ministers and even the Prime Minister and President of India to include visits to women's associations in their tours of India.

In turn, the women's organizations serve as a vehicle for a minority community – the Brahmins – to organize themselves, and maintain some links with the loci of power. At the same time, the channels of the organizations and the welfare boards at state and central level provide one of the few ways in which *women* can achieve political power; for instance, the ex-secretary of one organization later chaired first the State and then the CSWB. As another chairman of the Tamilnadu Board told an audience of the Housewives' Association, 'only in social welfare do women get access to government'.

But the mainly Brahmin and Congress-dominated women's organizations in Madras have had to come to terms with the Dravidian nationalist governments – they take care to invite leading politicians from these parties as well as those from Congress. In their turn, the DMK and ADMK governments have learned to use the voluntary sector for their own ends, even if it is 'Brahmin and Congress-dominated'; they have simply found it too useful to dispense with.

This is not to say that the interests of all these sectors harmonize completely; plainly they do not. At a meeting of the Housewives' Association, the drafting of a letter to the Tamilnadu government, protesting at the income ceiling for subsidized food, was accompanied by remarks such as 'We have to defend the interests of the middle classes', and 'Yes, *we* are the downtrodden now, and those people [i.e. the working class] are coming up'. Measures taken by either the central or state governments which were considered to be 'socialistic' or primarily for the benefit of the lower castes and classes were criticized, and, in so far as possible, undermined or circumvented. In the case of their own children, this meant even greater struggles for better education, and help for poorer members of the Brahmin community through charity.

Conclusion: *cui bono?*

In whose interests, then, are women acting when they 'learn new things', make friends, or dispense charity through the women's organizations? On one level, of course, they are acting in their own individual interests – most enjoy what they do, and it provides a justification for a break from their domestic routines. At the same time, they are in many respects acting as members of families – they are engaging in what Papanek (1979) has called 'status production work', that is they are creating the culture and life-style appropriate to their class level. It is not surprising that many husbands, particularly of upper-class women, are supportive and encourage their wives to get involved.

On another level, the women are acting in the interests of their own community, particularly if they are Brahmins, for social welfare is one of the few areas (perhaps along with classical Carnatic music) in which Brahmins can organize by informal means. The same argument of 'ethnicity' might also be used of the north Indians who dominate the men's international service organization and its Wives' Auxiliary. Only the Brahmins, however, can at the same time benefit members of their own caste by helping them with scholarships, vocational training, and so on.

Third, women are acting in the interests of their own class *vis-à-vis* other classes – both those slightly lower than their own from which they seek to separate themselves, and from the lower classes as a whole. It is perhaps here that the interests of the state and of the women's organizations may diverge. The state, both at the centre (Union) and local level, seeks to use social welfare as a means of controlling the poor. In India it has sought to do this mainly through utilizing the voluntary sector. However, it has not always found this the most efficient means (see Chapter 7), and a case study of Madras city women's organizations gives some indications of why this may be. The women's organizations have many aims and interests and the objects of their charity may not at all be those to which the state gives priority. Nor can most women's organizations give charity on the scale which is probably needed if the masses are to be 'kept quiet'. It is thus not surprising that both Union and local state governments have come around to a point where they use the women's organizations directly, but themselves decide programmes and priorities, as in the case of the Tamilnadu Child Feeding Scheme (discussed in Chapter 7).

Both the (Congress) central government and the (Dravidian nationalist) state government have an interest in preserving the voluntary sector. The former has a special interest in the case of Tamilnadu, as already stated, since social welfare is an avenue through which it can gain some entree into state politics. The local state, on the other hand, has learned to welcome the 'respectability' it can accrue through co-operation with the social welfare establishment in Tamilnadu; this trend has of course been intensified by the alliance between the ADMK and Congress in recent electoral contests.

10
The ideology of gender and class

In a capitalist society the reproduction of labour power requires not only a reproduction of its skills but also a reproduction of submission to the ruling ideology for the workers, and the ability to manipulate this ideology correctly by the ruling class (Althusser 1972: 245–46).

India has been characterized as an 'ideologically highly developed nation' (Selbourne 1982: 148), and it is not infrequently suggested that the sophistication of its ideological apparatuses goes a long way towards explaining why its gross socio-economic inequalities continue to persist.

Recent studies of welfare in developed capitalist states have seen it as an important means of securing hegemony for the ruling classes (Ginsburg 1979; Gough 1979). The state is viewed by its citizens as beneficent, because it is supposed to cushion them against poverty, unemployment, and ill-health. A large part of the impact of the welfare state is then ideological in nature, although the financial and other benefits it gives are not, of course, inconsequential.

In India, the state and the voluntary sector disburse relatively fewer benefits and to a smaller proportion of the population than in the developed capitalist states. None the less, both the state and the ruling classes have a common interest in promulgating a view that they are concerned with the welfare of the masses, and doing something to alleviate their misery. Thus it is my contention that the ideological effects of voluntary social welfare are probably far more important than their effects in terms of concrete assistance rendered or improvements effected.

In this chapter, I examine some of the ideological statements made by voluntary social welfare organizations, and show how they serve at one and the same time to define particular classes, to explain poverty, and to justify the status quo, while perpetuating an ideology which places women firmly in the domestic sphere.

Rituals of hierarchy

Public ceremonies organized by the women's associations are numerous. They take place on such occasions as anniversaries of the association (particularly grandly on the tenth, twenty-fifth, and fifticth years), the inauguration of some new project or building, and at seminars and conferences. Such events, almost invariably referred to as 'functions' or 'celebrations', are highly ritualized, and they constitute an important reaffirmation of hierarchical principles.

This is clearly seen in the seating, where important personages and in particular the speech-makers sit up on a platform, while the audience sits in rows below facing them; the most important people in the audience sit in specially reserved seats in the front rows. At the centre of the platform party is the most important person, with others radiating out to the wings in descending order of importance.

The first event of the ceremony is usually a prayer, which is sung, often by a member of the association. Next, the chief guests on the platform are garlanded, again usually by members of the association. Garlands, which are made of flowers, are never worn, but removed immediately and handed to attendants. During the garlanding, photographs are usually taken by a professional photographer.

The person presiding over the event, who may be either an invited guest or a prominent member of the organization, then makes a speech to introduce the chief guest or guest of honour. The latter then proceeds to make a longer speech, sometimes known as the 'keynote address'. On some occasions, a eulogy or 'felicitation' in praise of the chief guest is read out by a member of the association. Next, the souvenir (described in more detail below) is 'released', sometimes by the chief guest, sometimes by another guest, and this also involves another speech. Finally, the 'vote of thanks' is given to the guests, usually by one of the association members. In all, then, there are rarely fewer than three speeches, and frequently there are more. The commonest language used is English, particularly for the larger and wealthier organizations, although Tamil is sometimes used in the smaller ones.

An example of such an event is provided by the 'function' organized by the Institute for Women for a visit of the Governor's wife in the early 1970s. The programme was as follows:

prayer	sung by Joint Secretary
welcome speech	by other Joint Secretary
garlanding	by one of the Vice-Presidents
veena concert	by members of the Institution's music class
prize giving	by the Governor's wife
gift of money★	by President of Institution to Governor's wife
performance	by *balwadi* children
gift of clothes to children	by senior committee member of Institution
speech	by Governor's wife
vote of thanks	by senior committee member
bhajans	

★ This was for the National Defence Fund

This occasion involved four speeches, but it was a relatively minor event compared with the Silver Jubilee of the same association. The minutes of the committee meeting that planned this event read as follows:

'The programme was tentatively fixed in the following manner to hold a seminar on "Reaching the Youth". There should be a leader report or speaker ... and the All-India Women's Conference Chairman would sum up and conclude [the seminar discussions]. It was decided to conclude the seminar by 4 p.m. so that the evening function could commence at 5 p.m. Dr X [a woman who had founded a social welfare institution and who is related to one of the Joint Secretaries] would be asked to preside, and His Excellency [the Governor] to release the souvenir, and his wife to present medallions to the office-bearers and members who have been closely associated for the past 25 years. Mrs Y [President of the largest social welfare organization in the city] and Mrs W [ex-Chairman of the CSWB] would speak about the institution and its invaluable service rendered for the past 25 years ... The Annual Report of the Jubilee year, as well as of the last 25 years, would be read, after which the function would conclude with a vote of thanks.'

In the case of this association, they were able not only to involve some of the most important people in Tamilnadu, including the Governor and his wife, but also to bring in two leading women's welfare figures from Delhi. This occasion raised a great deal of money: Rs 13,600 (£800) from advertisements for the souvenir and donations of over Rs 18,000 (£1,000), besides money from the sale of tickets, which brought in another Rs 1,000 (£60).

Functions like this are always conducted with solemnity. There is almost always reference to religion, not only in the form of an opening prayer, but quite often in other ways too, for instance the singing of *bhajans*. Since almost all music in south India is devotional in nature, the use of any music as what Cohen (1981) calls a 'dramaturgical technique' is not only aesthetic but also religious in nature.

Oratory is another such technique. Speakers are distanced from their audience by being on a platform, usually behind a table, and invariably, even in quite small gatherings, use is made of a microphone. Most speeches on such occasions are very similar; they praise the institution and its leaders for their good work, making use of past historical or mythological figures (particularly Gandhi) to drive home points, and extolling such virtues as generosity, social service, and national integration.

As Cohen has noted in his recent study of the Creoles of Sierra Leone, such ceremonies serve an important purpose: 'It is mainly in the course of such key dramatic performances that the symbolic order and the power order interpenetrate one another within the self to produce, and repetitively reproduce, the bivocality, and hence the mystificatory nature, of the major symbolic forms' (1981: 155). The symbolic order that is highlighted in such a ceremony is essentially one of hierarchy. If at all possible, the Governor and/or his wife will be invited, or at least a State Minister. Prominence is also given to senior members of the association, who are often called upon to make speeches. Thus hierarchy within the organization is also emphasized. Clients or beneficiaries, in whose name all this is taking place, rarely play any role at all, except that on occasion children of a *balwadi* may sing a few songs or do a dance.

On all such occasions, numerous photographs are taken by professional photographers and they too reflect the same notions of hierarchy. Most photographs are taken of prominent persons, very few of others, particularly beneficiaries. If the latter are photographed, their names rarely appear either in the newspapers or in the publications of the associations: they remain anonymous – 'a poor deserving bride', 'a paralysed man'. In this respect, they contrast sharply with donors, whose names invariably appear. In one typical souvenir, out of a total of 59 photographs, 32 were of 'distinguished visitors', 14 of the organization's buildings, 8 of anonymous inmates, and the remaining 5 of the committee members or founders.

Publications and their format

The ideology of the women's associations is manifest not only in the forms of rituals already described, particularly in the speeches, but also through the medium of the 'souvenir' booklets which are produced annually or for some important occasion. These contain, besides the advertisements which finance them, stories, poems, articles, and photographs. Some associations produce a regular souvenir, others bring out a regular newsletter. The dominant language, again, is usually English, although some associations may use a mixture of Tamil and English.

The format of most souvenirs and journals is remarkably similar. At the beginning is a photograph, the commonest being of the current Prime Minister, although Mahatma Gandhi ranks a close second, usually with a quotation from his writings. Then follows a list of the office-bearers and patrons of the association. Next come the 'messages'. It is customary to write to important personages on the occasion of the release of a souvenir, telling them of the event, and they respond with messages of goodwill; these are conventional in form, merely noting the event, congratulating the institution, and wishing it well for the future. However, the status of those from whom messages are received is a fair indication of the relative status of the organization. Messages, needless to say, are always arranged in strictly hierarchical fashion.

Many souvenirs or journals also contain thè names of visitors and their remarks about the association written in the visitors' book; these are always of a laudatory nature. In all the publications, there is an emphasis upon congratulation and upon the achievements of the members. There is very little about the beneficiaries or their problems, or indeed about any difficulties which the association may have encountered in seeking to fulfil its aims and objectives.

The content of oratory and publications: the language of gender and class

The two main themes that recur over and over again in speeches and written material are women and their role (i.e. gender) and social welfare; in the process of writing or speaking about the latter, many ideas about class also emerge. In spite of the differences in style between the associations discussed in Chapter 9, there is basically little discernible difference in their ideology, and they present a common view of both gender and class.

This ideology is not, of course, peculiar to the women's organizations – it is very much the dominant ideology in Indian society and is also reflected in the mass media (and 1975, which was International Women's Year, provided particularly rich sources) and even to some extent in academic sociological literature (Caplan 1979). Most of the discussion in this chapter, however, relates to the publications of the five organizations studied.

WOMEN

Articles, stories, and poems in the publications of the women's associations frequently lay down norms of conduct for women in their roles as wives, mothers, and daughters-in-law. Quite often such norms are reinforced by reference to mythical heroines, as in the following story from the *Mahabharata*,[1] quoted in an article in an Institute for Women's souvenir, which states what a good wife should be:

'Panjali told Satyanha that women should never do things which gave displeasure to their husbands. Sacrificing her own self, she should devote herself to the welfare of her husband. She should not eat before him. After finishing the work in the house, she should spend some pleasant time with him. Women should not waste their time standing at the door step and roaming about the garden. Controlling her anger and other evil habits, she should act according to his wishes. In his absence, she should not pay much attention to her dress and beauty, and train herself to develop a taste only for what he eats and drinks. She should obey her mother-in-law, and do the duties expected of her to their ancestors. She should take an interest in all her husband's activities and help him in his tasks. She should take charge of the household duties and accounts, and do her duties tirelessly. Women should go to bed only after their husbands and get up before them. Panjali had been practising these things and she was a very good and loyal wife.'

In short, then, wifely duty should know no bounds, and women should be self-sacrificing, patient, and totally attentive to their husbands, regardless of the latter's character and behaviour. In one story in a souvenir, a woman decides that she does not want any more children and so she refuses to sleep with her husband. He begins to stay away from home, and finally an elderly woman neighbour advises her to 'change her ways'. The wife resolves to act upon the advice, but finally when her husband does return, it is too late, for he is dying from the venereal disease he caught from visiting brothels. She is heart-broken and realizes that it has all been her fault.

Although the role of woman as wife seems to receive the greatest amount of attention (see also Wadley 1977), her function as a mother is also frequently mentioned: 'It is women who, by nature, are endowed with insight and sympathy; they have a better understanding of the problems and difficulties of children' (AIWC conference paper 1975); 'The domestic sphere should not be neglected and the present day trends of indiscipline warrant greater attention on the upbringing of children. If every mother accepts the responsibilities of supplying the Nation with disciplined children, the nation takes care of itself, and this is an impending and urgent need of the hour' (AIWC conference paper 1975). Women are therefore seen as 'naturally' fitted to bring up children, but they are also blamed if they do not instil discipline into them, for indiscipline is seen as the root of most of the nation's problems. In the Indian family system women do, of course, have responsibilities to kin other than husbands and children: 'In this context, women should not forget that "charity begins at home", and that they should not neglect an old ailing mother-in-law, a dependent father-in-law, a student daughter-in-law, or a needy sister-in-law' (AIWC conference paper 1975).

It is sometimes recognized that the joint family is a source of conflict, with the 'classic triangle' being the mother–son–wife relationship. None the less, it is always made clear that it is the duty of the wife to 'adjust' to her husband's family. A story in an Institute for Women's souvenir, for instance, is about a man who marries a woman who then fails to get along with his mother. Finally, the latter moves out of the house. Subsequently, the man becomes ill, loses his job, and realizes how much he needs his mother. She comes back to nurse him and the wife repents of her former behaviour. In this story, the wife is blamed because she failed to 'adjust' to her mother-in-law, and the husband is also blamed for allowing himself to put his wife before his mother.

It might be expected that the few articles that attempt to advocate some form of 'emancipation' for women might put forward new norms for women and for men too. But this is not the case. The sanctity of the family and the woman's overwhelming responsibility to it are still stressed. 'To a woman [the] family is very important. Unless she has a happy family, she will not be able to emancipate herself. [But] the emancipation should not have any adverse effect on family life' (article written by AIWC President). In the context of women's 'emancipation', there is considerable debate (already discussed briefly in Chapter 5) about whether or not women have the right to work for pay. For most of the organizations, women should be wives and mothers first, 'social workers' second, and have no need to seek other occupations:

> 'Why should a married woman earn? Does she not earn so that she and her husband and children should live more comfortably? But if her family life should suffer without any added advantage, then why should she go to work? ... What

is the state of our nation today? Widows, orphans, stranded women, fatherless families, and unemployed men abound. It would be commendable if women would gracefully give up their [job] opportunities to those who really need them. By doing so, many a sad tale of several families can be erased.'

(Article in Housewives' Association *Souvenir*)

Such an article is not unexpected in the publication of an organization that sees itself as primarily for housewives. It is, however, perhaps more surprising to hear it from members of the Professional Women's Association. At the 1975 All-India Women's Conference, from which I have already quoted extracts in Chapter 5, an unmarried librarian argued that:

> 'All women cannot take up professions. All men *have* to work, but women have their family for work, and cannot do two things at once. Only when their children grow up can they come out in the form of social service or self-employment ... We have to make sacrifices, we must sacrifice to the have-nots.'

Her paper resulted in an acrimonious debate, with many supporting her view. Another speaker argued that women should only work from economic necessity and should otherwise fulfil themselves in social service. Only a minority of women put forward a different view, one pointing out that, carried to its logical conclusion, such an argument would mean that men from wealthy families ought not to seek jobs either. The only 'radical' in the Madras branch (who subsequently left the organization) denigrated the constant glorification of women's self-sacrifice, and urged that not only should women have the right to work, but that fathers and husbands should help in the domestic sphere.

This latter view was extremely unusual. Even where the right to work is occasionally conceded, this is only where women can manage both their professional and domestic duties, and it is always made clear that domestic duties are paramount:

> 'Indian working woman's great strength lies in her psychological security which is related to her compliant nature. She accepts the family without question ... She likes to be needed and important to others. [The] Indian working woman adjusts herself to the life of her husband, helping him in all

ways that she can ... She wants to be a perfect partner in mind and temperament.'
(Article in Professional Women's Association *Souvenir*)

Any suggestion that men might participate in domestic duties, a suggestion which is in any case very rarely made, is opposed. At the seminar cited above, a medical specialist, at the top of her field, unmarried, and living with her natal family, stated firmly that she and her sisters did the housework, and that they would never allow her father and brothers to do anything, although she admitted that she did not know why she felt that way. A similar view was taken by a very well-known social worker: 'This sharing in the household work which is so prominent in the West ... we have been brought up in such a way that whenever I come home, whether it is as a [voluntary] social worker, or a paid worker, even though I be dead tired, I would never want the man to do the household work. We accept that it is our job.' She went on to tell me how she went to the International Women's Year conference in Mexico City in 1975, as an Indian representative. She and the other Indian delegates plus those from several Asian countries had clashed with western women over the issue of male participation in domestic chores. The former felt that 'there are certain small things for which we need not fight'.

In all of the articles and stories which refer to women in the publications of the women's association, the same words recur: women should be chaste, pure, unsullied, and modest as far as their sexuality is concerned, and sacrificing, suffering, compliant, docile, serving, devoted, and patient as far as their domestic roles are concerned. None of these terms is ever applied to males, although it is thought that through their possession of these qualities women can influence men for the better: 'The raging sea with its ever-rolling waves becomes subdued when the waves reach the shore. Like the waves, man, whatever his potential, has his nature subdued by the influence of woman. Women rule men through their good qualities, and enable them to perform their duties of ruling the world' (Institute for Women *Souvenir*).

This view is expressed in another way in the Professional Women's Association *Souvenir*: 'Today, the Indian woman faces the task of bringing about a revolutionary transformation in the society. She has to extend and enlarge the scope of the family to the dimensions of the whole society. She has to undertake the work of the conversion of men's minds and outlook.' In other words, it is thought that if women fulfil all the ideals already discussed, they can influence their husbands and children, and through them, society. Furthermore, women can 'come out' of their homes to bring their virtues into the world and so improve it. This is, of course, very much Gandhi's argument (see Chapter 6), and the reason he gave for bringing women into the nationalist struggle.

If we may discern any change in the norms advocated for women, it lies rather in an *extension* of their roles rather than in any qualitative change, while men's role, at least *vis-à-vis* women, remains totally unchanged and unchallenged. The extension of women's roles advocated is primarily that of voluntary social work; if women do take up paid work (which is not usually advocated), then this does not mean any diminution of their domestic roles.

A good deal of use is made of history in the women's associations' rhetoric, which tends to divide the past into three periods. The earliest of these is the Vedic, of which it is frequently said that at that time, Indian women had a high status: 'In the Vedic Age, when our country was vast in area, flourishing in prosperity, [it] was a Golden Age, where woman had a say in every venture of life; she was a dominant figure ... We had a glorious past, with customs and traditions of a beautiful culture' (speech by Governor's wife to Professional Woman's Association seminar). However, after the Vedic Age, women's status is said to have diminished, largely because of the 'foreign invasions', first by the Moghuls, and then by the British: the Governor's wife continued 'During that period, our women had to stay at home, were not allowed to educate themselves, and we had child marriages, with the result that the future of the woman was rather bleak, on account of British rule.'

The third period is said to have begun in the nineteenth century with the work of reformers like Ram Mohan Roy, who argued that what was needed was a return to the 'purity' of the Vedas, and a restoration to women of their rightful place in society, which had been corrupted by foreign rule. Gandhi is seen as the culmination of the reform movement, particularly as far as women are concerned: again, the Governor's wife says, 'And then came Mahatma Gandhi, the Father of the Nation, who was responsible for bringing women to the forefront.'

The support of Gandhi, the role of women in the freedom struggle, and the laws passed since independence are often cited by the women's organizations today as their achievements, as is the fact that women obtained the right to vote without opposition from men. Thus many articles, while extolling the past glories of the women's movement, tend to adopt what can only be described as an air of complacency. One well-known voluntary social welfare worker wrote:

> 'Wherever I go in the world, wherever I speak to the Women's Organisations, on the television, on the radio, I am so proud of being an Indian woman ... Just recently, when I was in America last year, at Philadelphia airport the Immigration Officer asked me whose guest I was. I said "Of women's clubs". Then he said "You have come to fight the liberation battle for our women as well as your women." I turned round to him and said "No, our liberation was given to us on a platter by our men and we never had to fight for it."'
>
> (AIWC *Souvenir*)

In short, it is generally thought that women have today obtained their emancipation, and that if they do not make use of it, it is largely their own fault:

> 'After Independence, many of us thought social legislation and economic independence of women will solve many ills of Indian women ... The social legislation in our country seems to be only an exhibit in a show case, rather than a utility weapon. The blame could probably be put squarely on the women.'
>
> (AIWC *Souvenir*)

Thus women are told that they have to rouse themselves out of their 'apathy' and utilize the opportunities which are said to be there in abundance. Since women are, or can be if they choose, 'emancipated', there is above all no need for a women's liberation movement in India.

> 'In the western countries ... women's movements are going strong, and women are carrying things too far to assert their

198 Class & Gender in India

rights ... Our women enjoy respect and freedom at home and outside ... they have advanced into all jobs without difficulty and the various Acts have given them all the freedom and opportunities to compete with men. In our country, women need not fight for their rights. Women are respected everywhere by everybody. We can take pride in this.'

(Neighbourhood Club *Souvenir*)

Any suggestion of criticism of the status quo is met with the accusation that this is 'women's lib' which is said to have led to such a decline in morals and the quality of family life in the west:

'When we discuss the contribution of women of India, we should not confuse ourselves with the women's lib or feminist movements in highly advanced countries which have their origins in the high divorce rate, sex scandals, large numbers of unmarried mothers, etc. They are the concomitants of a social structure which has been completely broken on account of their craze to substitute indulgence for independence and madness for change. Luckily, our social structure still retains its basic moral fibre, thanks to the sober and constructive attitude of the women of India.'

(Speech made by Governor of Tamilnadu
when opening an AIWC conference)

Thus the security and stability of Indian homes, and even Indian society, are contrasted with what is seen as the insecure and unstable nature of life in the west:

'So far life in India has been happy because of the family bondage, because of the concern for others, and because of acceptance of altruism as a code of conduct ... But western life is far from these things. Their main aim is physical comforts and material enjoyments. There is no deep attachment and the sacred feeling of living for one another's sake. The children, because of the frequency of divorce of parents, lack parental care and affection. Life is mechanical. Everybody lives for his own sake and not for the sake of the family.'

(Article in Neighbourhood Club *Souvenir*)

Indian women are constantly being told that the stability of the nation rests on the stability of family life, which in its turn rests on their shoulders. In one sense, their reward for conforming to all the norms discussed above is not only the respect of their families, and that of the wider society, but also a sense that they are the upholders of sacred values, and of ordered society. At the same time, any deviation from these norms threatens social stability and can lead to the situation which is supposed to exist in the west; this is usually caricatured as being so horrendous, that the only sensible option for women is to conform.

The ideology I have so far been discussing concerning women is not confined to the women's organizations – it is widespread in Indian society.[2] There is, for instance, a remarkable consistency between the values perpetuated by the women's organizations and the values of the mass media, not only in the content of the messages they give out, but also in the ideological mechanisms utilized.

One of these is 'naturalism': it is women's *nature* to be self-sacrificing, pure, a good mother, and so on. As Bromley (following Gramsci) has pointed out: 'Naturalisation is a key mechanism of common sense thought which closes knowledge, ends debate, and dissolves contradictions' (Bromley 1977: 5).

Another important mechanism is the use of religion and mythology. Apart from citing scriptures which directly pronounce on women's roles, such as the Manusmirti (cf. Bühler 1886), there is frequent allusion to various heroines in Hindu mythology, and certainly the majority of those commonly cited, such as Sita or Savithri, are shining examples of all the wifely virtues. As Mies (1975) has pointed out, other kinds of women, such as Draupadi, are less likely to be invoked.

Third, history, both ancient and more modern, is interpreted to validate relations between the sexes; the Vedic age, the colonial period, the reformist and nationalist movements, and Gandhi and his messages are all cited, both to show how much women's position has improved and to demonstrate that they are now totally 'emancipated' (or at least they could be if only they cared to take advantage of the numerous benefits men have conferred on them).

Finally, the use of contrasts with western society has recently become important, although to some extent this analogy has a long history (see Chapter 6). Whereas the west is often mentioned in India when it is desired to propagate scientific development, modernity, rationalism, and an emphasis upon the technology which it is hoped will cure India's ills, it is also used as a horrendous example of how a society can go wrong, particularly in relations between the sexes and in family life. In part, this encapsulates the view that many middle and upper-class Indians share, which is that they want 'modernization' in terms of affluence, more material goods, and so on (hence presumably the reasons for the massive exodus of upper middle-class skilled professionals from India to the west in recent years). At the same time, they want to retain their 'traditional values', which include religion and a stable family life. The only way to reconcile the perceived contradiction between the values of 'tradition' and 'modernity' is to assign the keeping of the former to women, thus reinforcing the stereotypes of the 'ideal' Indian woman. Hence also the appearance of the caricature of the 'women's libber'[3] which is nowadays so often invoked as a spectre to deter any woman who questions the dominant norms regarding women's roles and behaviour.

SOCIAL WELFARE

In many respects, social work is seen as peculiarly fitted for women. One reason is that 'It is their natural instinct to care for the welfare of others' (Institute for Women *Souvenir*). Another is that it is an extension of their domestic roles:

> 'Social service should also be taken up, as a duty to mankind along with her other duties. She can practise it in her leisure hours instead of indulging in sleep and vain gossip. It is wrong to think that an interest outside the family makes her neglect her family duties. She should strive for the welfare of her family first, then the nation as well.'
>
> (Institute for Women *Souvenir*)

A further reason is that it provides a justification for the education that upper-middle and upper-class women receive today: 'Our developing India offers many other tremendous challenges ... Here again is a vast area of work for the intelligent and educated woman who should strive hard to wipe out the material inadequacies and spiritual impoverishment, since women are bestowed [*sic*] with natural and instinctive stability' (speech by Tamilnadu

Minister's wife). This extract refers not only to the need for educated women to do social work, and to women's 'natural' endowments, but also provides a typical example of the conflation of material with spiritual poverty. Since women are in certain senses thought to be more spiritual than men, it is natural that their participation in social work will alleviate spiritual as well as material inadequacies. A reason for doing social work is often said to be religion. 'Only when religion and social service go hand in hand can some good be achieved. Society will deteriorate if we forget our religious duties and traditions. Education should be religiously based and social service organisations should have a good religious foundation with members who are well versed in religious matters' (article in Neighbourhood Club *Souvenir* written by well-known social worker). Religion then provides an incentive for doing social work. It also provides an explanation of why the poor are there in the first place. 'One should sympathise with the people who have sinned and share what we have with the have-nots' (President of Institute for Women). This quotation refers to the Hindu doctrine of *karma* – that sin in previous life leads to misfortune in a later life, such as birth in a low caste or poverty. Indeed, key concepts in Hinduism such as *dharma* (religion, correct conduct), *karma* (both fate, and the result of one's deeds in a previous life), and *maya* (illusion, or attachment to worldly things) explain inequality, legitimize it, and, at the same time, deny its importance by emphasizing spiritual over material values.[4] As one cynical Indian has remarked: 'Indian philosophy has learned very well to disperse objective reality by changing its definitions' (quoted in Wiebe 1981: 197).

Therefore the idea that the poor should be satisfied with what they have is often put forward through stories in the publications of the women's organizations. In one such story, a poor man wants to buy his wife a silk sari for Deepavalli. By chance he meets a wealthy friend in the bazaar, and confides in him. The friend insists upon buying the sari, going home with him, and obliging the wife to accept it, although she is reluctant to do so. Soon afterwards, however, the sari catches fire from the flame of a lamp burning at a domestic ritual. The wife is relieved because she feels that such a sari is not suitable for people like them.

Social work should always be performed on behalf of other

people, never on behalf of one's self. To agitate for one's own betterment can be constructed as lacking in selflessness or altruism (cf. Mayer 1981). It is always made very clear in the publications of the women's organizations that it is the upper classes who are the 'social workers' and the lower classes who are the beneficiaries. The Institute for Women, for instance, describes itself as working for the 'uplift of the poor and down-trodden in society' and takes as its motto 'To serve suffering humanity is to serve God.' In one of its reports to the Women's Indian Association, this institution states:

'We dedicate ourselves to work for the welfare and uplift of helpless women and children in economic, social and spiritual aspects. With the help of the benevolent members who are a little over a hundred in number, along with the assistance of the Central Social Welfare Board, the institution carries out its various activities in the respective fields.'

Similarly, the Neighbourhood Club describes its aims as 'social work, especially for the amelioration of the backward people and children'.

These two charters contain certain of the key terms that are constantly used to describe the beneficiaries of the social welfare agencies: *poor, suffering, helpless, backward,* and *ignorant* are the most frequently applied epithets. Such people are said to be in need of various remedies, generally referred to as *uplift, reform, rehabilitation, guidance,* and *enlightenment.* What the poor need, then, is a change in their habits which are seen as contributing towards their misfortunes: 'If those children who are being educated at the school are even marginally better off than their parents in their physical habits and mental attitudes, we would derive some satisfaction' (report on project funded by Wives' Auxiliary and Men's Service Organization).

One of the major changes of attitude that needs to be instilled in the poor is for them to adopt family planning. At the Annual General Meeting of the Wives' Auxiliary, for example, the National President's speech referred to this: 'Although we do social service by helping an orphanage, we should try to think about why children are there at all. The root causes are the need for family planning. But this is difficult. I have tried to persuade my servant to try it, but she replied "It [having children] is the only pleasure we have." I felt so sad that there should be such *ignorance* in a citizen of India.' Obviously, this woman saw no justification whatsoever in her servant's position, and felt she spoke merely from 'ignorance'.

It is clear from reading the publications of the women's organizations and listening to speeches made on public occasions, as well as talking to people, that many members of the upper middle and upper classes see India's rapid population growth as its major problem. Many voluntary social welfare agencies now have family planning programmes. Occasionally, connections between rapid population growth among the working class and the threats which it poses to the upper classes are made explicit: 'Every 1½ seconds, there is a new baby in India. If we don't do something about it, then those of us who are sitting in reasonable comfort will be swept away, so out of pure self-interest, we *should* do something about it ... It is the moral duty of service organisations and enlightened people like you to do something about it' (speech by Governor of Rotary to Annual Dinner of Professional Women's Association). Here too, we come across the epithet that is applied most frequently to the members of voluntary social welfare agencies – that they are *enlightened* in contrast to the ignorance of the beneficiaries.

Another area of ignorance on the part of the poor about which they are seen as needing enlightenment is drink. Prohibition is a favourite theme of the women's association publications (with the exception of the Wives' Auxiliary), and one of the few occasions in the recent past when women's voluntary organizations organized a political protest was when the government of Tamilnadu wanted to repeal the Prohibition Act in 1969. The Institute for Women made its feelings very clear:

'The General Body deplores and strongly objects to the removal of prohibition in Tamilnadu. It feels that such an act will result in the deterioration of moral values and standards of living. This will lead to the destruction of peaceful and happy homes, and women and children are bound to be the victims of this rash act. As such, the members request the Chief Minister of our state, who has a reputation for sympathy and understanding for the families of the poor, to reconsider this issue in the light of the welfare and security of women and children in Tamilnadu, and ensure the continuation of prohibition in the State.'

What is apparent in this extract from the Institute's minutes, and indeed in much of the literature on prohibition which emerges from the women's organizations' publications, is that upper-class women are worrying about lower-class women. It does not appear to bother them that it might be a problem that could affect the upper classes, in spite of the fact that even during the strictest periods of prohibition in the state there has always been provision for licences for drink to be granted 'on medical grounds' against the payment of a hefty licence fee.

Another area about which the poor need enlightenment is thought to be in their life-style. 'Our laboratory and check-up [in the clinic for the poor] is to warn individuals so that they may seek health care by way of exercise, diet and regulation of habits which are more valuable than swallowing medicines' (Professional Women's Association). Obviously, preventive medicine is preferable to curative, but since many of the beneficiaries of this organization earn as little as Rs 25 per month, they are in no position to try and improve their health by choosing a good diet. As has already been pointed out, the solution for the chronic malnutrition in so many children in Tamilnadu is often thought to be 'better education' of the mothers so that they may learn to choose the correct foods for their children (cf. Devadass 1972). However, as Katona-Apte has pointed out, the foods which they give their children and eat themselves are dictated by their income level, not by their ignorance; given a choice, most would in fact choose nutritious foods, but they are too poor to be able to do so (1978: 100). She concludes, 'It should be remembered that the health professionals belong to the middle class or above. They are highly educated and often far removed from the culture of the people they are working with' (Katona-Apte 1978: 108).

I have so far been discussing the poor as an undifferentiated mass. In most of the quotations cited, what is striking is the contrast drawn between the 'enlightened' social workers and the 'ignorant' poor. There is, however, one section of the poor that has something in common with the social workers, and that is poor *women*, who, like *all* women, ultimately need some form of protection. Poor women are thought to be in moral danger, particularly if they are unmarried, deserted wives, or widows. The solutions are not so much to alleviate their poverty but to 'protect' them, either by institutionalization or else by 'rehabilitation through marriage'. Many young girls find themselves institutionalized not only because they are orphans, but more commonly because their families are extremely poor, and particularly because their virtue cannot be guaranteed if they are living without a male protector such as a father. Ultimately, the only solution is to provide such a protector through marriage: 'They [upper-middle-class housewives] must help the uneducated and poor and help people to get married at the right age' (Neighbourhood Club *Souvenir*). As already shown in Chapter 9, large sums of charitable money are ear-marked to help poor girls get married, and even the Tamilnadu government has various schemes to encourage marriage or re-marriage for poor girls and women (see Chapter 7).

Once safely married, however, there are other problems. Allied to the risk of over-fertility already discussed, poor women are thought to make rather bad mothers:

'For the uplift of the weaker sections of the people, education has been rightly regarded as of the highest importance ... It is the welfare of the women and children and of the poor which is of the greatest importance ... Traditions require early marriage and lack of education often makes a married woman among the poorer classes, a rather ill-equipped and unintelligent mother ... A woman from the poorest class is limited in her mental horizon for lack of education ... Her knowledge of child care is poor ... Malnutrition is a problem ... The [government] Nutrition Plan ... aims at reducing infant and child mortality ... and achieving the much larger object of educating the mother about child care.'

(Oza 1974: 79)

This extract, written by a Secretary to the Social Welfare Department of the Tamilnadu government, is not untypical. When poverty enters the door, somehow a woman's 'natural instinct' to care for her child appears to fly out of the window. This view is not confined to social welfare organizations or departments of government. An editorial in the *Hindu* newspaper during the period of field-work stated that 'Both rural and urban working women tend to neglect the health and care of children' (17 December 1974). By 1981, this view did not appear to have changed much:

'These children [from working-class backgrounds] live in a restricted environment with no toys or books or materials which stimulate communication or expression. They live with people who are so obsessed with just making a living that they do not have any time for their children, their needs or interests. Actually, the home environment is one of unpredictable threats, fear, insecurity, suspicion and lack of trust.'
(Article on need for nursery education by Professor of Education in a university in Tamilnadu, *Hindu*, 22 February 1982)

The view held by members of the upper classes about poor women and their capacities as mothers is replete with contradictions. Besides the already stated conflict between women's biologically 'natural' qualities as a mother and the behaviour attributed to poor mothers, there is one contradiction which is even more glaring, and that is the fact that the institutionalization of children propagated by the voluntary social welfare institutions separates them from their mothers. Here then, we have an instance where the rules for the upper and lower classes are different – well-to-do women should not work because their domestic duties, particularly childcare, are paramount. Poor women, on the other hand, are 'helped' by having their children put in orphanages so that they may go and earn a living. It is, however, in the nature of ideology that it contains such inconsistencies and even contradictions.

DISCUSSION

The language and rhetoric of social work are largely a vocabulary of class. The beneficiaries are described as ignorant, weak, needy, and backward – more rarely as *poor*. Their needs are uplift, awakening, training, guidance, enlightenment, rehabilitation, discipline, betterment, amelioration. Voluntary social workers, on the other hand, are described most frequently as enlightened, experienced, dedicated, sincere, munificent, generous, devoted, keen, active, stalwart, pioneering, illustrious, eminent, dynamic, and as shining examples, torch-bearers, path-finders, and crusaders. Thus we find opposed sets of terms to describe the upper and lower classes:

social workers	*beneficiaries*
enlightened	ignorant
generous	deserving
munificent	grateful
forward	backward
active/dynamic	helpless

Such a terminology constitutes a rhetoric which has the function of political rhetoric in all societies; as Bloch (1975) has pointed out, by lifting the level of political discourse on to 'higher planes', arguments become difficult either to penetrate or to oppose.

The speeches and writings of the women's organizations and indeed of the wider society (particularly the mass media) are full of such rhetoric.

'As far as the development of society is concerned, what we require is strength. Food gives strength to the body and knowledge gives strength to the mind. What we want is a spiritual awakening. We have to have religion in practice in a secular way of life ... We want [an] education which would be sound in order to widen our horizons of sympathy, and intensify our social feelings for social service. And in that way, we want to develop our women ... unless we do that we cannot achieve the required targets. We are to shape the future generations. Instead of thinking in terms of privileges and rights, it is better we think of duties and obligations to society ... What we want is a real combination of heart and head. If we only join hand and heart, we would have emotions and feelings, and with mere hands and head, one may be an intellectual giant. We want a co-ordinated combination of hand, heart and head, and [it is] that [which] we must develop. It is not the standard of living, but the standard of life in us.'

(Speech by Governor's wife to
Professional Women's Association)

I have quoted this extract in some detail because it contains so many examples of the ideological mechanisms which are used in the rhetoric of social welfare; there are references to religion, to emotion and to the need for greater spiritual welfare. It is a perfect example of what Bloch has called 'formalised language', in which

the specific is merged into the eternal, and where 'disagreement is
ruled out since one cannot disagree with the right order' (Bloch
1975: 16). It is, as he says, a system of communication largely
lacking in creativity, and ruling out the possibility of contradiction.

The importance of ideology

Ideology is probably the most important aspect of the women's
organizations. It reaches a far larger number of people than those
directly involved, either as members or beneficiaries, through its
dissemination by the mass media which the organizations are, of
course, happy to utilize to the maximum. It is important because
in a very subtle way, it masks the nature of relations between the
classes, as well as between the sexes. Ultimately, the survival of any
inegalitarian system depends upon a disjunction between economic and political reality, and the surface appearance that such a
society presents to its members. Ideology is the crucial element
which disguises reality. The rhetoric of social welfare institutions
gives an impression both of concern for the poor and also of
working to ameliorate their conditions.

None the less, it is important to understand that there is a
difference between the ideology of the organizations which is the
subject of this chapter, and the motivations of individual members.
The vast majority of members of the social welfare organizations
do not consciously do social work merely as a panacea for society's
ills. They are fully aware that social work is often done out of
mixed motives:

> 'Much of social work is vanity. And it is also politics. I am
> very bitter about social work and women's organisations. I
> try to keep aloof now and do my work separately, otherwise
> one gets bogged down. Of course they are after publicity.
> Yes, their husbands like it too "My wife does such and such."
> I also feel that the social workers don't study what the real
> needs of the people are.'
> (Ex-committee member of Institute for Women)

> 'Yes, I am a member of the organisation. But I don't really
> like to be involved in such organisations because people are
> only concerned with the name. If her photo comes in the

paper, she wants to see her name there too. Such people have a craving for power.'

'My husband does not belong to the men's service organisation any more. Their motto is supposed to be "service before self", but in fact it is the other way round. He says that people only join for the contacts they can make and the prestige that it brings.'

(Secretary of a women's organization)

The quotations reveal a certain amount of cynicism and yet, at the same time, such accusations are generally made about *other* social workers and *other* voluntary organizations. Self-criticism, whether on an individual or group level, is much more rarely practised. Some voluntary social workers did tell me that at one time they had been disparaging about the usefulness of social work, but had changed their minds: 'Previously I was very much opposed to social service . . . Some people had convinced me that it was a waste of time – a drop in the ocean – a hopeless task' (secretary of Institute for Women); 'When I became Chairman of the State Board, I criticised institutions freely for not running properly. But with time, I came to think that any small accomplishment is a good thing' (ex-Chairman of SSWB).

The members of the women's organizations do not for the most part have any alternative perspective or world view, and their class position almost inevitably precludes this. For them, the poor will always be there, and any suggestion that things might change is viewed as 'political' or even 'communistic' (as in the conversation below). Radical change is seen as inevitably threatening their own position and all the values which they hold dear, and which are often articulated in terms of just rewards for their endeavours. If the old order is swept away, there will be chaos and violence, and religion and family life will be threatened. Few are able to or dare to contemplate what any radical re-structuring of the social system might entail – and their education, their reading of newspapers and magazines, and their participation in women's organizations does little to present them with a critical world view. They realize that all is not well with their society, but many of them feel (possibly with justification) unable to do anything about it, since the problems are just too huge and overwhelming. So they either do nothing, or content themselves with helping 'in some small way', 'within the limits of our capacities'. If they are asked for solutions, they generally answer in terms of the need for family planning and a general change in attitudes on the part of the poor, and more or better 'service' on the part of the better off.

Thus most of the members of the women's organizations are convinced by their ideology. But what about the beneficiaries? Inevitably, it is much more difficult to get any clear indication of what they feel about their situation as recipients of charity, or their relations with the members of the organizations. On the rare occasions when they are allowed to speak for themselves, they say very much what their listeners want to hear:

> 'I am grateful to X, Y and Z for their self-sacrifice in making me a useful teacher ... When I joined this Training School, I was very ignorant about the world. This school has wiped out the dark cloud of ignorance ... I have learned all the basic principles of life only in this school ... This training school prepares ignorant people [and turns them into] best teachers ... I thank the institution for the opportunity offered me.'
>
> (Written by a woman trained in an institution run by a WIA branch)

Sometimes, however, a different picture emerges, as the following excerpt from a taped conversation among a group of suburban housewives, suggests:

MRS R: I want to do something for the hill tribes.

MRS S: But there are so many people around here in the slums. Why shouldn't we tackle them first?

MRS R: They are all communist-minded. If you go and talk to them they will say 'You are living in bungalows [i.e. fine houses] – what have you got to do with us? You come and ask us questions, but nothing improves.'

MRS K: Yes, these people are impossible. If you give them a Slum Clearance Flat, the next day they will move out and sub-let it.

MRS R: I feel that we should help those who are *innocent* like the tribal hill people.

Many social workers whom I knew, both professional and voluntary, spoke of the problems of working with slum people; by this they often meant precisely what Mrs R said – that the slum people, many of whom are now politicized (cf. Wiebe 1981) would often tell them to go away and mind their own business, or else would ask them how they came to be handing out advice when they could know nothing of the sort of problems faced in the slums. When villagers, or slum people, do not accept the suggestions or programmes offered by voluntary agencies, there is resentment and criticism. 'This programme, although very useful, was not eliciting a *proper* response from the villagers' (my italics; report on a project funded by the Wives' Auxiliary and the Men's Service Organization).

Many of the beneficiaries of the social welfare organizations have themselves internalized the ideology the organizations propagate. Many do appear to regard themselves as lucky to receive some form of charity, and feel, quite rightly, that if they did not, their situation would be even worse than it already is. Unless they have been given (perhaps through contact with one of the populist political parties) some alternative view of society, they are unlikely to feel critical either of the voluntary organizations or of their members. In any case, those who feel such criticism may be unwilling to voice it, for fear of losing the benefits they obtain. In a society where all resources for the poor are in extremely short supply, one more *balwadi*, or free clinic, *is* perceived as being a positive help.[5]

DISCUSSION

Is this, then, a dominant ideology held by the upper classes and imposed on the lower classes, or does it in fact only convince the former, while the latter have their own world view? Does it, as Althusser (1972) suggests, transform its object, which is people's consciousness?

Most of the proceedings of the organizations are conducted in English, and even when they are in Tamil, few members of the lower classes are present to witness them. Souvenirs appear in both English and Tamil, but are unlikely to be read in either language by any but association members and their peers – partly because they are not bought by the members of the lower classes, who in any case would be unlikely to be able to read them, given the extremely high rates of illiteracy.

Abercrombie and Turner have argued that 'in most societies the apparatus of transmission of the dominant ideology is not very efficient, and in any event, is typically directed at the dominant rather than the subordinate class' (1978: 149). They thus criticize Gramsci's notion of hegemony (1971), and the work of such writers as Miliband (1969), who has suggested that in western society there is a process of massive indoctrination. On the contrary, they posit the existence of a dualistic character of working-class culture which has a fluctuating relationship between 'dominant' and 'subordinate' conceptions, and conclude that 'subordinate classes in contemporary capitalism do not *straightforwardly* adopt the dominant ideology' (Abercrombie and Turner 1978: 158).

Some work by anthropologists of India would also suggest a similar conclusion, even if their terminology might be different. Mencher (1974), for example, has argued that the caste system looks very different from the perspective of those at the bottom of it. They tend to see it much less in terms of pollution and purity than in terms of distribution of economic resources and power. Varadachar's study (1979: 135) of a slum in Madras notes that most outsiders tend to view slum dwellers as feckless, but the people characterize themselves in quite a different way. Similarly, the conversation quoted earlier in this chapter (see p. 210) suggests that not all recipients of charity are as grateful as their would-be benefactors might like. None the less, it may be in the immediate interests of the lower classes to appear to acquiesce and to act as if they had internalized the dominant ideology, whether this comes from the state or the caste system.

In any case, as has already been shown in the previous chapter, many of the beneficiaries of social welfare programmes are not members of the working class, nor are they of low-caste status – social welfare is often a means of helping fellow caste members, and of enabling members of the lower middle class to maintain quasi-respectability, or even possibly to achieve social mobility.

What of gender ideology? It is striking that much of the rhetoric of the women's organizations discussed here differs very little from the rhetoric of half a century or more ago. As was seen in Chapter 6, use was made then, just as it is today, of a very selective interpretation of Indian history, religion, and mythology, of assertions about women's special nature and therefore special needs, and of the suffragette movement in the west (which was attacked then just as today's women's movement is now). The arguments in the pre-independence era were used to justify women's right to vote and to education, and to attack such 'social evils' as child marriage, the prohibition on widow re-marriage, and the institution of devadasis. Today, much of what the early campaigners fought for is enshrined in legislation, although it is perhaps more frequently honoured in the breach than the observance. Why, it may be asked, do the women's organizations continue to propagate this kind of ideology? Is it merely a hollow shell?

On some levels, it may be argued that the organizations are fighting a rear-guard action against competing ideologies and roles for women. New and more radical women's organizations are arising in India which focus on issues like rape, dowry deaths, and self-help for poor working women, although such organizations as yet only touch a tiny minority of women, and more so in the northern cities than in Madras. Another competing model for upper middle-class women is of course that of the professional career woman. Although relatively few such women enter the job market, their numbers are growing; whereas few young women seem to be engaging in voluntary social work. In part, of course, this is because the demands of their reproductive role are greatest at this time, but it seems clear that for some of them voluntary social work is not as attractive as a professional career.

Do then such women really believe all that is said in the souvenirs and speeches of their associations? By and large, they certainly speak in private as if they did, although paradoxically, their behaviour, or at least that of some of them, tends to contradict it. Maria Mies, in a study of educated upper-class Indian women, observed that such women are in fact often able to deviate from the ideal norms precisely because they never challenge them (1975: 58; 1979). This could perhaps be said of a small number of my informants, chiefly those belonging to the Professional Women's Association, but they constitute only a minority. The vast majority of middle-class Indian women do place their husbands and children at the centre of their lives, although this is not to say of course that frequently such women are not the holders of real power within their homes, even while they accord public deference to their husbands.

Such discrepancies could of course be adduced almost any-where. There are bound to be gaps and contradictions between ideal and reality, between ideology and behaviour. But the fact remains that, by and large, norms regarding gender are not being challenged in practice, much less in theory, by members of these organizations.

If the women of the upper classes are convinced by their own rhetoric, what of lower-class women? In India, as has been stated, the censuses reveal a decreasing female participation in the work force up to the 1971 census, and only a very tiny rise in the 1981 census. Much of the ideology propagated by the women's organizations helps to justify this situation by making it explicit that women ought not to work outside the home, unless in cases of dire economic necessity. Even then, it is thought preferable for married women to have jobs that can be done either at home or nearby, and for unmarried women to get husbands, and for husbands to be helped to get work. It would seem that the creation of an ideology of domesticity, like that of social welfare, is historically specific, and that the two are inter-linked, for it is philanthropy which is often the vehicle for the transmission of an ideal of domesticity as will be shown in Chapter 11.

Althusser (1972) has accorded primacy to the educational institutions as ideological state apparatuses under capitalism. There is little doubt that these are also important in a peripheral capitalist state such as India, but they obviously work much less efficiently when education is not universal. Similarly, although the mass media, such as the radio, newspapers, magazines, and cinema (television is still confined very much to the affluent urban upper classes), are becoming increasingly important, they are not as pervasive nor, perhaps, as sophisticated in their ideological messages as those in the west. For this reason then, other 'apparatuses', such as voluntary social welfare institutions, also serve an important role in disseminating ideology.

Notes

1 The *Mahabharata* is one of the two major Hindu epics, the other being the *Ramayana*; the former is basically an account of the war between the Pandavas and Kauravas. Many incidental stories also occur, like the one from which the extract in the text is quoted.

2 This view is also shared by politicians. The Chief Minister of Tamilnadu, while opening a new women's college (named, incidentally, after a man) said that: 'The opening of more women's colleges should

be welcomed, firstly because educated women would be able to organise their homes better, and secondly, these institutions [for women] were free from [student] strikes' (*Hindu*, 17 October 1974).

3   'That we in India need a women's movement of some kind is true beyond doubt. But what kind of a movement? ... or to put the question another way, what makes a woman liberated? One who follows the stereotype of ragged jeans, hairy underarms, legs and upper lip, working for the extermination of man? ... More important, can one in a dismally backward country like ours, afford to follow women's liberation in isolation?'

(*Sunday Express*, 1 November 1981)

4   A fairly typical example is the following extract from a booklet produced by the Chinmaya Mission: 'The source of joy is not in the external world of objects, but is deep within us ... The desire for objects creates disturbances which shatter our real nature of *Shanti* – peace'; 'To herald in a true *Ramarajyam* [golden age] we have to make every human being live the enduring spiritual values of renunciation and desirelessness' (n.d.: 8, 10–11).

5   None the less, a study in Bombay, which asked low (under Rs 500 per month) and middle (Rs 500–1,000 per month) income families about what kind of services they preferred, revealed that: 'It is seen that a very large percentage of the respondents is in favour of the *official* agencies for conducting these services ... the percentage of respondents who mention the [voluntary] welfare agencies is not high' (Khandekar 1974: 103). In part this may be a reflection of preferences, in part of the relatively small number of beneficiaries that the voluntary agencies are able to serve.

11
Conclusion

This book has focused on the relationship between gender and class. It has not been meant simply as another attempt to 'integrate' women into the class structure of a particular society, by stretching and pulling concepts such as mode of production. Rather, it has argued that in order to understand properly what is meant by class, we must pay as much attention to reproduction, including the sphere of the family,[1] as we do to production. This involves abandoning a narrowly economistic definition of class and considering class in terms of culture, including ideology, as well as economy.

In Part Two of this book, I tried through an examination of reproduction and production to show how there is a clear interrelationship between these areas. Most women in India are not 'producers', largely because they have been assigned specific reproductive tasks which form an integral part of the total social system.

Part Three of the book has considered voluntary organizations, and looked particularly at their social welfare activities. This is a field that highlights the relations between the dominant and subordinate classes, as well as between the former and the state. It also produces rich data on ideology, for this indeed would appear to be one of the main aspects of social welfare – that it provides a form of control, which is often hidden behind a facade of philanthropy; where this is purely voluntary in nature it is all the more effective (Stedman-Jones 1971). However, it would be misleading to consider voluntary social welfare as nothing more than ideological in nature; it has important economic implications too, in providing a cheap form of social welfare which might otherwise have to be funded by the state from its own resources.

At the same time social welfare provides women with a 'sphere of their own', an arena in which they can form organizations, and play a significant role in an area of life which is seen to be both public and political. Just as it has been argued by some that social welfare in advanced countries is a product not only of the desire of the state and the ruling class to control the poor, but also of the struggles of the poor themselves, similarly women's involvement in the sphere of philanthropy can be viewed as an achievement, as the outcome of their strivings to 'do something', as they often put it.

It seems likely that much of the analysis of India in this book might well be true of other capitalist societies, in different times and places, depending upon their specific stage of historical development. In the following section, I look briefly at the development of social welfare in England during the nineteenth and early twentieth centuries, and suggest that there are close parallels between India now and England then. In other words, there are trends in social welfare, and particularly in the association between women and welfare, which both countries have in common. This suggests that even while there are important cultural differences, the development of social welfare is a historically specific process in the growth of capitalism.

Women and charity in
nineteenth-century England

England in the nineteenth century resembled in many ways the India of the last several decades. There was a growing population, particularly in the cities, some of which grew by as much as 30–40 per cent per decade.[2]

The reasons for this were not dissimilar from those in India at a more recent period. The late eighteenth century in England may be viewed as a period of primitive accumulation during which the producer was divorced from the means of production. In many cases this meant the expropriation of the land of peasants during the period of the enclosures, and the creation of a large pool of landless labour. This new class of 'free labour' migrated to the cities in search of work. Ginsburg draws attention to the role of the state in this process, with laws to protect private property and 'terrorise the nascent proletariat . . . such as forms of forced labour . . . as well as flogging, imprisonment, the stocks etc.' (1979: 30).

Young and Ashton point out that conditions had never changed as much, before or since, as in the period 1800 to 1850 (1956: 8–15). The new towns were filthy, with poor housing for the working classes, and very little schooling. Job conditions for men, women, and children were deplorable in the main, with low wages and long hours. Ten per cent of the population lived in acute poverty, although this is less than the current estimates for Indian society, which range between 40 per cent and 70 per cent (cf. Chapter 1).

Mid-nineteenth-century England saw the rise of the new middle classes, whose consumption of food, furniture, china, and other luxuries increased rapidly, as did their numbers of servants (Davidoff 1973; Hall 1979). Entry to the top echelons was carefully guarded (cf. Davidoff's (1973) study of the etiquette of the upper classes), although the new middle classes rapidly developed their own culture, just as they have done in India, and much of this cultural production was the work of women.

An important aspect of the culture of the middle classes was based on an ideology of domesticity for women, facilitated by the separation of the home from the work-place, and the increasing confinement of women of this class level to the former area. An idealized view of home grew up, described in terms like 'a place apart, a walled garden, in which certain virtues too easily crushed by modern life could be preserved' (Houghton 1957: 343), or 'a temple of purity, a haven of peace in a hostile and impure world' (Basch 1974: 7).

This is not dissimilar from the view of the Indian urban upper-middle classes. Here however, culturally specific notions of purity and impurity, which have a long history in Indian thought, have come to be associated in certain respects with the domestic sphere, for it is only there that rules of food preparation and commensality can be strictly observed nowadays. In India too, the confinement of women to an interior private space has long been a dominant norm in such institutions as purdah. The more recent 'domestication' of women draws upon these traditional ideas, but invests them with new meaning.

The person in charge of the domestic sphere in both Victorian England and in modern India is the women – the 'angel in the house' as she was sometimes described in the nineteenth century. Davidoff suggests that domesticated women, isolated in their homes, acted as particularly effective 'boundary markers'. The fact that they did not work for pay clearly demonstrated their class position; they provided a 'haven of stability, of exact social classification in the threatening anonymity of the surrounding economic and political upheaval' (Davidoff 1973: 5). In India women have, of course, long served as caste boundary markers and, increasingly, as this study has shown, are now acting as class boundary markers too.

Writers on the Victorian period have suggested that women in the home performed two important kinds of work. One was to supervise the ever-growing army of servants, particularly in the fight against dirt, which Davidoff suggests separates in an important way the middle classes from those below them, i.e. the 'Great Unwashed' – the working classes, who in many instances were represented as untamed nature, while culture was epitomized by the life-style of the middle classes. This is not dissimilar to the situation in modern urban India, where western notions of dirt and hygiene have been added to already existing ideas about purity and pollution. Here too, the lower classes are frequently represented by the middle and upper classes as 'dirty' in their habits and their environment, and hence partly at least responsible for their own plight.

The second kind of work for which nineteenth-century middle-class women were largely responsible was religious observance. A number of writers have remarked on the importance of evangelical protestantism among the middle classes in nineteenth-century England (e.g. Hall 1979). It was a version of Christianity which has been described as 'narrow and bigoted ... and more concerned with respectable behaviour than theological niceties' (Young and Ashton 1956: 16).

Indian women too, as I showed in Chapter 4, have increasingly taken on much of the tasks associated with religious observance, particularly in the home, although they are also more assiduous in attending places of worship, such as temples, than are men.

In both instances, then, already existing norms of female behaviour and an indentification with the domestic sphere have intensified under capitalism. The home has become an increasingly private arena, separate from the world of production.

Some authors writing on the Victorian period have pointed out that there was a wide gap between theory and practice, with the ideal that every woman should be dependent upon a man and should stay at home often conflicting with the reality of large numbers of unsupported women. Even in the middle classes, many had no alternative but to become governesses (Basch 1974: 14; Harrison 1966). The ideal was also of course contradicted by the fact that many lower-class women worked for pay. The 1851 census in Britain showed that three-quarters of unmarried women of all classes were in employment, and by 1865, one-third of all women over the age of twenty-one were workers (Basch 1974: 105). Thus even as the capitalist class was propagating domesticity for women, it was employing them in its factories and its homes.

In India there are few women classified as workers in the censuses, although there are probably far more engaged in productive labour than the figures would suggest, since rural women who work in the family's fields, or urban women in the informal sector, are often not classified as productive. There are also, of course, enormous numbers of female servants and women home-workers, many of whom work part-time and of whom the census figures do not take account.

In Victorian England, as Hall (1979) points out, the ideal that women should be dependent upon men was a cardinal tenet of middle-class ideology, and no woman who worked for pay could be called a 'lady'. A contemporary source states that 'My opinion is that if a woman is obliged to work, at once, although she may be Christian and well bred, she loses that peculiar position which the word *lady* conventionally designates' (quoted by Davidoff 1973: 101).

In India too, the strictures against women working are severe. Girls are not trained vocationally, and appear to find greater difficulty than males in obtaining employment in many spheres. However, the sphere of unpaid voluntary social work is open to women of the upper classes, and indeed, may be an important way of demonstrating the family's status and so encouraged.

Victorian women became increasingly involved in charity during the nineteenth century, often in the face of considerable opposition from men.[3] Prochaska, for instance, states that conservative churchmen in nineteenth-century England claimed that such women were neglecting their families. However, as women began to show their fund-raising capacities, they were allowed to become members of charitable societies, although the managing committees long remained almost exclusively male (Prochaska 1980: 25).

What did *not* happen in Victorian England, however, was a growth in separate organizations for women as happened later in India; in this respect Indian women may have profited from the long-standing norms of segregation of the sexes. Furthermore, whereas Indian women became central in the field of charitable work in India, women in Britain for a long time existed on its fringes, usually working as 'home-visitors' on an individual unorganized basis (Summers 1979) or purely as fund-raisers. Davidoff notes that this factor probably reinforced the limitations of their social experience (1973: 75).

Later in the nineteenth century, however, the view that women should 'extend their sphere', thereby 'uplifting and purifying' the wider society, began to be widespread. This was perhaps a rationalization of the fact that many men were now too preoccupied with making money to spend a great deal of time on philanthropy, and were content to leave this sphere increasingly to their wives.

Whatever the merits of the ideological arguments, women did play an increasingly important part in charitable activities in England in the latter part of the nineteenth century – Prochaska (1980) states that almost every woman who did not receive charity was likely to dispense it. A survey of 1893 estimated that about half a million women worked in philanthropy continuously and semi-professionally, out of a population of 11.5 million women aged over ten in 1891; apart from domestic service, no other female occupation came near to this (Prochaska 1980: 225).

There were a number of reasons for the attractiveness of charitable work for women. A major one was the enormous increase in leisure for women at this class level, thanks to the number of servants. For such women, stifled in the ideology of Victorian femininity and domesticity, to engage themselves in philanthropic works was exciting. Although fancy fetes and bazaars, a major means of fund-raising, were often the target of satirical references, 'There were so few opportunities for many middle-class girls and women to take part in any sort of organised public event that these functions were highly prized, despite masculine ridicule' (Davidoff

1973: 54). 'Charitable work, free from chaperones and prying relatives, represented deliverance from the stitch–church–stitch routine of female experience. It was adventure' (Prochaska 1980: 11). Simey too notes that women were supporters of charitable work because it was carried out in groups, and this gave them an opportunity to belong to something other than their families (1951: 125).

The work women did might be sneered at by many men, but it often required a good deal of organization and initiative. Bazaars for example, were usually large events, and rarely made less than £1,000 each time (Prochaska 1980: 64).

The above arguments for women engaging in charitable activity remind us that whether in nineteenth-century England or in modern India, the skills and energies which women bring to bear on such work, limited as its effects may be, should not be underrated. In Victorian England, women first learned organizing skills, which they were later to use in suffrage campaigns, through philanthropy. In India, women learned such skills in the process of the freedom struggle and the campaign for suffrage, and then were able to use them in social welfare to create a public 'sphere of their own'.

For women, then, the field of social welfare is a contradictory one. On the one hand, it can and does mean an enlargement of their arena. In nineteenth-century England, some women who were active in philanthropy were outstandingly successful public figures: Louisa Twining, who campaigned for women to become workhouse visitors; Octavia Hill, who was one of the founders of the large and influential Charity Organisation Society (cf. Mowat 1961); and Josephine Butler, who led a campaign against the treatment of prostitutes.[4] In India too, some women have been able to use 'social work' as a stepping stone to a political career, and few of India's women politicians have failed to do their stint as social workers in their early days (cf. Wolkowitz 1983: 201, 284, 314–15, 389).

In these circumstances, it is not surprising that such women should resist the incursions of the state into the field of social welfare. In late nineteenth-century England, although such resentment was voiced in terms of a kind of *laissez-faire* version of social welfare, many women to whom charitable works were an important part of their lives must have been afraid that their role would decrease or even disappear if the state took over completely. They need not have worried. Most of the measures adopted by the British state in the early part of the twentieth century were predicated upon the assumption that there would continue to be an army of unpaid female charitable workers (Summers 1979: 57). Indian women likewise have resisted to some extent the entry of the state into social welfare, although they have of course been co-operating with it since the inception of the CSWB. Voluntary social workers in India have, it is plain, felt threatened by the growth in the number of professional social workers and, in Tamilnadu, were also initially threatened by the election of anti-Brahmin governments. However, they too seem to be achieving a *modus vivendi* with the state, which is increasingly realizing, as the British state did earlier, that volunteers and voluntary social welfare work are indispensable.

One of the major arguments of this book has been about the relationship between women and class, and particularly how charity defines and separates classes. At the same time, philanthropic activities serve as a means of social mobility, particularly for the new industrial bourgeoisie. Plainly this was also the case in Victorian England (Harrison 1966: 364). Most charities were run as private committees, access to which was in the hands of social leaders. In this way, charity work could bring opportunity for mixing with higher social strata, as many *nouveau riche* families realized (Davidoff 1973: 54). Harrison also comments on the 'numerous charity balls, philanthropic dinners and conversaziones, pretentious central offices, the pages of print devoted to lists of subscribers, the elegant membership cards' (1966: 363). Not everyone of course was impressed by this. A nineteenth-century columnist in a Liverpool paper is quoted as writing: 'The fashionable amusement of the present age is philanthropy ... No small number of these benevolent persons are philanthropic because it is the fashion to be so; because it brings them into contact with this Bishop or that Earl' (in Simey 1951: 66). (The same cynical columnist on another occasion warned his readers that unless they could buy themselves off with a large subscription, they might actually have to do some work.) There seems little doubt that the long lists of donors, which took up the bulk of the annual report, were a sign of status seeking (Prochaska 1980: 40).

However, charitable activity does not only define and separate classes (and assist some in social mobility), it also creates vertical links between the classes (cf. Stedman-Jones 1971: Chapter 5). This is particularly true of the kind of activities in which women engage, whether in Victorian England or modern India. Summers's study of women as 'home visitors' points out that 'Relations within the household [i.e. master/mistress and servants] offered a model for relations between rich and poor outside it. Much of the content of home visiting in the 19th century can be seen as the attempt to transpose the values and relations of domestic service to a wider class of the poor' (Summers 1979: 38).

Indeed, not a small part of the net result of this 'visiting' was the creation of a large pool of reliable domestic servants. Visiting societies were especially useful in the big cities which were short of medical facilities, especially for the poor, and Prochaska concludes that 'They bolstered that network of relations between the classes which, for better or for worse, gave England a semblance of social order in the early years of the 19th century and after' (Prochaska 1980: 102).

It can be similarly argued in India that one of the main forms of vertical ties between classes, apart from the mistress–servant relationship, is that between 'social workers' and recipients of charity. One important effect of this is to soften relations between the classes, and, of course, many upper and middle-class women do indeed feel pity for their 'unfortunate sisters'. In nineteenth-century England such feelings were, however, frequently expressed in an attempt to impose their own values, particularly domestication for women, on to the working classes. This is precisely what has been happening in the field of social welfare in India since independence. Here we have to consider the relationship between women and the labour market for it is scarcely surprising to find women being encouraged to 'stay at home' when the market for their labour is shrinking.

Another major theme of this book has been the ideological importance of philanthropy. Part of its ideological effectiveness lies in its explanation for poverty. This does not differ greatly between Victorian England and modern India – it is seen to lie not so much in social conditions, but rather in individual failure. It was for this reason that the skills of women, religious and domestic, were thought to be ideally suited to the moral reformation of character said to be necessary prerequisites for improvement in the lot of the poor (Owen 1964: 211; Prochaska 1980: 7). Young and Ashton comment of Victorian England:

> 'The common belief then was that many of the poor were afflicted because of their own perversity. Even widows and orphans, the handicapped, or sufferers from bad health who were in poverty were not in every case regarded as deserving; for were there not many in like pass who did not become parasites on the community; or who through their own strength of character and resourcefulness had overcome the dangers of poverty and dependence?'
>
> (Young and Ashton 1956: 67)

It has been suggested by some writers that a motive for Victorian charity was guilt (Simey 1951: 57), or that charity was often the bridge between the business and commercial dealings of the middle classes and their Christian consciences, since what mattered was not how wealth was *acquired* but how it was *spent* (Young and Ashton 1956: 30). However, others have disagreed. Beatrice Webb claimed that many involved in charity had no 'consciousness of collective sin', but rather thought that modern capitalism was the best of all possible ways of organizing industries and services (Webb 1926: 177–78). After all, the opportunity to be charitable in the first place depended on social inequality (Prochaska 1980: 125); the middle classes tended to quote only those parts of the work of philosophers and economists which justified their own increasing prosperity (Young and Ashton 1956). In India too, there is rarely any questioning of the status quo by the middle and upper classes, as I showed in Chapter 10. There is however, a certain amount of fear of the poor, and parallels can be found in Victorian England. Charity was sometimes seen as the ransom which the wealthy paid for their security, and charities often got more financial contributions after disturbances such as a riot (Harrison 1966; Stedman-Jones 1971; Thompson 1976). However, while the middle classes were willing to give of themselves, and some of their money, they were not willing to countenance any major change in the social conditions which made charity necessary in the first place (Young and Ashton 1956: 30). Indeed, philanthropy helped to validate existing social institutions by highlighting the generosity of the rich and the inadequacies of the poor (Harrison 1965). As Owen points out, 'The priorities of the philanthropists were not to achieve social reform but to preach uncomplaining submission as an injunction of Divine law' (Owen 1964: 95). In India, too, religion is often used much in the same way as in Victorian England, to encourage the poor to hope for better conditions in their next life, rather than trying to change them in this one. The ideology of charity, then, explains the status quo; at the same time it also perpetuates certain ideas about women. Chastity was a dominant value in Victorian England, just as it is in India. The middle classes in both countries shared a common set of ideas regarding women – that they should be sexually pure, dependent upon a man, and primarily in the home, although they might engage in philanthropic work as an extension of their domestic sphere. Although it is true that female chastity has an extremely long history as an important ideology in India (cf. Jacobson 1978), and particularly in Tamilnadu (cf. Hart 1973; Wadley 1980), it has acquired new meanings when linked with the process of domestication of women already discussed. It has even been suggested that the dominant norms regarding Indian women owe less to the *Manusmirti* than to Victorian ideals (Mies 1975), although such norms are justified by Hinduism as well. Given the close historical connections between England and India, it is perhaps not surprising that aspects of the ideology of one should have been transplanted to the other.

Social welfare, the state, and the development of capitalism

At one point in carrying out research for this book, I assumed, somewhat naively, that there was a linear progression in the development of social welfare – as Meillassoux puts it 'The cost of maintaining and reproducing this labour power had to be resolved by setting up equalisation mechanisms more and more sophisticated as the proletariat became more fully integrated into capitalist relations of production. Charity gave way to public assistance and finally – while the workers tried different forms of mutual aid – to social security' (1981: 108). In fact the situation is not nearly so simple, as an examination of various situations of different historical stages of development in India and Britain shows clearly.

Walton's study of women in social work in Britain shows how

the profession grew between the war years, but 'At the same time as more paid workers were being appointed . . . there were still far more voluntary workers to be found in our large cities' (1975: 146). He concludes that even in the period following the Second World War,

'It is arguable that one of the greatest inhibiting factors in the development of professional social work in this country is the exaggerated official patronage at central and local government levels given to the virtue of voluntary effort. This has led to inadequately staffed statutory social services. The poverty of our statutory social welfare provisions meant that a key part would be played by voluntary organisations and voluntary workers.'

(Walton 1975: 181)

Although the Beveridge Report (1942) provided the foundation stone for the welfare state, which came into existence in Britain after the Second World War, by setting up a state scheme of social insurance, Lord Beveridge himself also strongly supported the continuation of voluntarism in his later report *Voluntary Action*. Here he stated that 'The reasons for it have not been diminished and will not be destroyed by the growing activities of the state' (Beveridge 1948: 306) and concluded that 'The State should encourage Voluntary Action of all kinds for social advance' (Beveridge 1948: 318). This philosophy was to be continually echoed in subsequent official reports.

The 1968 Seebohm Report on the social services recommended greater use of volunteers, not to replace professionals or to perform menial tasks that professionals do not want to do, but to give 'to infirm or inadequate people, in their own homes, practical help of a kind which they can clearly be seen to need'. The Aves Report of 1969 on the voluntary worker in the social services recommended that even more use be made of volunteers.

Some statutory services in Britain today are provided by voluntary organizations, like the NSPCC (National Society for the Prevention of Cruelty to Children), and other organizations also receive government funding to carry out specific welfare tasks, like the Women's Royal Voluntary Services, which provides 'meals on wheels' to housebound elderly people.

In more recent years, government policies in Britain have meant severe cuts in resources available for the social services, and an increasing rhetoric regarding the virtues of 'community care'. As has already been pointed out, this generally means more unpaid work for women (see e.g. Weir 1974; EOC 1982a,b).

In the late 1970s, the Social Science Research Council commissioned a study of research on the voluntary social welfare sector, which would explore 'alternative patterns' of social welfare. A workshop held in 1980 concluded that there is a need for a more integral role for the voluntary services for a whole variety of reasons, 'reinforced by the election . . . of a government committed to reducing the role of the State' (Hadley and Hatch 1980).

Thus, the relationship between charity and the voluntary sector on the one hand, and the state and statutory services run by professional social workers on the other, fluctuates. Until relatively recently in the west, most historical accounts implied that the state had intervened increasingly since the beginning of this century, and that voluntarism and private philanthropy had become much less important (e.g. Woodroofe 1962). But while the nature of charity and its exact relationship to the state may have changed over time, it still remains extremely significant. As one investigates the social services in Britain, one finds that voluntary helpers play a crucial role in filling gaps, complementing statutory provision, and even providing statutory services themselves (cf. also Newton 1976: 71–3; Wolfenden 1978). It would seem likely that even greater use is to be made of voluntarism in the near future than at any time since the last century.

The position in the USA, another advanced capitalist society, shares certain features with Britain in this respect. During the late 1960s, at a time when the number of welfare recipients reached an all-time high of almost 2.5 million people, and money spent on welfare annually was around 15 billion dollars (Piven and Cloward 1972), the monetary worth of volunteer social work in the country was estimated by one study as worth 14.2 billion dollars annually (Gold 1971).

In 1971, the Nixon administration prepared a media campaign to persuade citizens to offer their services, so that the government could cut social welfare spending in order to cover its increased defence expenditure (Gold 1971). Gold argues that volunteers have been responsible for considerable savings in the private and public sectors. Most of these are of course women, and she attributes to them much the same motivations as I have done for Indian women – seeking status outside the home and forming groups with women from a similar background (Gold 1971: 539). None the less, although such women and their families do derive benefits from their volunteerism, Gold sees them as exploited – in reality underpaid employed workers. Similarly, Gittel and Shtob find it ironic that the US Administration was trying to institutionalize voluntary service organizations by creating a cabinet level committee on volunteerism at the same time as the feminist movement in North America was first calling into question the values of volunteerism for women (Gittel and Shtob 1980: 77).[5]

If then we compare the situation in India with that in Britain and the USA, there are many similarities, although they are more striking for England of the nineteenth century than for present-day Britain. Even so, the processes that can be discerned in the development of welfare under capitalism are of a great unevenness, with many contradictions present. The state is under conflicting pressures for the allocation of its resources. There are periods when relatively large amounts are devoted to welfare, and these tend also to be periods when greater emphasis is placed on professional agencies and workers. However, even during such periods, voluntary workers and agencies continue to play a vital role, as can be shown from an examination of Britain or the USA in the 1960s and 1970s. By injecting relatively small funds into the voluntary sector, the state can revitalize it at times when it desires to cut government spending in this field, as is happening in Britain and the USA today. In any case, the ideological aspects of voluntary social welfare work make it too useful for it to be done away with, even if state provision is plentiful.

We may return, then, to the question posed at the beginning of this chapter, and ask whether social welfare is an intrinsic part of a capitalist society. It certainly seems to be the case for the examples so far examined. What of peripheral capitalist states at a lower stage of development than India?

Other peripheral capitalist states and social welfare

Although information is not plentiful in this area, a number of recent studies suggest that there is likely to be a development of a voluntary social welfare sector, probably with links with government, in post-colonial capitalist states. A study by Audrey Wipper (1975) of the Kenyan women's organization *Maendeleo ya Wanawake* shows that in spite of its progressive beginnings, this association has turned into a philanthropic association. It has become part of a system of patronage in its gift-giving and charity, and the women who are its leaders are closely linked to leading politicians in terms of kinship and marriage. Wipper notes that 'in Kenya, there are the beginnings of an established elite – old families bound together by shared beliefs, interests and wealth ... the government, by having its "own women" in the top leadership positions [of the organization], can assure itself of moderation, cooperation and the stifling of dissent' (Wipper 1975: 116). In other words, here too there is a process of class formation, and women of the bourgeoisie are performing the work of social reproduction, and defining and separating out their own class from others through the medium of charity.

On the other side of the African continent, Bujra cites her experience of the Gambian Women's Federation which she studied in 1976. She reports that its members came from several other organizations, the most important of which was a leading girls' secondary school situated in the capital. The President of the Federation said that its main concerns were with charity work, finding employment for educated girls, and preventing female juvenile delinquency (a euphemism for prostitution) (Bujra 1983: 23). Similarly, Abner Cohen's study of the Creoles in Sierra Leone finds women from this elite ethnic group operating philanthropic associations to help the 'poor, sick and ignorant' (1981: 80). Chipp's (1970) study of the All-Pakistan Women's Association shows that its primary role is that of a social welfare agency, and most of its leaders are the wives of prominent government people.

Indeed, wherever we look, we find evidence that at certain historical periods in the development of capitalism voluntary social welfare organizations are likely to be formed, and they are most likely to be run by women of the upper classes for those of the lower.

Conclusion

The conclusion then would seem to be that social welfare of some kind is a necessary adjunct of capitalism, but there is no necessary historical progression from private charity to state welfare. Even in situations of apparent maximum state intervention, use seems to be made of volunteers on a large scale, not to mention, of course, the unpaid welfare work carried out by kin and neighbours. And charitable foundations, which I have not had space to consider in this book, do, of course, provide a significant financial input into this field in developed capitalist states, and even in some states of the periphery, such as India (cf. Arnove 1982; Whitaker 1974). The relationship between the state and the voluntary sector is a fluctuating one, but the impact of the latter on the former sector, as well as the importance of their relationship, is often concealed under an apparently *laissez-faire* philosophy, as is the case in India. In fact the state can, and often does, intervene cheaply and effectively by injections of a judicious mixture of funding and ideology, and so direct and profit from the policies of the voluntary social welfare sector. At various times, the state co-opts women's organizations and women volunteers, particularly in times of crisis such as war, famine, or flood,[6] or when the state has decided to put its priorities into fields other than social welfare and cuts such expenditure.

This would seem to be the likely course which many advanced and peripheral capitalist nations are likely to take in the foreseeable future – encouraging the voluntary organized welfare sector, as well as attempting to revive kinship ('the family') as a provider of welfare.

All this is likely to have significant effects on women. Social welfare sits at the site of the articulation of production and reproduction. It is a form of public reproduction, and like domestic labour (which is similarly mainly the concern of women) it reproduces the conditions of existence, including the classes which are so clearly defined by the exercise of charity.

Notes

1 It is interesting to note that much male work on reproduction has focused on the state and its apparatuses (e.g. Althusser 1972; Bourdieu and Passeron 1977), whereas most work by women has concentrated

upon the family, and the way in which it articulates with capitalism (cf. Barrett and McIntosh 1982).

2 For example, between 1821 and 1831, Liverpool expanded in size by 45 per cent, Manchester and Salford by almost as much, and Leeds, at 47 per cent, by even more.

3 There has been a great neglect of the study of women and philanthropy in the nineteenth century until very recently. Owen's seminal study (1964), for example, restricts the term 'philanthropist' to donors, the vast majority of whom he states are male, thereby excluding women from his book for the most part. However, Prochaska's later work, which looks mainly at women, states that women gave as much as men did, and that a *higher* proportion of women than men left their estates to charity (1980: 35).

4 During the nineteenth century, prostitution flourished as never before. Prochaska (1980), for instance, quotes estimated figures for prostitutes in London alone during the 1850s as between ten and eighty thousand, but as Houghton says, this was scarcely surprising, given 'The growth of industrial cities providing a cover of secrecy, the starvation wages of women at the lowest economic level, the maintenance of large armed forces, and the social ambition which required a postponement of marriage until a young man could afford to live like a gentleman' (Houghton 1957: 366).

5 The NOW (National Organization of Women) position on volunteerism is that it is an extension of unpaid housework, reinforces a woman's low self-image, and is society's solution for those for whom there is little real employment choice.

6 See Walton (1975) for information on Britain in the Second World War; Chipp (1970) for Pakistani women during the Indo–Pakistani war; and Godden (1945) for British women in India during the Second World War.

References

Abercrombie, N. and Turner, B. S. (1978) The Dominant Ideology Thesis. *British Journal of Sociology* 29 (2).

Ahmad, K. (1979) Studies of Educated Working Women in India: Trends and Issues. *Economic and Political Weekly* 14:1435–440.

AIWC (All-India Women's Conference) (1970) *Souvenir*. Delhi.

Aiyar, C. P. Ramaswami. (1963) *Annie Besant*. Builders of Modern India series. New Delhi: Publications Division, Ministry of Information and Broadcasting.

Allen, M. (1982) The Hindu View of Women. In N. Allen and S. N. Mukherjee (eds) *Women In India and Nepal*. ANU Monographs on South Asia no. 8. Canberra, Australian University Press.

Althusser, L. (1972) Ideology and Ideological State Apparatuses. In B. R. Cosin (ed.) *Education: Structure and Society*. Harmondsworth: Penguin.

Appadurai, A. (1981) Gastro-politics in Hindu South Asia. *American Ethnologist* 8 (3).

Arnove, R. F. (ed.) (1982) *Philanthropy and Cultural Imperialism*. Bloomington, IN: Indiana University Press.

ARTEP (1981) *Women in the Indian Labour Force: Papers and Proceedings of a Workshop*. Asian Employment Programme: Asian Regional Team for Employment Promotion (ARTEP) and ILO Bangkok.

Aves, G. (1969) *The Voluntary Worker in the Social Services*. Report of a Committee jointly set up by the National Council of Social Service and the National Institute for Social Work Training. London: Allen & Unwin.

Baghuna, S. (1980) Protecting the Sources of Community Life: Women's Non-violent Power in the Chipko Movement. *Manushi* 6 (July–August).

234   Class & Gender in India

Baig, T. A. (1974) *Sarojini Naidu*. Builders of Modern India series. New Delhi: Publications Division, Ministry of Information and Broadcasting.

—— (1976) *India's Woman Power*. New Delhi: Chand.

Bailey, F. G. (1971) The Peasant View of the Bad Life. In T. Shanin (ed.) *Peasants and Peasant Societies*. Harmondsworth: Penguin.

Balse, M. (1976) *The Indian Female: Attitude towards Sex*. New Delhi: Chetana.

Barnett, M. R. (1976) *The Politics of Cultural Nationalism*. Princeton, NJ: Princeton University Press.

Barrett, M. (1980) *Women's Oppression Today: Problems in Marxist Feminist Analysis*. London: Verso.

Barrett, M. and McIntosh, M. (1982) *The Anti-Social Family*. London: Verso.

Basch, F. (1974) *Relative Creatures – Victorian Women 1837–67*. London: Allen Lane.

Basu, Amrita (1981) Two Faces of Protest; Alternative Forms of Women Mobilization in West Bengal and Maharashtra. In G. Minault (ed.) *The Extended Family*. Delhi: Chanakya.

Basu, Aparna (1976) The Role of Women in the Indian Struggle for Freedom. In B. R. Nanda (ed.) *Indian Women*. New Delhi: Vikas.

Basu, S. (1971) Women in Four Important Professions – Social Work. In YWCA *Educated Women in Indian Society Today*. Bombay: Tata McGraw-Hill.

Batliwala, S. (1982) Rural Energy Scarcity and Nutrition: A New Perspective. *Economic and Political Weekly* 17 (9).

Berreman, G. (1981) *The Politics of Truth*. New Delhi: South Asian Publishers.

Besant, A. (1894) *An Autobiography*. London: Fischer, Unwin.

Beteille, A. (1977) *Inequality among Men*. Oxford: Basil Blackwell.

Bettelheim, C. (1968) *India Independent*. London: MacGibbon & Kee.

Beveridge, Lord W. H. (1942) *Report on Social Insurance and Allied Social Services*. London: HMSO.

—— (1948) *Voluntary Action: A Report on Methods of Social Advance*. London: Allen & Unwin.

Bhatia, B. M. (1965) Growth and Composition of Middle Class in South India in 19th Century. *Indian Economic and Social History Review* 2 (4).

Bland, L., Harrison, R., Mort, F., and Weedon, C. (1978) Relations of Reproduction – Approaches through Anthropology. In Women's Studies Group, Centre for Contemporary Cultural Studies *Women Take Issue – Aspects of Woman's Subordination*. London: Hutchinson.

Bloch, M. (ed.) (1975) Introduction. In *Political Language and Oratory in Traditional Society*. London: Academic Press.

Bose, A. (1975) A Demographic Profile. In D. Jain (ed.) *Indian Women*. New Delhi: Publications Division, Ministry of Information and Broadcasting.

Boserup, E. (1970) *Women's Role in Economic Development*. London: Allen & Unwin.

Bourdieu, P. and Passeron, J. C. (1977) *Reproduction in Education, Society and Culture*. London: Sage.

Bromley, R. (1977) Natural Boundaries; The Social Function of Popular Fiction. *Red Letters* 7.

Bühler, G. (1886) *Manu (Dharma-Sastra)*. Sacred Books of the East Vol. XXX. Oxford; Clarendon Press.

Bujra, J. (1983) Urging Women to Redouble their Efforts: Class, Gender and Capitalist Transformation in Africa. Paper given at British Sociological Association conference, Cardiff.

Caplan, L. (1976) Class and Urban Migration in South India: Christian Elites in Madras City. *Sociological Bulletin* 25 (2).

—— (1977) Social Mobility in Metropolitan Centres: Christians in Madras City. *Contributions to Indian Sociology* 2 (1).

—— (1984) Bridegroom Price in Urban India: Class, Caste and 'Dowry Evil' among Christians in Madras. *Man* 19 (2).

Caplan, P. (1973) Review of Orenstein's Book *Gaon*. In *Women's Anthropology Workshop*. (Mimeo) London.

—— (1977) Women in Professions in India. *Women Speaking* July–September.

—— (1978) Women's Organisations in Madras City, India. In P. Caplan and J. Bujra (eds) *Women United, Women Divided*. London: Tavistock.

—— (1979) Indian Women: Model and Reality: A Review of Recent Books. *Women's Studies International Quarterly* 2:4.

—— (1980) Joiners and Non-joiners: A South Indian City Suburb and its Women's Club. *Sociological Bulletin* 29 (2).

Chakrabortty, K. (1978) *The Conflicting Worlds of Working Mothers: A Sociological Enquiry*. Calcutta: Progressive Publishers.

Chakravarthy, R. (1980) *Communists in Indian Women's Movement*. New Delhi: People's Publishing House.

Chari, T. V. R. (1982) Vistas of Employment for Needy Women and Disabled: Spotlight: CSWB's Economic Programme. *Social Welfare* 28 (11 February).

Chattopadhyay, K. (1975) The Women's Movement. Then and Now. In D. Jain (ed.) *Indian Women*. New Delhi: Publications Division, Ministry of Information and Broadcasting.

Chaudhary, R. (1961) *Hindu Woman's Right to Property, Past and Present*. Calcutta: K. L. Mukhopadhyay.

Chen, L. C. (1982) Where Have the Women Gone? Insights from Bangladesh on Low Sex Ratio of India's Population. *Economic and Political Weekly* 17 (10).

Chinmaya Mission (n.d.) *Source of Joy*. New Delhi: Chinmaya Mission.

Chipp, S. A. (1970) *The Role of Women Elites in a Modernizing Country: The All-Pakistan Women's Association*. PhD thesis, University of Syracuse, NY.

Chowdhry, D. P. (1971) *Voluntary Social Welfare in India*. New Delhi: Sterling.

Cohen, A. (1981) *The Politics of Elite Culture: Explorations in the Dramaturgy of Power in a Modern African Society*. Berkeley, CA: University of California Press.

Cohen, G. (1978) Women's Solidarity and the Preservation of Privilege. In P. Caplan and J. Bujra (eds) *Women United: Women Divided*. London and New York: Tavistock.

Counter Information Services (1981) *Women in the 80's*. London: CIS.

Cousins, J. and Cousins, M. (1950) *We Two Together*. Madras: Ganesh.

Cousins, M. E. (1947) *Indian Womanhood Today*. Allahabad: Kitabastan.

CSWB (Central Social Welfare Board) (1978a) *Directory of Social Welfare Agencies in India Tamilnadu*, vols I and II. New Delhi: CSWB.

—— (1978b) *Report of the Silver Jubilee Celebrations*. New Delhi: CSWB.

—— (1980) *Annual Report, 1979–80*. New Delhi: CSWB.

—— (n.d.) *Programmes of Assistance: Policy and Procedure*. New Delhi: CSWB.

Dandekar, K. (1975) Why Has the Proportion of Women in India's Population been Declining? *Economic and Political Weekly* 10 (42):1663–667.

Dandekar, V. M. and Rath, M. (1971) *Poverty in India*. Bombay: Indian School of Political Economy.

Das, V. (1976) Indian Women: Work, Power and Status. In B. R. Nanda (ed.) *Indian Women from Purdah to Modernity*. New Delhi: Vikas.

Davey, B. (1975) *The Economic Development of India*. Nottingham: Spokesman Books.

David, M. E. (1980) *The State, The Family and Education*. London: Routledge & Kegan Paul.

Davidoff, L. (1973) *The Best Circles: Society, Etiquette and the Season*. London: Croom Helm.

Desai, A. S. (1981) Social Work Education in India. In T. K. Nair (ed.) *Social Work Education and Social Work Practice in India*. Association of Schools of Social Work in India.

Desai, P. B. (1967) Variations in Population Sex Ratios in India, 1901–61. In A. Bose (ed.) *Patterns of Population Change in India 1951–61*. Bombay; Allied.

Devadass, R. (1972) *Nutrition in Tamilnadu*. Madras: Sangam.

Driver, E. and Driver, A. (1982) Social Class and Voluntary Associations in South India. *Sociological Bulletin* 31 (2).

D'Souza, S. (1980) The Data Base for Studies on Women: Sex Biases in National Data Systems. In A. de Souza (ed.) *Women in Contemporary India and S. Asia* (2nd edn). New Delhi: Manohar.

D'Souza, V. S. (1980) Family Status and Female Work Participation. In A. de Souza (ed.) *Women in Contemporary India and S. Asia*. New Delhi: Manohar.

Dumont, L. (1970) *Homo Hierarchicus*. London: Weidenfeld & Nicolson.

Dutt, G. S. (1929) *A Woman of India: Being the Life of Saroj Nalini*. London: The Hogarth Press.

Edholm, F., Harris, O., and Young, K. (1977) Conceptualising Women. *Critique of Anthropology* 9/10.

Egnor, M. (1977) A Tamil Priestess. Unpublished paper presented at a panel on Sacred and Secular Images of Women at the American Anthropological Association Meeting, Houston, Texas.

—— (1980) On the Meaning of Sakti to Women in Tamilnadu. In S. Wadley (ed.) *The Powers of Tamil Women*. Syracuse, NY: Syracuse University Press.

Ehrenreich, B. and English, D. (1979) *For Her Own Good: 150 Years of the Experts' Advice to Women*. London: Pluto Press.

Engels, F. (1972) *The Origin of the Family, Private Property and the State*. London: Lawrence & Wishart.

EOC (Equal Opportunities Commission) (1982a) *Caring for the Elderly and Handicapped: Community Care Policies and Women's Lives*. Manchester: EOC.

—— (1982b) *Who Cares for the Carers? Opportunities for those Caring for the Elderly and Handicapped*. Manchester: EOC.

Everett, J. M. (1979) *Women and Social Change in India*. New Delhi: Heritage.

Felton, M. (1966) *A Child Widow's Story*. London: Victor Gollancz.

Ferro-Luzzi, E. (1974) Women's Pollution Periods in Tamilnadu, India. *Anthropos* 69.

Flandrin, J-L. (1979) *Families in Former Times: Kinship, Household and Sexuality*. London: Cambridge University Press.

Fonseca, A. J. (1971) *Challenge of Poverty in India*. New Delhi: Vikas.

Forbes, G. (1979a) Women and Modernity: The Issue of Child Marriage in India. *Women's Studies International Quarterly* 2 (4).

—— (1979b) The Women's Movement in India: Traditional Symbols and New Roles. In M. S. A. Rao (ed.) *Social Movements in India* vol. 2. New Delhi: Manohar.

—— (1979c) Votes for Women: The Demands for Women's Franchise 1917–37. In V. Majumdar (ed). *Symbols of Power*. Bombay: Allied.

—— (1980) Goddesses or Rebels? The Women Revolutionaries of Bengal. *The Oracle* 2 (2).

—— (1981) The Indian Women's Movement: A Struggle for Women's Rights or National Liberation? In G. Minault (ed.) *The Extended Family*. New Delhi: Chanakya.

—— (1982) From Purdah to Politics: The Social Feminism of the All-India Women's Organisations. In H. Papanek and G. Minault (eds) *Separate Worlds: Studies in Purdah in South Asia*. New Delhi: Chanakya.

Forrester, D. B. (1970). Kamaraj: A Study in Percolation of Style. *Modern Asian Studies* 4 (1).

—— (1976) Factions and Filmstars: Tamilnadu Politics since 1971. *Asian Survey* 16 (3).

Fuller, C. J. (1980) The Divine Couple's Relationship in a South Indian Temple: Minakshi and Sundaresvara at Madurai. *History of Religions* 19.

Gadgil, D. R. (1965) *Women in the Working Force in India*. Bombay: Asia Publishing House.

Gandhi, M. K. (1942) *Women and Social Injustice*. Ahmadabad: Navajivan.

Gangrade, K. D. and Varma, R. M. (1981) Community Development. In T. K. Nair (ed.) *Social Work Education and Social Work Practice in India*. Association of Schools of Social Work in India.

Ginsburg, N. (1979) *Class, Capital and Social Policy*. London: Macmillan.

Gittell, M. and Shtob, T. (1980) Changing Women's Roles in Political Volunteerism and Reform of the City. Special supplement on Women and the American City. *Signs* 5 (3).

Godden, R. (1945) *Bengali Journey*. London, Bombay, Calcutta, Madras: Longmans Green.

Gold, D. B. (1971) Women and Volunteerism. In V. Gornick and B. K. Moran. *Women in Sexist Society: Studies in Power and Powerlessness*. New York: Basic Books.

Good, A. (1980) Elder Sister's Daughter Marriage in S. Asia. *Journal of Anthropological Research* 36 (4).

Goody, J. (1976) *Production and Reproduction: A Comparative Study of the Domestic Domain*. London: Cambridge University Press.

Gore, M. S. (1965) *Social Work and Social Work Education*. Bombay: Asia Publishing House.

Gough, I. (1979) *The Political Economy of the Welfare State*. London: Macmillan.

Government of India (1974) *Towards Equality*. The Report of the Committee on the Status of Women in India. New Delhi: Department of Social Welfare, Ministry of Education and Social Welfare.

Government of India, Planning Commission (1953) *First Five Year Plan, 1951–56*. New Delhi: Publications Division, Ministry of Information and Broadcasting.

References 239

—— (1968) *Encyclopaedia of Social Work in India*. New Delhi: Director of Publications.

—— (1971) *Study of the Working of Voluntary Agencies in Social Welfare Programmes*. Mimeo.

—— (1978) *Draft Five Year Plan, 1978–83*. New Delhi.

Government of Tamilnadu, Directorate of Social Welfare (n.d.) *A Note on Schemes for the Welfare of Handicapped, Children, Women*. Madras.

Gramsci, A. (1971) *Selections from Prison Notebooks*. London: Lawrence & Wishart.

Guhan, S. (1981) *A Primer on Poverty: India and Tamilnadu*. Popular Series no. 2. Madras: IDS.

Gulati, L. (1975) Occupational Distribution of Working Women. *Economic and Political Weekly* 10 (43).

Gupta, R. L., Haksar, N., and Sivadas, C. (1982) The Delhi Nari Niketan – Protection Worse than Imprisonment. *Manushi* 10.

Hadley, R. and Hatch, S. (1980) *Research on the Voluntary Sector*. Report to Sociology and Social Administration Committee. London: Social Science Research Council.

Haksar, N. (1981) Ak Sata Ho, Hum Mandir Banayenge: Countering Attempt to Revive Sati. *Manushi* 7: 32–3.

Hall, C. (1979) The Early Formation of Victorian Domestic Ideology. In S. Burman (ed.) *Fit Work for Women*. London: Croom Helm.

Hanchett, S. (1975) Hindu Potlaches: Ceremonial Reciprocity and Prestige in Karnataka. In H. Ullrich (ed.) *Competition and Modernization in South Asia*. New Delhi: Abhinav.

Hardgrave, R. L. (1965) *The Dravidian Movement*. Bombay: Popular Prakashan; New York: The Humanities Press.

Harper, E. P. (1969) Fear and the Status of Women. *South-western Journal of Anthropology* 25.

Harris, O. and Young, K. (1981) Engendered Structures; Some Problems in the Analysis of Reproduction. In J. Kahn and J. Llobera (eds) *The Anthropology of Pre-capitalist Societies*. London: Macmillan.

Harrison, B. (1966) Philanthropy and the Victorians. *Victorian Studies* 9.

Hart, G. (1973) Women and the Sacred in Ancient Tamilnadu. *Journal of Asian Studies* 32 (2).

Hindess, B. and Hirst, P. Q. (1975). *Pre-capitalist Modes of Production*. London: Routledge & Kegan Paul.

Houghton, W. E. (1957) *The Victorian Frame of Mind 1830–70*. New Haven, CT: Yale University Press.

Hyma, B. (1971) *The Rural–Urban Fringe of a Growing Metropolis: Madras, An Indian Example*. PhD thesis, University of Pittsburgh.

Institute of Social Studies (Jain, D.) (1981) *Catalogue of Agencies reaching the Poorest Women in India.* New Delhi: Institute of Social Studies, for Swedish International Development Agency.

Irschik, E. F. (1969) *Politics and Social Conflict in South India: The Non-Brahmin Movement and Tamil Separatism 1916–29.* Berkeley and Los Angeles, CA: University of California Press.

Jacobson, D. (1976) Women and Jewelry in Rural India. In G. R. Gupta (ed.) *Main Currents in Indian Sociology* vol. ii, *Family and Social Change in India.* New Delhi: Vikas.

—— (1978) The Chaste Wife: Cultural Norm and Individual Experience. In S. Vatuk (ed.) *American Studies in the Anthropology of India.* New Delhi: Manohar and American Institute of Indian Studies.

Jagannadham, V. (1978) 'Key-note Address' in Central Social Welfare Board *Report of the Silver Jubilee Celebrations of the Central Social Welfare Board.* New Delhi: CSWB.

Jain, D. (1975) *From Dissociation to Rehabilitation The Report of an Experiment to Promote Self-employment in an Urban Area.* New Delhi: Indian Council for Social Science Research.

—— (1980) *Women's Quest for Power: Five Indian Case Studies.* Ghaziabad: Vikas.

Jain, S. P. and Krishnamurthy Reddy (1979) *Role of Women in Rural Development – A Study of Mahila Mandals.* Hyderabad: National Institute of Rural Development.

Jayaraman, R. (1981) *Caste, Class and Sex: The Dynamics of Inequality in Indian Society.* New Delhi: Hindustan Publishing Corporation.

Jeffers, H. (1981) Organizing Petty Women Traders and Producers: A Case Study of Working Women's Forum, Madras. Thesis for Master of City Planning degree, University of California, Berkeley.

Jeffreys, P. (1979) *Frogs in a Well.* London: Zed Press.

Kalanidhi, M. S. (1973) Problems of Job Satisfaction among Women Workers in Industry. In T. E. Shanmugan (ed.) *Researches in Personality and Social Problems.* University of Madras.

Kalpagam, U. (1981) Labour in Small Industry: Case of Export Garments Industry in Madras. *Economic and Political Weekly* 16 (48).

Kapur, P. (1970) *Marriage and the Working Woman in India.* New Delhi: Vikas.

—— (1974) *The Changing Status of the Working Woman in India.* New Delhi: Vikas.

Katona-Apte, J. (1978) Urbanisation, Income and Socio-Cultural Factors Relevant to Nutrition in Tamilnadu. In A. de Souza (ed.) *The Indian City.* New Delhi: Manohar.

Kaur, M. (1968) *Role of Women in the Freedom Movement 1857–1947.* New Delhi: Sterling.

Khandekar, M. (1974) *Utilization of Social and Welfare Services in Greater Bombay*. Bombay: Tata Institute of the Social Sciences.

Khare, R. S. (1976) *The Hindu Hearth and Home*. New Delhi: Vikas.

Khinduka, S. K. (ed.) (1965) *Social Work in India*. Allahabad: Kitab Mahal.

Kirkpatrick, J. (1978) Themes of Consciousness among some Educated Working Women of Bangladesh. In R. Ray *et al.* (eds) *Role and Status of Women in Indian Society*. Calcutta: Firma KLM Private.

Krygier, J. (1982) Caste and Female Pollution. In M. Allen and S. N. Mukherjee (eds) *Women in India and Nepal*. ANU Monographs on South Asia no. 8.

Kulkarni, P. D. (1981) Social Policy and Social Welfare Administration in India. In T. K. Nair (ed.) *Social Work Education and Social Work Practice in India*. Madras: Association of Schools of Social Work in India.

Kurien, C. T. (1974) *Poverty and Development*. Madras: Christian Literature Society.

Lalitha, N. V. (1975) *Voluntary Work in India: A Study of Volunteers in Welfare Agencies*. New Delhi: National Institute of Public Co-operation and Child Development.

Lam, M. J. (1973) *Women in India: A General Survey of their Condition, Status and Advancement*. New Delhi: AIWC.

Lanchester, H. V. (1918). *Report on Madras Town*. Government of Madras.

Land, H. (1976) Women: Supporters or Supported? In D. L. Barker and S. Allen (eds) *Sexual Divisions and Society: Process and Change*. London: Tavistock.

—— (1980) The Family Wage. *Feminist Review* 6.

L'Armand, K. and L'Armand A. (1978) Music in Madras: the Urbanization of a Cultural Tradition. In B. Nettle (ed.) *Eight Urban Musical Cultures*. Urbana, IL: University of Illinois Press.

Leonard, K. I. and Leonard, J. G. (1981) Social Reform and Women's Participation in Political Culture: Andhra and Madras. In G. Minault (ed.) *The Extended Family*. New Delhi: Chanakya.

Lewandowski, S. (1980) *Migration and Ethnicity in Urban India: Kerala Migrants in the City of Madras 1870–1970*. New Delhi: Manohar.

Lewis, P. (1978) *Reason Wounded: An Experience of India's Emergency*. London: Allen & Unwin.

Luthra, B. (1976) Nehru and the Place of Women in Indian Society. In B. R. Nanda (ed.) *Indian Women*. New Delhi: Vikas.

Lynch, O. M. (1969) *The Politics of Untouchability*. New York: Columbia University Press.

—— (1979) Potters, Plotters, Prodders in a Bombay Slum: Marx and Meaning or Meaning versus Marx. *Urban Anthropology* 8 (1).

Maclay, S. (1969) *Women's Organisations in India. Voluntary Associations in a Developing Society.* PhD thesis, University of Virginia.

Madan, T. N. (1970) Doctors in a North Indian City: Recruitment, Role Perception and Role Performance. In R. Fox (ed.) *Urban India: Society, Space and Image.* Durham, NC: Duke University Press.

Madras School of Social Work (1967) *Impact of Grant-in-Aid from CSWB on Social Welfare Agencies in Madras City.* Madras.

—— (1970) *Working Mothers in White Collar Occupations.* Madras.

Malkani, N. R. (1968) Voluntary Agencies for Social Welfare. In Government of India, Planning Commission *Encyclopaedia of Social Work in India.* New Delhi: Director of Publications.

Marx, K. (1954) *Capital* vol. 1. London: Lawrence & Wishart.

—— (1968) Preface to *Critique of Political Economy.* In *Marx/Engels: Selected Works.* London: Lawrence & Wishart.

Mauss, M. (1967) *The Gift: Forms and Functions of Exchange in Archaic Societies* (first published 1925). New York: Norton.

Mayer, A. (1981) Public Service and Individual Merit in a Town of Central India. *Culture and Morality.* New Delhi: Oxford University Press.

Mazumdar, V. (1976) The Social Reform Movement: from Ranade to Nehru. In B. R. Nanda (ed.) *Indian Women.* New Delhi: Vikas.

—— (ed.) (1979) *Symbols of Power: Studies on the Political Status of Women in India.* Bombay: Allied.

McIntosh, M. (1979) The Welfare State and the Needs of the Dependent Family. In S. Burman (ed.) *Fit Work for Women.* London: Croom Helm.

Mehta, B. H. (1968) Leadership. In Government of India, Planning Commission *Encyclopaedia of Social Work in India.* New Delhi: Director of Publications.

Mehta R. (1975) *The Divorced Hindu Woman.* New Delhi: Vikas.

Meillassoux, C. (1981) *Maidens, Meal and Money.* London: Cambridge University Press.

Mencher, J. (1974) The Caste System Upside Down, or the Not So Mysterious East. *Current Anthropology* 15 (4): 469–93.

Midgley, J. (1981) *Professional Imperialism: Social Work in the Third World.* Studies in Social Policy and Welfare. London: Heinemann Educational.

Mies, M. (1975) Indian Women and Leadership. *Bulletin of Concerned Asian Scholars* 7:56–66.

—— (1979) *Indian Women and Patriarchy.* New Delhi: Concept.

Miliband, R. (1969). *The State in Capitalist Society.* London: Weidenfeld & Nicolson.

Miller, B. D. (1981) *The Endangered Sex: Neglect of Female Children in Rural North India.* Ithaca, NY: Cornell University Press.

References **243**

Minattur, J. (1980) Women and the Law; Constitutional Rights and Continuing Inequalities. In A. de Souza (ed.) *Women in Contemporary India*. New Delhi: Manohar.

Minault, G. (1981) The Extended Family as Metaphor and the Expansion of Women's Realm. In *The Extended Family*. New Delhi: Chanakya.

Misra, B. B. (1961) *The Indian Middle Classes: Their Growth in Modern Times*. London: Oxford University Press.

Mitra, A. (1978) *India's Population: Aspects of Quality and Control*. A Family Planning Foundation Book. New Delhi: Abhinav.

—— (1979a) *The Status of Women: Literacy and Employment*. Indian Council of Social Science Research Programme of Women's Studies II. New Delhi: Allied.

—— (1979b) *Implications of Declining Sex Ratio in India's Population*. Indian Council of Social Science Research Programme of Women's Studies I. New Delhi: Allied.

Mitra, A., Srimany, A. K., and Pathak, L. P. (1979c) *The Status of Women: Household and Non-Household Economic Activity*. Indian Council of Social Research Programme of Women's Studies III. New Delhi: Allied.

Moorthy, M. V. (1981) Philosophy of Social Work in Changing India. In T. K. Nair (ed.) *Social Work Education and Social Work Practice in India*. Madras: Association of Schools of Social Work in India.

Mowat, C. L. (1961) *The Charity Organization Society, 1869–1913*. London: Methuen.

Muthulakshmi Reddy, S. (1930) *My Experience as a Legislator*. Madras: The Current Thought Press.

—— (1956) *Mrs Margaret Cousins and Her Work in India*. Adyar Madras: WIA.

—— (1964) *Autobiography*. Published privately. Madras.

Nader, L. (1974) Up the Anthropologist: Perspectives gained from Studying Up. In D. Hymes (ed.) *Reinventing Anthropology*. New York: Vintage Books.

Nair, T. K. (1978) *Social Welfare Manpower in Tamilnadu*. Madras School of Social Work.

—— (1981) *Social Work Education and Social Work Practice in India*. Madras: Association of Schools of Social Work in India.

Nambiar, P. K. (1961) *Slums of Madras City* vol. 9 (Madras) Part XI-C. Census of India. Government of India.

Nanavathy, M. C. (1968) The Social Work Profession. In Government of India, Planning Commission *Encyclopaedia of Social Work in India*. New Delhi: Director of Publications.

Narang, S. (1974) Social Welfare in the Plans. *Social Welfare* 20 (11).

Nath, K. (1965) Urban Women Workers. *Economic and Political Weekly* 17 (37): 1405–412.

Nehru, J. (1972) *Selected Works of J. Nehru* vol. VII. New Delhi: Orient Longman.

Nelson, N. (1979) *Why Have the Women of Village India been Neglected?* Oxford: Pergamon Press.

Nethercot, A. H. (1960) *The First Five Lives of Annie Besant*. London: Rupert Hart-Davis.

—— (1963) *The Last Four Lives of Annie Besant*. London: Rupert Hart-Davis.

Newton, K. (1976) *Second City Politics*. Oxford: Clarendon Press.

O'Brien, M. (1981) *The Politics of Reproduction*. London: Routledge & Kegan Paul.

Omvedt, G. (1973) Gandhi and the Pacification of the Indian Nationalist Movement. *Bulletin of Concerned Asian Scholars* 5.

—— (1975a) Rural Origins of Women's Liberation in India. *Social Scientist* 4 (4/5).

—— (1975b) Caste, Class and Women's Liberation in India. *Bulletin of Concerned Asian Scholars* 7.

—— (1978) Women and Rural Revolt in India. *Journal of Peasant Studies* 5.

—— (1981) Capitalist Agriculture and Rural Classes in India. *Economic and Political Weekly* 16 (52).

Owen, D. (1964) *English Philanthropy 1660–1960*. Cambridge, Mass.: Belknap Press.

Oza, D. K. (1974) Policies and Programmes of Social Welfare. (Special issue on Tamilnadu.) *Social Welfare* 20 (11).

Pandey, R. (1969) *Hindu Samskaras*. New Delhi: Motilal Banarsidas.

Papanek, H. (1979) Family Status Production: The 'Work' and 'Non-Work' of Women. *Signs* 4 (4):775–81.

Patil, B. R. (1978) *Economics of Social Welfare in India*. Bombay/New Delhi: Somaiya Publications Private.

Pearson, G. (1981) Nationalism, Universalization and the Extended Female Space in Bombay City. In G. Minault (ed.) *The Extended Family*. New Delhi: Chanakya.

Piven, F. F. and Cloward, R. A. (1972) *Regulating the Poor; The Functions of Public Welfare*. London: Tavistock.

Prasad, K. V. (1979) Education and Unemployment of Professional Manpower in India. *Economic and Political Weekly* 14 (20).

Prochaska, F. K. (1980) *Women and Philanthropy in 19th Century England*. Oxford: Clarendon Press.

Rama, K. G. (1974) *Women's Welfare in Tamilnadu*. Madras: Sangam /MIDS.

Ranade, S. N. (1968) Personnel in Social Work. In Government of India, Planning Commission *Encyclopaedia of Social Work in India*. New Delhi: Director of Publications.

Ranade, S. N. and Ramachandran, P. (1970) *Women and Employment.* Bombay: Tata Institute.

Rani, K. (1976) *Role Conflict in Working Women.* New Delhi: Chetana.

Ranson, C. W. (1938) *A City in Transition: Studies in the Social Life of Madras.* Madras: The Christian Literature Society for India.

Rau, I. M. (n.d.) *The Women's Swadeshi League.* Unpublished paper.

Ray, R. (1968) History of Social Welfare Development since 1947. In Government of India, Planning Commission *Encyclopaedia of Social Work in India.* New Delhi: Director of Publications.

Reynolds, H. B. (1980) The Auspicious Married Women. In S. Wadley (ed.) *The Powers of Tamil Women.* Syracuse, NY: Syracuse University.

Rogers, B. (1980) *The Domestication of Women: Discrimination in Developing Societies.* London and New York: Tavistock.

Ross, A. D. (1961) *The Hindu Family in its Urban Setting.* University of Toronto Press.

Roy, M. (1975a) The Concepts of 'Femininity' and 'Liberation' in the Context of Changing Sex Roles: Women in Modern India and America. In D. Raphael (ed.) *Being Female.* The Hague: Mouton.

—— (1975b) *Bengali Women.* London: University of Chicago Press.

Rubin, G. (1975) The Traffic in Women. In R. Reiter *Towards an Anthropology of Women.* New York: Monthly Review Press.

Rudolph, L. I. (1961) Urban Life and Populist Radicalism: Dravidian Politics in Madras. *Journal of Asian Studies* 20 (May).

Rudolph, L. I. and Rudolph, S. H. (1967) *The Modernity of Tradition: Political Development in India.* Chicago, IL: University of Chicago Press.

Rudolph, S. and Rudolph, L. I. (1966) Barristers and Brahmins in India: Legal Cultures and Social Change. *Comparative Studies in Society and History* 8.

Sachs, A. (1978) The Myth of Male Protectiveness and the Legal Subordination of Women. In C. Smart and B. Smart (eds) *Women, Sexuality and Social Control.* London: Routledge & Kegan Paul.

Sahlins, M. (1974) *Stone Age Economics.* London: Tavistock.

Sangari, K. and Vaid, S. (1981) Sati in Modern India: A Report. *Economic and Political Weekly* 16 (31).

Sastri, K. R. R. R. (1972) *S. Srinivasa Iyengar* Builders of Modern India series. New Delhi: Publications Division, Ministry of Information and Broadcasting.

Sau, R. (1981) *India's Economic Development: Aspects of Class Relations.* Hyderabad: Orient Longman.

Seebohm, Lord (1968) *Report of the Committee on Local Authority and Allied Personal Social Services.* Cmnd 3703. London: HMSO.

Selbourne, D. (1982) *Through the Indian Looking-glass.* London: Zed Press.

Sen, S. N. (1960) *The City of Calcutta: A Socio-Economic Survey 1954–55, 1957–58.* Calcutta: Bookland.

Sengupta, P. (1960) *Women Workers of India.* Bombay: Asia Publishing House.

Shah, K. T. (1947) *Women's Role in Planned Economy.* Bombay: Vora.

Sharma, K. (1983) Interactions between Policy Assumptions and Rural Women's Work – A Case Study. Paper presented at International Congress of Anthropological and Ethnological Sciences, Vancouver.

Sharpe, S. (1976) *'Just like a Girl': How Girls Learn to be Women.* London: Penguin.

Simey, M. B. (1951) *Charitable Effort in Liverpool in the 19th Century.* Liverpool: Liverpool University Press.

Singer, M. (1971) *When a Great Tradition Modernizes.* New York: Praeger.

Singh, A. M. (1975) The Study of Women in India: Some Problems in Methodology. In. A. de Souza (ed.) *Women in Contemporary India.* New Delhi: Manohar.

—— (1976) *Neighbourhood and Networks in Urban India.* New Delhi: Marwah.

Singh, K. P. (1979) *Status of Women and Population Growth in India.* New Delhi: Munshiram Manoharlal.

Singh, R. R. (1981) Social Work Practice and Education in the Area of Family, Child and Youth Welfare. In T. K. Nair (ed.) *Social Work Education and Social Work Practice in India.* Madras: Association of Schools of Social Work in India.

Singh, S. R. (1968) *Nationalism and Social Reform in India, 1885–1920.* New Delhi: Rampart.

Smart, C. and Smart, B. (eds) (1978) An Introduction. In *Women, Sexuality and Social Control.* London: Routledge & Kegan Paul.

Sopher, D. E. (1980) Sex Disparity in Indian Literacy. In D. Sopher (ed.) *An Exploration of India.* London: Longman.

Spratt, P. (1970) *DMK in Power.* Bombay: Nachiketa.

Stedman-Jones, G. (1971) *Outcast London.* London: Oxford University Press.

Stein, D. (1978) Women to Burn: Suttee as Normative Institution. *Signs* 4 (2).

Stivens, M. (1978) Women and their Kin. In P. Caplan and J. M. Bujra (eds) *Women United: Women Divided: Cross-cultural Perspectives on Female Solidarity.* London and New York: Tavistock.

—— (1981) Women, Kinship and Capitalist Development. In K. Young, C. Wolkowitz, and R. McCullagh (eds) *Of Marriage and the Market.* London: CSE Books.

Stone, L. (1977) *The Family, Sex and Marriage in England 1500–1800.* London: Weidenfeld & Nicolson.

Summers, A. (1979) A Home from Home: Women's Philanthropic Work in the 19th Century. In S. Burman (ed.) *Fit Work for Women*. London: Croom Helm.

S. V. (1978) Keeping the Home Fires Burning. (On dowry deaths.) *Economic and Political Weekly* 14 (25):1038.

Swaminathan, M. (1975) Chellamna: An Illustration of the Multiple Roles of Traditional Women. In D. Jain (ed.) *Indian Women*. New Delhi: Ministry of Information and Broadcasting.

Thane, P. (1982) *The Foundation of the Welfare State*. London: Longman.

Tharu, S. and Melkote, R. (1981) Living Outside the Protection of Marriage: Patriarchal Relations in Working Women's Hostels. *Manushi* 9.

Thompson, E. P. (1976) Folklore, Anthropology and Social History. *Indian Historical Review* 3.

Thorner, D. (1980) *The Shaping of Modern India*. Bombay: Allied.

Varadachar B. D. (1979) The Bottom View Up: Some Cognitive Categories. Slums in Madras. In M. N. Srinivas, A. M. Shah, and E. A. Ramaswamy (eds) *The Field Worker and the Field*. New Delhi: Oxford University Press.

Vatuk, S. (1971) On a System of Private Savings among North Indian Village Women. *Journal of African and Asian Studies* 6.

—— (1972) *Kinship and Urbanization*. Berkeley and Los Angeles, CA: California University Press.

—— (1975) The Ageing Woman in India: Self-Perceptions and Changing Roles. In A. de Souza (ed.) *Women in Contemporary India*. New Delhi: Manohar.

Visaria, P. M. (1967) The Sex Ratio of the Population of India and Pakistan and Regional Variations During 1901–61. In A. Bose (ed.) *Patterns of Population Change in India, 1951–61*. Bombay: Allied.

Wadley, S. (1975) *Shakti: Power in the Conceptual Structure of Karimpur Religion*. Studies in Anthropology No. 2. University of Chicago.

—— (1977) Women and the Hindu Tradition. In Wellesley Editorial Committee *Women and National Development: The Complexities of Change*. Chicago, IL: University of Chicago Press.

—— (1980) The Paradoxical Powers of Tamil Women. In *The Powers of Tamil Women*. Syracuse, NY: Syracuse University Press.

Walton, R. G. (1975) *Women in Social Work*. London: Routledge & Kegan Paul.

Watson, W. (1964) Social Mobility and Social Class in Industrial Communities. In M. Gluckman (ed.) *Closed Systems and Open Minds: the Limits of Naivety in Anthropology*. London: Oliver & Boyd.

Webb, B. (1926) *My Apprenticeship*. London: Longmans.

Weir, A. (1974) The Family, Social Work and the Welfare State. In S. Allen, L. Sanders and J. Wallis *et al. Conditions of Illusion.* Leeds: Feminist Books.

Whitaker, B. (1974) *The Foundations: An Anatomy of Philanthropic Bodies.* Harmondsworth: Penguin.

WIA (Women's Indian Association) (1967) *Golden Jubilee Souvenir: 1917–67.* Madras: WIA.

Wiebe, P. D. (1981) *Tenants and Trustees: A Study of the Poor in Madras.* Delhi: Macmillan.

Wilson, E. (1977) *Women and the Welfare State.* London: Tavistock.

Wipper, A. (1975) The Maendelo ya Wanawake Organisation. The Co-optation of Leadership. *African Studies Review* 18 (3).

Wolfenden Committee (1978) *Report on the Future of Voluntary Organisations.* London: Croom Helm.

Wolkowitz, C. (1983) *Gender as a Variable in the Political Process: A Study of Women's Participation in State-Level Electoral Politics in Andhra Pradesh, India.* DPhil. thesis, University of Sussex.

Woodroofe, K. (1962) *From Charity to Social Work.* London: Routledge & Kegan Paul.

Young, A. F. and Ashton, E. T. (1956) *British Social Work in the Nineteenth Century.* London: Routledge & Kegan Paul.

Zaretsky, E. (1976) *Capitalism, the Family and Personal Life.* London: Pluto Press.

Name index

Subject index

activities of organizations 148, 154–61
adolescence 40–1
agencies, voluntary 124–45; and Central Social Welfare Board 127–30; programmes run by 133–38; and the state 125–26
All-India Women's Conference (AIWC) 105, 112, 116, 123, 194, 197–98
Anna Dravida Munnetra Kazagham (ADMK) 25, 136–40, 184
anthropology ix, 8–9, 13
Aves Report (1969) 227

babies 56–7
balwadis 148, 157, 164, 175–77
barrenness 55–6
beneficiaries of welfare 125–26, 136–37, 173–85; and ideology 210–11
Beveridge Report (1942) 227
bhajan groups 28–9, 35, 81
Brahmins: in organizations 32–3, 151–52, 183–85; in politics 23–6
breast-feeding 56–7
budgets, household 64–5

capitalism 6–7, 225; development of 226–31; ideology of 186; and reproduction 12–15, 18; and welfare 186, 226–31; and women 14–16
caste: beneficiaries of welfare 175–83; members of organizations 148, 151–52; and politics 23–6
Central Social Welfare Board (CSWB) 126, 127–30, 133, 143, 163
Centre for Contemporary Cultural Studies 13
ceremonies, organization 187–90
chaddangu 40–1
charity: England, nineteenth-century 217–26, 232; Hindu philosophy 174; see also organizations; voluntary work
chastity 5, 226
Child Feeding Scheme, Tamilnadu 140, 185
childhood 39–41
childlessness 55–6
children: babies 56–7; balwadis 148, 157, 164, 175–77; bearing 55–7; care of 73–7, 94–5, 176–79;